A NEST OF NINNIES

A NEST OF NINNIES

and Other English Jestbooks
of the Seventeenth Century

Selected and Edited by
P. M. ZALL

UNIVERSITY OF NEBRASKA PRESS • LINCOLN

Publishers on the Plains

UNP

Copyright © 1970 by the University of Nebraska Press

All Rights Reserved

International Standard Book Number 0–8032–0723–9

Library of Congress Catalog Card Number 70–88091

Manufactured in the United States of America

For Jon

Contents

The Blending of Wit and Jest: An Introduction ix

Selections from *Wits, Fits, and Fancies* (1614), by ANTHONY
   COPLEY 1
A Nest of Ninnies (1608), by ROBERT ARMIN 15
Selections from *Jests to Make You Merry* (1607), by GEORGE
   WILKINS and T. D. 73
Selections from *Tarlton's Jests* (1611) 89
Selections from *Scogin's Jests* (ca. 1680) 103
Selections from *Wit and Mirth* (1629), by JOHN TAYLOR 119
Selections from *Conceits, Clinches, Flashes, and Whimzies*
   (1639), by ROBERT CHAMBERLAIN 151
Selections from *A Banquet of Jests* (1633–1660) 159
Tales and Jests of Hugh Peters (1660) 185
No Jest Like a True Jest (ca. 1670) 215
Selections from *Oxford Jests* (1671), by WILLIAM HICKS 235
Selections from *The Wise and Ingenious Companion* (1700),
   by ABEL BOYER 249

An Introduction

The Blending of Wit and Jest

THIS sampling of a dozen seventeenth-century jestbooks is a sequel to an earlier book, *A Hundred Merry Tales and Other Jestbooks of the Fifteenth and Sixteenth Centuries*. That book showed how small volumes of merry tales and witty remarks flourished between 1484 and 1584 as subsoil for the luxuriant growth of Elizabethan prose fiction and comedy. But where the earlier book could reprint virtually all the sixteenth-century survivors in their entirety, now we have room for only representative samples; there are some fifty seventeenth-century jestbooks in the Huntington Library alone. The large increase in number reflects the fact that the making of jestbooks became an industry in the seventeenth century, expanding with the development of a larger reading public. Jestbooks flourished throughout the land, feeding one upon another in a happy self-sustaining cycle. Badly printed, crudely written, they were welcome alike in parlor and pulpit, playhouse and pub. Aside from their value in sparkling conversation and repartee, they provided preachers with pithy parables, pundits with pungent wit, and a rising middle class with instant culture. It would not be surprising, then, if more people read jestbooks than read the works of Chaucer, Spenser, and Milton combined.

A legion of nameless hackwriters during the previous century had patiently turned out collections like *A Hundred Merry Tales* and *The Jests of Skelton*. In the seventeenth century they worked on quietly industrious as ever, with such results as are represented here by the *Banquet of Jests* and the books about Scogin, Tarlton, Peters, and Hind. But now came a new kind of jestbookmaker from a growing group of entertainers proud of their authorship and eager to capitalize on the advertising of their skills that would accrue from such popular publication. There were semi-professional entertainers also, university wits and impoverished gentlemen, for whom jest-books might have made the difference between abject and genteel poverty. The identifiable authors represented here, then, make up a highly diversified cast of characters:

> Anthony Copley, impoverished gentleman, distant relative of Queen Elizabeth (but a secret agent in the service of the King of Spain), whose *Wits, Fits, and Fancies* provided a well-stocked larder for jestbookmakers throughout the century.

> Robert Armin, comedian in Shakespeare's company, an innovator in comic acting, whose *Nest of Ninnies* used jests as a means to study comic character types.

> George Wilkins and Thomas Dekker, among the foremost hackwriters of the day, for whom jestbooks were part of their stock in trade—and collaboration, as in *Jests to Make You Merry*, part of their way of life.

> John Taylor the Water Poet, a professional entertainer in verse and prose, whose *Wit and Mirth* was another fruitful repository from which other writers, and he himself, drew for later books.

> Robert Chamberlain, university wit of meager means, whose *Conceits* may well have been the first jestbook in English to specialize in puns.

> Captain William Hicks, a pseudo-university wit, a tapster in an Oxford tavern, whose *Oxford Jests* applied the brevity of puns to the telling of tales.

> Abel Boyer, lexicographer and pedant, whose *Ingenious Companion*, with its French and English texts on facing pages, made ingenious use of jests and, through its wide ranging selection, in effect recapitulated the history of jests to the end of the century.

This new breed of jestbookmaker brought a new approach to the writing of jests. Not content, as conventional jestbookmakers had been (and continued to be), with simply reprinting old jests and perhaps changing only names and places, they searched for new sources and reworked the old ones. Copley, for instance, translated a compendium of jests from the Spanish and added many more picked up during his travels on the Continent and in England. Dekker, Wilkins, and Armin exploited theatrical sources. Taylor, openly rejecting bookish sources, plucked his jests from the air of metropolitan London, while Chamberlain and Hicks plucked theirs from university common rooms and taverns. Still, the bulk of their jests were traditional, reworked in a more artful way.

The new approach was not innovative so much as representative of a different tradition of jests, one that we can call classical as distinct from the medieval tradition of conventional jestbooks. This distinction is less historical than stylistic, for the two traditions were coeval. Medieval jests, on the one hand, are discursive, diffuse, explanatory, and emphasize deeds rather than words. Classical jests are direct, concise, more subtle, and emphasize words rather than deeds. The difference is seen in this comparison between a classical jest from Copley and a Medieval jest from *Scogin*:

> In the North of Ireland, where they eat but Oaten-cake bread, there was a Kern's mother, hearing that her son was slain in fight against the Englishmen, came the morrow after into the field, and finding her dead son there, after much moan and lamentation over him, she chanced to cast her eye aside and thereby espied a dead Englishman. Then up she rose and, much accursing our nation for the death of her son, in the end she stripped him of his apparel and chanced to find a stale loaf of bread in his breeches—which was of the provision he brought with him from the English pale—which after she had a good while well viewed and wondered at, in the end burst forth into fresh tears and said, "No marvel though my dear son be slain by one that voids so hard and huge a turd!"
>
> (from Copley, *Wits, Fits, and Fancies*)

> Scogin had a great Hare's skin that was new killed, and he went to a Wheatland that was an handful and a half high and did lay there a foul great Mard (they that can speak French can tell what a Mard is), and couched the Hare's skin over it, and set up the Hare's ears. And then he came to Oxford and said to them that used hunting that he had found a Hare sitting. They ran for their Greyhounds to kill the Hare, and Scogin went with them to the land where the Hare did sit. At last, one espied the ears and the head of the Hare and said, "So how!" "Stand you there," said the other, "and give her the law of the game."
>
> Scogin got him home to Oxford, and one that came to see the game was bid to put up the Hare. And when he came almost at the Hare, "Up whore!" he said, "or I will prick you in the buttock by and by."

But the Hare did not stir. At last, when he came to the place, he thrust his staff at the Hare's skin and did turn it over, and under it was a great Mard. He returned again as if he had a flea in his ear to Oxford. "Why," said they, "do you not put up the Hare?" "Go put her up yourself, with a vengeance," said he and went home in a fury.

They that held the Greyhounds did marvel what he meant, and that Scogin was gone. They went to see where the Hare should sit, and they found a Hare's skin and a great Mard. "Well," said they, "we can never beware of Scogin's mocks and jests. Would part of this Hare were in his mouth." And so they departed. Whereby you may see that fair words make fools fain.

(from *Scogin's Jests*)

The differences seen here flourished side by side throughout the century, but there was a strong tendency for the medieval and classical elements to blend, combining the exuberant story-telling quality of the one with the concise economy of the other, producing a hybrid with roots centuries deep.

Typical of the ancestry of the medieval style was the collection of erotic stories called Milesian Tales that were extremely popular in the ancient world. Barbarian chiefs were shocked when they found that Roman legionaries carried such tales into battle, but by the eleventh century they were considered decent enough to hold a steady place in Peter Alphonso's *Disciplina Clericalis*, or Priest's Handbook. In this vehicle they were carried throughout the western world, wherever missionaries wandered, from Spain to Iceland. Embellished with appropriate moral taglines, they served as the root stock of every medieval preacher's collection of "exempla," and every story-teller's collection of merry tales. Versified, they spread into more formal literature as fabliaux and, with the coming of printing, they were translated back into prose for jests in vernacular French, German, Spanish, and English.

Coeval with collections of such realistic, often scatalogical tales were collections of verbal wit accumulating especially in textbooks on the art of rhetoric, where rules for effective public speaking were illustrated by the practice of past masters. In an age when education consisted chiefly of rhetorical training, no educated man could escape being exposed to such examples as these, from Cicero's *De Oratore*: A citizen, hearing about the death of his neighbor, exclaims, "What a fool! Just as he starts making money he dies." A politician, pointing graciously at his opponent, asks, "What does this noble man lack—except cash and character?" It was only a question of time before such examples would be accumulated for their own sakes as collections of bons mots, repartee, choice insults, and witty remarks. Some collections specialized, like the tenth-century manuscript now known as *The Jests of Hierocles* (about Hierocles rather than by him), consisting of one- or two-line profiles of an absent-minded professor: told that a friend's ancestors drank from a deep well, the hero says, "My, what long necks they had!" He meets a friend reported to have died, and the friend cannot convince him that the report had been exaggerated; our hero persists, "The man who told me so was much more reliable than you."

During the Middle Ages, the more leisurely merry tales spread across the land while collections of concise, witty jests lay dormant. But the classical jests bloomed again in the Renaissance, especially after the appearance of Poggio Bracciolini's *Facetiae* in 1477. Poggio, discoverer of some of the finest classical manuscripts in northern Italy, renewed Cicero's emphasis on epigrammatic economy, applying it to both merry tales and witty sayings. Thus in sixty words we hear the wily father assuring the prospective suitor that his daughter is neither too young nor too innocent to wed, having already had three children by the parish clerk. And we hear of the sad husband whose wife has fallen into a rushing stream, looking for her upstream rather than downstream, because he knew her to be the most perverse woman alive. Disseminated more widely than ever thanks to printing, such pointed jests served subsequent generations of Humanists as a vehicle for wit and wisdom. Many of them, like Erasmus and More, turned classical epigrams into prose jests and prose jests into classical epigrams as a means to practicing a clean Latin style; others used merry tales as a vehicle for spreading "the new learning," mixing classical wit and medieval tales for sweetness and light. Towards the end of the sixteenth century the cosmopolitan Copley had little trouble in quickly compiling 1125 classical jests for *Wits, Fits, and Fancies*.

The dramatic quality of the classical jest was of course congenial to theater people like Dekker, Wilkins, and Armin, with their knack for dialogue, irony, and colloquial language:

> "Dear heart," said a Gentleman to his bride, "shall we have our pleasure or our dinner first?"
> "Do just as you like, dear, and then we can dine."
> (Poggio, Facetiae, 1477)

> One called a Captain coward and said he had no heart. "It's no matter," quoth the Captain, "I have legs."
> (Wilkins and Dekker, Jests to Make You Merry, 1607)

Their knack for scene and dialogue expanded simple jests into comic skits, modern "blackouts." A jest of Copley's reads:

> One being in danger of drowning, another standing on the shore said unto him, "Get to yonder stooping tree and you are safe."
> "Tut," he answered, "tell not me of getting or gaining, for I care only to save myself at this time."

Wilkins and Dekker's *Jests to Make You Merry* renders it thus:

> A couple of Servingmen, having drunk hard in Southwark, came to take water about ten or eleven of the clock at night at Saint Maryovary's stairs. But the moon shining, and a puddle of water lying before them which they could not perfectly discern (without better eyes) by reason that their shadows hid it, one of them fell in, laboring with his hands and feet as if he had been a-swimming.
> His fellow stood (so well as a man in his case could stand) looking upon him and said, "Art thou gone? Art thou gone? Jesus receive thy soul. Yet if thou canst but get the Temple stairs, there's some hope thou shalt do well enough."
> "Tush," says the other that was down, "I look not to *get*. So I may save myself, I care for no more."

Such skilful use of scenic detail boded well for the development of artistry in jests that would have combined the story-telling appeal of the medieval tradition with the style of the classical tradition.

But the wordplay of the classical tradition attracted popularity for its own sake. By 1639 Chamberlain's *Conceits* accumulated close to 150 one- or two-line puns: "Smiths of all handicraftsmen are the most irregular, for they never think themselves better employed than when they are addicted to their vices." Little dramatic quality here, and no narrative, yet its brevity must have been considered ample compensation, and over the century we can see a developing preference generally for economy at any cost. The effect is apparent in this comparison:

> Two Countrymen keeping company till night, it happened that one of the Countryman's heels were lighter than his head; and going under a Signpost this Countryman lifted his leg very high. The other demanded why he did so. He told him it was to go over the stile, and pointed to the Sign.
> "Stile!" quoth his friend, "thou fool, it is a Sign!"
> "A Sign?" quoth he. "What Sign?"
> "Marry," quoth he again, "a sign that thou art terribly drunk."
>
> (from *A Banquet of Jests*, 1633)

> A drunken fellow coming by a shop asked a 'prentice boy what their sign was. He answered, it was a sign he was drunk.
>
> (from *A Choice Banquet of Witty Jests*, 1660)

Those responsible for this kind of epitome were interested more in what was said than in how it was said, but fortunately there were also writers like Taylor, Hicks, and Boyer who tried for a more artful balance. They adapted the direct style and subtlety of classical jests to medieval jests, imposing order, point, and thus effective economy with happier results. And, incidentally, they developed a plain, simple narrative style that helped to prepare the tastes of a growing body of readers for the higher art of Defoe, Swift, and Fielding in the ensuing years. It is instructive that one of Boyer's best jests would hold place in the most influential jestbook of them all, *Joe Miller's Jests* (1739) with hardly any change:

> A modest Gentlewoman being compelled to accuse her Husband of defect and being in the Court, she humbly desired the Judge that she might write what she durst not speak for Modesty. The Judge gave her that liberty and a Clerk was presently commanded to give her Pen, Ink, and Paper; whereupon she took the Pen without dipping it into the Ink, and made as if she would write. Says the Clerk to her, "Madam, there is no Ink in your Pen."
> "Truly, Sir," says she, "that's just my Case, and therefore I need not explain myself any further."

A style like this blends the best of the classical and medieval traditions.

There was a comparable development in integrating classical and medieval traditions in jest-biographies, those jestbooks that focused their jests on the words and deeds of one man. Diogenes Laertes' *Lives of the Philosophers* (Ca. 250 A.D.), a typical progenitor of the classical tradition, compiled all known anecdotes about historical figures like Diogenes the Cynic, providing us with such well-known jests, for example, as Diogenes warning a bastard who was throwing rocks into a crowded street, "Be careful, lad, the man you hit may be your father." Written with the economy of classical jests, such episodes acquire a certain integrity from being focused on one consistent personality. By contrast, *Howleglas* (the English version of *Til Eulenspiegel*) makes no pretense of fact or integrity. A random collection of medieval jests is hung about the hero's neck, and he plays a variety of inconsistent roles—now a fool, then a shrewd peasant, next a rogue, and then a country bumpkin or a pilloried apprentice. The only element holding one jest to another, besides the hero, is his passage from the cradle to the grave. *Scogin's Jests* is representative of such medieval jest-biographies.

Armin's *Nest of Ninnies* is an attempt early in the century to bring some balance into jest-biographies, combining the conciseness and plausibility of the *Lives of the Philosophers* with the lively story-telling of *Howleglas*. Fortunately we have the *Nest of Ninnies* in three successive stages and can see how the author transformed it from an earlier jestbook entitled *Foole upon Foole*, achieving integrity of six different biographies by imposing upon them the linking dialogue between the cynical Puritan Sotto and the lively lady named World. By some such process as this, jest-biography was easily absorbed into fictional biography, a genre that became increasingly popular as the century wore on, culminating in *Robinson Crusoe* and *Moll Flanders*.

Meanwhile, however, more conventional jest-biography continued popular also. *Tarlton's Jests* and the books about Hind (*No Jest Like a True Jest*) and Peters, even though concerned with nationally known figures only recently dead, still mix traditional jests with historical fact. But when the jests are treated in a style associated with the classical tradition, they are given the appearance of historical truth, making such jest-biography a natural tool for propaganda. A mixture of jest and factual record could easily create a noble rogue or a vicious monster. The books about Hind, the Cavalier hero, and Peters, the Puritan regicide, are clear cases in point. Modern conceptions of both men derive from their jest-biographies, even though there is ample evidence to prove them calculated myths.

In random collections as well as in jest-biographies it became increasingly harder to separate man from myth, especially when their styles no longer gave a clue to which was which or who was who. Pseudonymous jestbooks continued popular, and so did the practice of assigning jestbooks to notorious figures like Long Meg of Westminster or Mother Bunch. But now in the boldness born of competition, booksellers carelessly assigned jestbooks to people still living, like the court jester Archee Armstrong. As with Hind and Peters, the myth has outlived the man and Archee's modern repu-tation as a jolly good fellow derives from his association with the *Banquet of Jests*—a mythical association spawning another myth, since Archee was neither jolly nor good nor the author of the *Banquet of Jests*.

Because of the emphasis placed upon the personality of the real or attributed collector, some professional or semi-professional enter-tainer is associated with every jestbook represented in this edition. For that reason each selection is prefaced by a brief biographical note which tries to separate fact from fiction, former from performer. At the end of each note parenthetical references identify the copy text for each selection according to A. W. Pollard and G. R. Red-grave, *Short-Title Catalogue of Books Printed in England, Scotland, and Ireland . . . 1475–1640* (London: Quaritch, 1926), and Donald Wing, *Short-Title Catalogue of Books Printed in England, Scotland, and Ireland . . . 1641–1700* (New York: Columbia University Press, 1945). Addi-tional information may be found in summary articles by Margaret Schlauch and Charles C. Mish in *Studies in Short Fiction*, III (1966), 404–411; VI (1969), 259–270. Some jestbooks that might have been represented have been omitted because they are available in modern editions such as E. A. Horsman, ed., *Dobson's Dry Bobs* (New York: Oxford University Press, 1955) or M. E. Lawlis, ed., *Elizabethan Prose Fiction* (New York: Odyssey Press, 1967).

The texts represented here are based on books at the Huntington

Library, except *Nest of Ninnies* (Folger Library) and Chamberlain's *Conceits* (Houghton Library). The *Nest of Ninnies* and the books about Peters and Hind are given in their entirety; the others are represented by about a quarter of their total texts, with the jests numbered to show their relative positions in the original. Brackets indicate emendations and, in *Nest of Ninnies*, insertions. All the texts have been modernized in typography, paragraphing, and use of quotation marks, but the original capitalization is generally retained. Spelling and punctuation are modernized also, according to the *Webster's New Collegiate Dictionary*, based on *Webster's New International Dictionary*, second edition. Glosses are added to define words not found in that dictionary or used in special senses. Ken Winebrenner helped with the glosses, Elisabeth Zall prepared the original copy texts. Others assisting included Anne Hyder, J. Kent Clark, George Mayhew, Gilbert McEwen, and J. M. Steadman, III.

P. M. ZALL

Selections from

ANTHONY COPLEY

WITS, FITS, AND FANCIES
(1614)

The biography of Anthony Copley is understandably hazy because of his activities as a secret agent for the King of Spain. Son of the leader of English recusants abroad, he entered the Spanish King's service in 1586 and returned secretly to England in 1590. Imprisoned as a secret agent, he had sufficient ties among powerful people (as a distant relative of Queen Elizabeth) to obtain release within two years, but he was thereafter watched closely by government counteragents who reported him to be "the most desperate youth that liveth," shooting at gentlemen, drawing daggers in church, and engaging in other nefarious pastimes. Yet he survived at liberty at least until 1607 when he left England for the English College of Rome and passed out of sight for good.

It is hard to say whether Wits, Fits, and Fancies was written as pastime or hack work. Copley wrote pamphlets and poems also, but nothing so successful as this jestbook. It is mostly a translation of Melchor de Santa Cruz's Floresta Española de Apotegmas, o Sententias Sabia y Graciosamente Dichas de Algunos Españoles (1574), totaling 1125 jests in the first edition of 1595 and 1100 in the second edition of 1614, which is the basis for the following text. Whoever prepared the second edition took the trouble to delete those jests that turned on Spanish puns (which Copley had explained) and also added several new English jests to complement those Copley himself had added to Santa Cruz's work. The large bulk of Wits, Fits, and Fancies remained unchanged, however, from the first to the second edition.

The book is divided into seven "parts," and these are subdivided according to social types, except for the seventh part which organizes the jests according to kind of word play. Plays on words, however, are interspersed throughout the book, for Copley's emphasis is on quibbles with words and sense, and he is concerned very little with establishing situation or character. His jests in general follow the strategy of his Spanish model, itself following the epigrammatic strategy of humanists like Erasmus and Thomas More. They are brief and to the point, often concluding with a "switch," or sudden surprise, and therefore seem modern.

(STC 5741)

23.

Henry the Third, King of France, the very same morning that he had murdered the Duke of Guise in Blois, coming to the old Queen, his Mother, with the news and asking her how she liked thereof, she answered, "It is well done, Son, if it be well done."

98.

A Gentleman came hungry home and called for dinner, and his man answered that it was but new stroken ten. "Tut," said the Gentleman, "tellest thou me of ten by the clock, being twelve by my stomach?"

106.

A virtuous Gentleman, seeing a malicious person look down on the ground and continue gazing thereon a good space, said, "Questionless, either some mischief is befallen yonder man or some good to some other body."

125.

One asking a Gentleman what he thought of one that was newly taken in adultery, he answered, "Taken tardy."

129.

One that had lain first with the mother and then afterward with the daughter, asked a Ruffian mate what that fact might resemble, who answered, "All one as if you should eat the hen first and the chicken after."

132.

A Gallant was brought before a merry Recorder of London for getting a maid with child, and the Recorder said, "It is a marvel, Master L., that you being a Gentleman of good quality, would venture to get a maid with child." The Gentleman answered, "Nay, rather were it a marvel if a maid had gotten me with child."

145.

Two companions went to a wenching-house and the Lass was not yet come according to appointment, whereupon one of them began in the meantime to conceit the old Vicaress of that hell, there present, which the other seeing said unto him, "Are you so hungry that you will eat up the halter before the hay come?"

187.

A Gallego[1] of Spain went to the wars and was shot with an arrow into the head. The Surgeon, searching the wound, said that he could not possibly live, for that the arrow had pierced his brain. The Gallego answered, "That cannot be, for I have no brain at all. Had I had brains I trow I had never come to the wars."

198.

A Soldier was a-telling how that in a battle in which he was, the enemy's Arrows were so infinite in the air that they darkened the Sun over them, whereunto another answered, "Then had you the odds, to fight with them in the shade."

211.

Two Travelers met together at an Inn, and a fat Capon was served up to their board. At dinner time, one asked the other whether he had a father living or no. He answered, no, and withal told him a long discourse how and where and how long since his father died. Meantime the other eat up all the best of the Capon, which the tale-teller at last perceiving, half angry, said unto him, "Now that you have heard the discourse of my father's death, I pray you tell me, have you also e'er a father living?" He answered, no. "Now, I pray you then, tell me," quoth the other, "how he died."

He very earnest at his victuals, briefly answered, "Suddenly, very suddenly."

213.

A Mastiff dog flew upon a passenger and he with the pike of his staff ran him into the guts and killed him. The owner of the dog hereupon commenced his action against the party, and the matter being brought to the upshot, the Judge asked him why he did not rather strike the dog with the wood end of the staff than with the

[1] *Gallego*] Galician; i.e., from the provinces.

pike. He answered, "And like your Honor, he flew at me with his teeth, not with his tail."

220.

One traveling on a frosty morning through a country village, was set upon by a Mastiff. He, stooping for a stone to throw at him and feeling it hard frozen to the earth, said, "A pox on the country where the stones are tied and dogs let loose."

222.

A Traveler affirming that he saw a Colewort so monstrous huge that five hundred men on horseback might stand in her shade, another answered, "And I for my part did once see a Cauldron so wide that three hundred men wrought therein, every one distant twenty yards from other." Then the Colewort liar asked him to what use the Cauldron was made. He answered, "To seethe your Colewort in."

232.

A Ship sailing toward Peru, a mighty storm arose and endangered it, whereupon the Captain charged every man to throw into the sea the heaviest thing he could best spare, to the end to lighten somewhat the ship. A passenger that had his wife there, offered then to throw her overboard, but the company rescued her. And being asked what he ailed so to do, he answered, "She is the heaviest thing I have, and I can best spare her."

282.

Pope Adrian the Sixth was minded to have thrown Pasquin's Image[2] into Tiber, thereby to take away all occasion of libelling, which was then used in Rome in the person of that Image; whereunto the Duke of Sesa answered, "If your Holiness throw Pasquin into Tiber, out of doubt he will turn to a Frog, and then will he croak both day and night, whereas now his clamor is but only in the daytime."

[2] *Pasquin's Image*] In sixteenth-century Rome, this ancient statue was traditionally pasted over with satirical poems.

331.

A Friar following a many Gentlewomen in the street who with their long trains raised up a great dust after them—at last they, seeing the Friar near behind them, for reverence stood still and made him way—who as he passed along by them said, "Know ye, Gentlewomen, that the dust of the sheep is a lodestar to the Wolf."

335.

It was a great controversy in the University of Leyden between the Physic and Law Doctors whether of them should take place foremost at the Commencements; and a merry Chancellor, being deputed Judge of the difference, asked them whether at an execution the felon or the hangman ought to go foremost to the gallows. They all answered, the felon. "Even so," replied the Chancellor. "Then, ye Lawyers, go ye foremost as thieves, and ye Physicians, follow ye after as hangmen."

360.

A Scholar presented a gratulatory New Year[3] unto Sir Thomas More in prose, and he reading it and seeing how barren and senseless it was, asked him whether he could turn it into verse. He answered, yes. With that Sir Thomas More delivered it him again so to alter, who, within a two days after, came and brought it him all in verse—which Sir Thomas More reading and noting the rhyme said, "Aye, marry, now is here rhyme, I see, whereas before was neither rhyme nor reason."

371.

One used to say that a fool and a dancer differ but in this, that a fool is a fool all his life and a dancer but whiles he danceth.

377.

A Gentleman that played very well upon the Bandore[4] and had but a bad voice, played and sung in an Evening under his Mistress's

[3] *gratulatory New Year*] New Year's greeting.
[4] *Bandore*] an instrument like a bass guitar.

window, and when he had done, asked her how she liked his music. She answered, "You have played very well, and you have sung too."

394.

A Physician riding over Shooters Hill in Kent was afraid of Thieves, and by chance saw afar off a troop of people afore him, whereupon he bid his man ride toward them to discover what they were. Meantime, he hid himself close behind a bush. The fellow, coming unto them, understood that they conducted a murderer to execution, whereupon (being a mad knave) he straight set spurs to the Horse and galloped back again amain toward his master, still beckoning unto him all the way as he posted, to be gone and shift for himself—which the Doctor perceiving, away he flings back again towards London, as though he had had a devil at his tail. And being alighted at his Inn, he there attended his man's coming—who, eftsoons arrived, all panting and blowing, said unto him, "Happy you, master, that are so well escaped. Gog's nouns,[5] he to be hanged for killing only one man! What would they have done with you, I trow, who have slain so many in your days!"

429.

A Portugal wonted to say that fine love consists only in talking, dancing, and feasting with fair Ladies—the rest Asses can do as well as men.

457.

A man had a shrewd wife, and he one day broke her head, the cure whereof cost him dear expense afterward; insomuch that his wife in regard thereof said on a time unto her Gossips, "Faith, my husband will not dare give me no more broken heads in haste, considering how dear he finds them in the cure."

Her husband, hearing of such her braves,[6] sent the next day for the Surgeons and Apothecaries, and in her presence paid them all their bills and gave each of them twenty shillings over and above, saying, "Hold this, Sirs, against the next time."

[5] *Gog's nouns*] God's wounds, an expletive.
[6] *braves*] boasts.

470.

One wonted to say, "If your wife bid you throw yourself out at a window, pray God that it be not far to the ground."

483.

A Gentleman, seeing a Gentlewoman garter her stocking in the street, said, "Gentlewoman, you have a good leg."

"Sir," said she, "I have two."

Then said he, "Be they twins?"

"Not so," said she, "for there was a man borne between."

498.

A notable lewd Gentleman saying to a Gentlewoman that he loved her as his soul, she answered, "I had rather you said you loved me as your body."

529.

A Countryman came to ask for a Gentleman in a place where were many other Gentlemen besides, and it was his chance to ask the Gentleman himself, who answered, "My good friend, he that you ask for was hanged many a day ago."

"And wherefore, I pray you, Sir?" replied the stranger.

"Marry," he answered, "for a robbery."

"A robbery!" quoth the stranger. "O, the ungracious man, was he not content to be a cuckold all his life, but he would also prove himself a thief in the end?"

567.

Two Gentlemen came to break their fast in a Tavern, and a Bagpiper stood piping at the door. At last in came one and set them down a couple of eggs, whereat one of the Gentlemen excepted, and said, "Hath all this cackling been but for these two poor eggs?"

589.

In the North of Ireland, where they eat but Oaten-cake bread, there was a Kern's mother, hearing that her son was slain in fight against the Englishmen, came the morrow after into the field, and finding her dead son there, after much moan and lamentation over him, she chanced to cast her eye aside and thereby espied a dead Englishman. Then up she rose and, much accursing our nation for the death of her son, in the end she stripped him of his apparel and chanced to find a stale loaf of bread in his breeches—which was of the provision he brought with him from the English pale—which after she had a good while well viewed and wondered at, in the end burst forth into fresh tears and said, "No marvel though[7] my dear son be slain by one that voids so hard and huge a turd!"

714.

One asked a Painter how it chanced he drew so fair pictures and begot so foul children. He answered, "I paint by day and beget children by night."

821.

A Countryman lent his neighbor an Ass, and he neglected to return him home at the day appointed, so as the party was fain to go fetch him himself—who, when he came, the other denied that the Ass was yet come home, and made many flim-flam excuses to detain him a while longer. In the meantime the Ass brayed in the stable, whereby his master knew that there he was, who then waxed very angry with his neighbor for so abusing him; whereunto the other in a rage answered, "Gog's nails, neighbor, will you believe your Ass before me?"

837.

A Countryman was lopping off a tree, and down he fell and broke his neck. The clown his man straight ran home and told his dame of it. And telling her a long tale, both how he advised him to stand fast and how dangerously he stood upon the tree, and how he fell down with the Axe in his hand, at last he concluded, "And I assure you, Dame, it was a fair Grace of God that he cut not himself with the Axe."

7 *though*] if.

839.

A Country maid coming to market, her mare stumbled in the market place and down she fell over and over, showing all that ever God sent her, and then at rising up again, she turned her round about unto the people and said, "Sirs, did you ever see the like before?"

848.

A Countryman standing at a mark, an arrow lighted on his nose and spitted it through. At last the Archer coming to the mark to take up his arrow, the swain met him with it in his hand and asked him whether it were his arrow. "Yea," he answered. "Where had ye it?"

"Marry, see here," replied the swain pointing to his nose. "You have made me a proper nose, so you have. Indeed if you serve me so anymore, I'll break your arrow."

852.

A Countryman passing through a street in London stumbled and his tail fell to the ground. A 'Prentice, seeing it, fell a-laughing and said, "See, see, fellow how fine London is? It brooks no such swains as you."

With that, the Countryman turned back and answered, "As fine as it is, it hath kissed my tail for this once."

862.

A Smith had slain one and was to be condemned for the fact. Then his Parishioners came in and besought the Judge to spare him, affirming that they had no more smiths but him, nor any one near them of many a mile. They further alleged that besides he was a good Farrier, he could also make locks and keys and all manner of Ironage belonging either to cart or plow. Whereunto the Judge answered, "My masters, I have heard your allegations, but on the other side, a man is slain and how shall Justice then be performed?"

They replied, "Marry, and like your Lordship, we have here a couple of Weavers amongst us, and one of them will serve our turns well enough. We pray you therefore hang the other Weaver and save the Smith."

878.

One did a robbery in one shire and was taken in another and, being brought before the Justice there, the Justice thought good to return him back again to the other shire where he committed the robbery; whereupon the thief said unto him, "I pray, sir, if that be the Law let me ask you one question: How if a man be taken abed tonight with his neighbor's wife, ought he to be sent thither again the next night too?"

937.

One used an improper term to a Falconer, saying that his Hawk dunged. The Falconer told him that he should have said Muted. Anon after, this fellow stumbled and fell into a Cow-shard, and the Falconer asking him how he came so berayed,[8] he answered, "In a Cow mute."

978.

A Doctor of physic advised a great Drunkard that had but one eye to beware of wine, lest he lost the other. He answered, "Nay, better destroy a window than a whole house."

979.

One advised a great Drunkard still to mingle water with his wine. He answered, "If that were good, God would have done it in the Grape."

1007.

A poor man's eye was stroken out with a stone, and it hung only by a little string. Going presently to a Surgeon to have it put in again, he, while the Surgeon was busy about his preparatives and trinkets, said unto him, "How think you, I pray, shall I lose my eye?"

[8] *berayed*] dirtied.

"No," answered the Surgeon, "for, behold, I have it here in my hand."

1047.

One that had a white head and a black beard, another asked him how it came to pass. He answered, "Marry, the hair of my head is twenty years older than my beard."

1096.

A Spanish Earl was a great swearer, and hunting one day in a Forest and having lost his company, ranging up and down in the dark, chanced to fall horse and man into a very deep Mine pit where he remained all that night, not forgetting in the meantime to bethink himself of a many good thoughts. And namely, among the rest, he was right penitent of his sin in swearing, vowing that if it pleased God to deliver him out of that pickle, he would never while he lived swear more.

By chance his Spaniel being with him when he fell, was so kind as he would not depart from the place but there remained bawling and howling all the while, till at last certain Passengers traveling that way the next morning and overhearing the Dog's piteous clamor, made to the place and there looking down into the pit espied the Earl, and then with such tackles as they had about them drew him up and set him on firm ground. Then he looking down into the hole to see how deeply he had fallen, and seeing it very deep, rapped out a legion of huge oaths, saying, "Gog's nouns and his passion, is this a fit place for a Nobleman to fall into?"

ROBERT ARMIN

A NEST OF NINNIES
(1608)

This is the third edition of Robert Armin's Foole Upon Foole *but with enough major structural differences to constitute a new book. The first edition of* Foole Upon Foole *appeared in 1600 and the second, with minor verbal changes, in 1605. Both editions consisted of six discrete jest biographies introduced by rhymed descriptions. A* Nest of Ninnies *(1608) retains the biographies and rhymes but adds a framing dialogue between Sotto, the Puritan philosopher, and the World, represented as a lusty wench in search of excitement. The dramatic frame ties the biographies together and adds a satiric dimension as Sotto imposes his absurd allegories on the various jests.*

Armin (1568–1614) was a goldsmith turned pamphleteer and actor. He joined Shakespeare's company about 1600 as a replacement for Will Kempe. Kempe's clowning had been in the tradition of Richard Tarlton and earlier British clowns, emphasizing boorishness and abuse of language such as we see in Dogberry and Costard. Armin introduced a different style, emphasizing the wit and polish that we see in Touchstone and Feste. In view of Armin's interests it is easy to see Foole Upon Foole *as an attempt to analyze the styles of six different kinds of comic characters, an analysis preparatory to developing his own style.* Nest of Ninnies, *however, transcends this level of comic case-book to become a prose satire. The text below incorporates phrases from* Foole Upon Foole *that help to clarify the narrative. These phrases are indicated by brackets. Editorial emendations in this section are therefore indicated by footnotes. The subtitles are also from* Foole Upon Foole.

(STC 775)

To the youthful and rightly compleat in all good gifts and graces, the generous Gentlemen of Oxenford, Cambridge, and the Inns of Court, *Robert Armin* greeting:

> You first-born brothers of the highest skies,
> Twins of best *Jove* by blest *Memoria*,
> From whom our glories and our livings rise,
> Brothers and sons to him that brings the day
> (Phoebus) whom none can see but by your eyes,
> You only and you ever I shall pray
> (And praising ever) that your Sunny shine
> May beautify our GLOBE in every line.

But what higher strain am I in when yourselves have set my tongue lower?

Most liberal and well affected, I am brazed by your favors and made bold in your ostended[1] courtesies. I have seen you both ways as the Hare that squints on either side—marry, to look foreright[2] I cannot because judgment outlooks me. But as the Philosopher squeaned[3] at his curst wife in some fear because of quiet, so I fearful presume not to look into the millstone lest I gravel my eyesight. I have seen the stars at midnight in your societies and might have Commenced like an Ass as I was, but I lacked liberty in that. Yet I was admitted in Oxford to be of Christ's Church while they of All Souls gave aim[4] (such as knew me remember my meaning). I promised them to prove mad, and I think I am so, else I would not meddle with Folly so deeply, but *similis similem*,[5] etc. If I do offend, as I make no question, my Pardon is signed, I doubt not. Marry, there is an Execution yet behind, and I long till I pass my plunge— that is, Censure. They say he goes in colors as one strangely affected, and I go in Motley making my own cloak-bag ready.[6] If he prove porter and bear with me, I shall rest beholding. If not, I am his Martyr and suffer extremely.

I have, Gentlemen, in this book gone through Ireland. If I do stick in the bogs, help me out, not with your Skeen[7] head me—that's the way to spoil all—but with your goad prick me on to the true tract. And you of our Inns of Court, nimble-brained brands that burn without smoking, I challenge of you neighborly nearness and therefore dare say *sumus in toto*.[8] If you should fly out like rank riders, or rebel like the Irish, 'twere much because my presumption

---

[1] *ostended*] evident.
[2] *foreright*] forward.
[3] *squeaned*] squinted.
[4] *gave aim*] encouraged.
[5] *similis similem*] like attracts like.
[6] *They say . . . ready*] Censure wears a coat of many colors, suited to his wayward notions, but the narrator's is of motley. Motley, like tweed, was a rough cloth also of mixed colors but from the threads rather than the patterns of material. It was also used to make cloak bags. See Leslie Hotson, *Shakespeare's Motley* (New York: Oxford University Press, 1952), p. 10.
[7] *Skeen*] a possible triple pun, since the word could refer to a dagger, a sharp glance, and a pad on which a vessel rests when it is carried on the head.
[8] *sumus in toto*] we're all one.

challenges better being in you. But since all is one, and one all that's cared for, singleness hath such regard, I make a question which, if you easily answer, I am satisfied, otherwise buried quick. However, my love loses not his labor—an University fire in the Winter and a Temple pot may warm good liquor in which you may drink to me and I'll pledge you. I may live to make you amends; if not, no more but this—such a one died in your debt, and that's a Countertenor many a one sings. *Vale.* As for *vide* and *vici,* let Caesar at his next arrive so salute you.

Yours ever affected,
ROBERT ARMIN

Introduction

The World wanton sick,[9] as one surfeiting on sin (in morning pleasures, noon banquets, after riots, night's moriscoes,[10] midnight's modicums, and abundance of trash tricked up to all turbulent revelings), is now leaning on her elbow, devising what Doctor may deliver her, what Physic may free her, and what antidotes may antisepate[11] so dangerous a Dilemma. She now begins to grow bucksome as a lightning before death, and gad she will. Riches, her chamberlain, could not keep her in; Beauty, her bedfellow, was bold to persuade her; and sleepy Security, mother of all mischief—tut, her prayers was but mere prattle. Out she would, tucks up her trinkets like a Dutch Tannakin[12] sliding to market on the ice, and away she flings.

And whither, think you? Not to the Law, that was too loud; not to the Church, that was too proud; not to the Court, that was too stately; nor to the City, she was there lately; nor to the Camp, that was too keen; no, nor to the Country where seldom seen—she deigns her a friendly eye. But, of all, into a Philosopher's cell, who, because he was always poking at Fortune with his forefinger,

---

[9] *wanton sick*] i.e., sick from overindulgence.
[10] *moriscoes*] morris dance.
[11] *antisepate*] make antiseptic.
[12] *Tannakin*] girl.

the wise wittily named him Sotto—as one besotted, a grumbling sir, one that was wise enough and fond enough and sold all for a glass prospective because he would wisely see into all men but himself, a fault general in most, but such was his—who thus busied was took napping by the weal public, who smiles upon him with a wapper[13] eye, a jealous countenance, and bids him "All hale!"

"Mistress," says Sotto, "I will not say welcome, because you come ill to him that would be alone. But since you are come, look for such entertainment as my folly fits you with, that is, sharp sauce with bitter diet, no sweetness at all, for that were to mingle your pills with sugar. No, I am all one—Winter in the head and frost in the foot; no summer in me but in my smiles, and that as soon gone as smiles. The bauble I play with is men's estates, which I so tumble from hand to hand that, weary with it, I see (gluttingly and grievedly, yet mingled with smiles too) in my glass prospective what shall become of it."

The World, curling her locks with her fingers and anon scratching her brain with her itching pin, as one little regarding, answers, "What then?"

"Marry," says Hodge,[14] "I'll show thee. See, World, in whose bosom ever hath abundance been poured, what thy imps of impiety be, for are they all, for the most part, as these which I will present to thee in my glass prospective. Mark them well, and see what thou breedest in thy wantonness—six Children like thee, not the Father that begat them.

"Where were they nursed? In folly. Fed with the flotten[15] milk of nicety and wantonness, curdled in thy womb of water and blood, unseasoned, because thy mother-bearing temper was ever untrue, far from the relish of right breed. And it is hard that the taste of one Apple should distaste the whole lump of this diffused Chaos. But mark me and my glass. See into some (and in them thyself) whom I have descried or described these six parts of folly in thee. Thou shalt see them as clear as day, how mysty thy clouds be and what rankness rains from them."

13 *wapper*] bleared.
14 *Hodge*] i.e., Sotto.
15 *flotten*] skim.

The World, queasy-stomached as one fed with the earth's nectar and delicates, with the remembrance of her own appetite, squinnies at this and looks as one scorning yet beholding what will follow; at length espies a tall black man, jeering like himself, a fool in motley, muckender[16] hung, ever and anon wipes his nose, at whose girdle hanged a small blackjack of a quirt, his usual draft, his finger on his tongue as if he blamed Nature that cut not the strings of it in more large manner. But, hindered by defect, he still did guess at wisdom though seldom attaining it. Well, he was gouty, big, post-legged, and of years something many, as in the right sequel followeth:

> This Fool was tall, his face small,
> His beard was big and black,
> His neck was short, inclined to sport,
> Was this our dapper Jack;
> Of nature cursed, yet not the worst,
> Was nasty, given to swear,
> Toilsome ever, his endeavor
> Was delight in Beer.
> Gouty great, of conceit
> Apt and full of favor,
> Cursed yet kind, and inclined
> To spare the wise man's labor;
> Known to many, loved of any
> Cause his trust was truth,
> Seen in toys, apt to joys,
> To please with tricks of youth;
> Writh'd i'th knees, yet who sees
> Faults that hidden be?
> Calf great, in whose conceit
> Lay much game and glee;
> Big i'th small, ankle all,
> Footed broad and long,
> In Motley coats goes Jack Oates
> Of whom I sing this song.

The World, ready to disgorge at so homely a present, asked if it were possible such breathed hers to command. "O," saith our Philosophical Hodge, "hear his jests and what an unknown habit lives in him, then return judgment. Mark our application."

[16] *muckender*] bandanna, handkerchief.

How Jack Oates played at Cards all alone

Jack Oates, sitting at Cards all alone, was dealing to himself at Videruff[17] (for that was the game he joyed in) and as he spied a Knave, "Ah, knave, art there?" quoth he. When he spied a King, "King, by your leave," quoth he. If he spied a Queen, "Queen, Richard art come," quoth he and would kneel down and bid God bless her Majesty (meaning indeed the then Queen, whom he heard Sir William Hollis, his Master, so much to pray for). But here is the Jest:

Jack, as I say, being at Cards all alone, spying a Knave and saying, "Ah, Knave, art there?" a simple Servingman being in the Hall waiting his master's coming, walking by and hearing him say so, thought he had called him Knave—took the matter in dudgeon and miscalled the Fool. Another Servingman, more foolish than both, took Jack's part, so that in short time they two fell together by the ears, who, being parted, Jack Oates gives them each one a hand and so takes them into the Buttery to drink.

The Knight comes in, seeing the Hall not yet quiet, asked the matter. Jack comes. "I'll tell thee, Willy," quoth he. "As I was a-playing at Cards, one seeing I won all I played for, would needs have the Knave from me—which as very a Knave as he seeing, would needs bear him Knave for company. So to bid them both welcome to thy house, I have been to entreat the Knave thy Butler to make them drink."

"Aye," says Sir William, "and you like a knave made them fall out."

"Aye," answered Jack, "and your drink, Sir Knave, made them friends."

Sir William laughing departed.

How Jack hit a Nobleman a box on the ear

News came to Sir William that such a Nobleman was coming to his house. Great provision was made for his welcome, and amongst

---

[17] *Videruff*] i.e., Vie the Ruff, or bet the trump, the ancestor of modern bridge.

all, Jack Oates put on his new Motley coat, clean Muckender, and his new shoes. Much preparation was made which were too long to tell, for I'll assure ye it was one of the greatest Earls in England, unfit to name here. But the Knight and his Lady met him at the gate to entertain him.

Sir William with a low congé saluted him. The good Lady, as is the Courtly custom, was kissed of this Nobleman. Jack Oates, seeing him kiss his Lady, on the sudden gives the Earl a sound box on the ear. "Knave," quoth he, "kiss Sir Willy's wife?"

The good Knight, amazed at this, caused him to be whipped, but the kind Nobleman, knowing simplicity the ground of his error, would not suffer it, but putting it up, left him and entered the house.

Jack, seeing they were sad and he had done amiss, had this wit in simplicity to shadow it: He comes after and asked the Earl where his hand was. "Here," quoth he. With that, he shakes him by it and says, "I mistook it before, knowing not your ear from your hand, being so like one another."

Jack thought he had mended the matter, but now he was whipped indeed and had his payment altogether. Thus fools thinking to be wise become flat foolish. But all is one, Jack never repented him.

How a Minstrel became a fool artificial and had Jack Oates his reward for his labor

At a Christmas time, when great logs furnish the Hall fire, when Brawn is in season, and indeed all Reveling is regarded, this gallant knight kept open house for all comers, where beef, beer, and bread was no niggard. Amongst all the pleasures provided, a Noise of Minstrels and a Lincolnshire Bagpipe was prepared—the Minstrels for the great Chamber, the Bagpipe for the Hall—the Minstrels to serve up the Knight's meat and the Bagpipe for the common dancing. Jack could not endure to be in the common Hall, for indeed the fool was a little proudly minded, and therefore was altogether in the great Chamber at my Lady's or Sir William's elbow.

One time being very melancholy, the Knight to rouse him up

said, "Hence, fool, I'll have another fool. Thou shalt dwell no longer with me."

Jack to this answered little, though indeed ye could not anger him worse. A Gentleman at the board answers, "If it please you, sir, I'll bring ye another fool soon."

"I pray ye do," quoth the Knight, "and he shall be welcome."

Jack fell a-crying and departed mad and angry down into the great Hall, and, being strong armed (as before I described him), caught the Bagpipes from the Piper, knocked them about his pate that he laid the fellow for dead on the ground, and all broken carries the pipes up into the great Chamber and lays them on the fire.

The Knight knowing by Jack that something was amiss, sends down to see. News of this jest came. The Knight angry (but to no purpose, for he loved the fool above all, and that the household knew, else Jack had paid for it, for the common people's dancing was spoiled) sent down Jack and bade him out of his sight. Jack cries, "Hang, Sir Willy, hang, Sir Willy," and departs.

Sir William, not knowing how to amend the matter, caused the Piper to be carried to bed, who was very ill, and said, "I would now give a gold noble for a fool indeed to anger him thoroughly."

One of the Minstrels whispers a Gentleman in the ear and said if it pleased him he would—whereat the Gentleman laughed. The Knight demanded the reason of his laughing: "I pray you tell me," quoth he, "for laughing could never come in a better time. The fool hath madded me."

"If it please you," says the Gentleman, "here is a good fellow will go and attire him in one of his coats and can in all points behave himself naturally like such a one."

"It is good," says the Knight, "and I prithee, good fellow, about it. And one go call Jack Oates hither that we may hold him with talk in the meantime."

The simple Minstrel, thinking to work wonders, as one overjoyed at the good opportunity, threw his Fiddle one way, his stick another, and his case the third way, and was in such a case of joy that it was no boot to bid him make haste. But, proud of the Knight's favor, away he flings as if he went to take possession of some great Lordship. But whate'er he got by it, I am sure his Fiddle with the fall fell in pieces, which grieved his master so that in love and pity he laughed till the water ran down his cheeks. Besides, this good Knight was like to keep a bad Christmas, for the Bagpipes and the Music went to wrack, the one burnt and the other broken.

In comes Jack Oates and, being merry, told the Knight and the rest that a Country wench in the Hall had eaten Garlic and there was seventeen men poisoned with kissing her—for it was his use to jest thus. By and by comes in a Messenger, one of the Knight's men, to tell him that such a Gentleman had sent his fool to dwell with him.

"He is welcome," says the Knight, "for I am weary of this fool. Go bid him come in. Jack, bid him welcome."

They all laughed to see Jack's color come and go, like a wise man ready to make a good end. "What say you to this?" says the Knight.

Not one word says Jack. They tinged with a knife at the bottom of a glass, as tolling the bell for the fool, who was speechless and would die (than which nothing could more anger him, but now the thought of the new-come Fool so much moved him that he was as dead as a doornail), standing on tip-toe looking toward the door to behold his arrival, that he would put his nose out of joint.

By and by enters my artificial Fool in his old clothes, making wry mouths, dancing, and looking asquint—who, when Jack beheld, suddenly he flew at him and so violently beat him that all the Table rose but could scarce get him off. Well, off he was at length. The Knight caused the broken ones to be by themselves. My poor Minstrel with a fall had his head broke to the skull against the ground, his face scratched; that which was worst of all, his left eye put out; and withal so sore bruised that he could neither stand nor go.

The Knight caused him to be laid with the Piper, who was also hurt in the like conflict—who lacked no good looking to, because they miscarried in the Knight's service. But ever after, Jack Oates could not endure to hear any talk of another Fool to be there, and the Knight durst not make such a motion. The Piper and the Minstrel being in bed together, one cried, O his back and face; the other, O his face and eye; the one cried, O his Pipe; the other, O his Fiddle. Good Music or broken consorts, they agree well together, but when they were well, they were contented for their pains. They had both money and the Knight's favor.

Here you have heard the difference 'twixt a flat fool natural and a flat fool artificial: one that did his kind and the other who foolishly followed his own mind, on which two is written this Rhyme:

> Natural Fools are prone to self-conceit;
> Fools artificial with their wits lay wait
> To make themselves Fools, liking the disguise
> To feed their own minds and the gazer's eyes;
> He that attempts danger and is free,
> Hurting himself, being well cannot see,
> Must with the Fiddler here wear the Fool's coats
> And bide his penance sign'd him by Jack Oates;
> All such, say I, that use flat Foolery
> Bear this, bear more—this flat Fool's company.

How Jack Oates eat up a Quince Pie, being of choice provided for Sir William

Jack Oates could never abide the Cook, by reason that he would scold him out of the Kitchen. Upon a time, he had a great charge from his Lady to make her a Quince Pie of purpose for Sir William's own eating, which the Cook endeavored to do and sent to Lincoln of purpose to the Apothecary's for choice Quinces. Jack, being at this charge given, thought to be even with the Cook and waited the time when this Pie was made.

It happened so the Cook could get no Quinces. My Lady (for it was the Knight's desire to have one) sent about to Boston and all the chief towns, but all in vain—the season served not; but rather than Sir William should be unfurnished, sent to Lincoln again to buy up many Quinces ready preserved at 'Pothecaries, which she had, though with great cost.

The Knight asking his Lady for his Pie, she told him with much ado she had prevailed, but with no little pains in seeking Quinces; for she was fain to buy them ready preserved and to make a virtue of necessity that way. Sir William, seeing it was so, said it should be as well eaten, and sent for his Friends, Gentlemen and others of no small account. There was other great cheer provided to furnish up this sumptuous Feast, and, as he invited them, he told them it was a Quince Pie which he would have eaten.

The day drew on and the Gentles were come and all was in a readiness, and still Jack forgot not the Pie but stood faintly sick and refused his meat. The Knight, sorry that his best dish failed him, made no small account of his welfare, asked him, "Jack," says he, "where lies thy pain?"

"In my mouth," says he (meaning indeed his mouth hung for the Quince Pie). A Barber was sent for from a Market town hard by, who searched his mouth and could find no cause of pain. But Sir William, thinking the Fool wanted wit to tell his grief (though not wit to play the thief), bade the Barber depart.

Asking Jack what he would eat, he said, "Nothing." What he would drink? He said, "Nothing"—which made Sir William doubt much of his health, refusing his liquor when it was usually his practice and the Knight joyed in it too. Asked him if he would [walk? He said, "No." If he would] lie down? Still answering, "No," but would stand by the Kitchen fire, the Knight, that knew he never came there but he did some exploit, forgetting that, led him by the hand (so much he made of him) and bade the Cook see he wanted nothing.

Jack, standing still, groaned and said if he died he would forgive all the world but the Cook. "Hang, Fool," says the Cook, "I care not for thee, die tomorrow if thou wilt" and so followed his business. They knocked to the Dresser,[18] and the dinner went up.

Jack had a sheep's eye in the Oven. Anon the second course came, the Pie was drawn, set by, and among other baked meats was to be sent up, but wanting Sugar, the Cook[19] stepped aside to the spicery to fetch it. And Jack, in the meantime, catcheth the Pie and claps it under his coat and so runs through the Hall into the Yard, where was a broad Moat. And as he ran, the hot Pie burned his belly. "Aye," says Jack, "are ye so hot, Sir Willy's Pie? I'll quench ye anon, Sir Willy's Pie," says he, and straight very subtilely[20] leaps into the Moat up to the armpits and there stood eating the Pie.

[18] *knocked to the Dresser*] signaled to the servants.
[19] *the Cook*] editorial insertion.
[20] *subtilely*] cunningly.

The Cook comes in, misses the Pie, withal misses Jack, cries out, "The Pie!" Sir William's Pie was gone, the Author of that feast was gone, and they all were undone. A hurly burly went through the house, and one comes and whispers the Lady with the news. She tells Sir William how Jack Oates had stolen the Pie. Jack was searched for and anon found in the Moat. It was told the Knight where the Fool was eating it. "Gentlemen," quoth he, "we are disfurnished of our feast, for Jack my Fool is in my Moat up to the armpits eating of the Pie." They laughed and ran to the windows to see the jest.

There they might see Jack eat, the Cook call, the people hallo, but to no purpose. Jack fed, and feeding greedily (more to anger the Cook than disappoint Sir William), ever as he burnt his mouth, with haste dipped the Pie in the water to cool it.

"O," says the Cook, "It is Sir William's own Pie, sirrah!"

"O," says Jack, "Hang thee and Sir Willy, too, I care not. It is mine now."

"Save Sir William some," says one. "Save my Lady some," says another. "By James, not a bit," says Jack, and ate up all—to the wonder of the beholders, who never knew him eat so much before but drink ten times more.

At length out comes Jack dropping dry and goes to get fire to dry him. The Knight and the rest all laughed agood at the jest, not knowing how to amend it. Sir William sends for the Cook, who came up with a sorrowful heart and, lamentably complaining, said it was the Knight's fault for placing him in the Kitchen, where he never was but he did like villainy. The Knight, not satisfied with the Cook's answer, presently discharges him of his service and sent him to live elsewhere. "Go," says he, "truss up your trinkets and be gone." The Cook, seeing no remedy, departed.

Jack, being dry, up he comes and, knowing he had offended, tells a jest (for it was his manner so to do) how a young man brake his codpiece point and let all be seen that God sent him, or such fooleries. But that was not enough, and to chide him was to make of things worse than 'twas, and to no purpose neither. Sir William demanded why he ate the Pie. "Because I had a stomach," says Jack.

"Would nought else serve, "says the Knight, "but my Pie?"

"No, Willy," says he. "Thou would not be angry then, and the Cook had not been turned away. But all is well. Thou art rich enough to buy more."

The Knight, perceiving the Fool's envy, sent for the Cook and did let him enjoy his place again. So all parties well pleased but the young big-bellied woman who, perchance, longed for this long-looked-for Pie—but if she did, though long-looked-for comes at last, yet they shoot short that aim to hit this mark, for Jack Oates had eaten the Pie and served himself.

This was a flat Fool, yet now and then a blind man may hit a Crow, and you know a fool's bolt is soon shot—out it goes, happen how it will. Had Jack kept his own counsel, the Cook had been still out of service, and had been revenged; but now being in his place again may live to cry quittance for the Quince Pie.

"These," quoth the World, "are pretty toys."

"Aye," quoth the Philosopher, "but mark the appliance: By Jack Oates is morally meant many described like him, though not Fools natural yet most artificial. They card hence what their Parents spin, and do such Apish tricks that rapine, ruin, and a thousand inconveniences follow. By the Knight is meant maintainers of Foolery; by the Hall, the Inn where cards of vanity causeth many to be bewitched—as appears in the servingmen who, busy in others' brawls, are as easily made friends as they were set together by the ears.

"By the second is meant reaching at Stars, aiming at honor, lighting sometime on the ear of memory but ill taken (because badly meant is rewarded with a deserved whipping). By the third is called to question most that musically fret their time out in idle baubling, and will become artificial Fools to outbrave Fools indeed, but stick often in their own quicksands and are got out with repentance. But the fourth and last shows the devouring of devotion's diet—however come by, yet they will stand up to the armpits in danger rather than to lack their wills, to slack or rebate the edge of their appetites."

With this, the World a little hummed and hey'd, said she was not pleased that such lived, and did promise some amendment, but

desired to see further. Now our Philosophical Poker poked on, and
pointed to a strange show—that flat Fool not so tall but this fat Fool
as low, whose description runs in meter thus:

> This Fat Fool was a Scot born, brought up
> In Sterling, twenty miles from Edinborough,
> Who being but young was for the King caught up,
> Serv'd this King's Father all his lifetime through;
> A yard high and a nail, no more his stature,
> Smooth fac'd, fair spoken, yet unkind by nature;
> Two yards in compass and a nail, I read,
> Was he at forty years, since when I heard not
> Nor of his life or death, and further heed
> Since I never read, I look not nor regard not;
> But what at that time Jemy Camber was,
> As I have heard I'll write and so let pass:
> His head was small, his hair long on the same,
> One ear was bigger than the other far;
> His forehead full, his eyes shined like a flame,
> His nose flat and his beard small, yet grew square;
> His lips but little, and his wit was less,
> But wide of mouth, few teeth I must confess;
> His middle thick, as I have said before,
> Indifferent thighs and knees, but very short;
> His legs be square, a foot long and no more,
> Whose very presence made the King much sport;
> And a pearl spoon he still wore in his cap,
> To eat his meat he lov'd and got by hap;
> A pretty little foot, but a big hand,
> On which he ever wore rings rich and good;
> Backward well made as any in that land,
> Though thick, and he did come of gentle blood;
> But of his wisdom ye shall quickly hear,
> How this Fat Fool was made on[21] everywhere.

The World, smiling at this Rhyme describing so unseemly a
portrait, gave leave to the rest and desired greatly to be satisfied
with something done, as one longing to know what so round-trussed
a lump could perform. The poking arts master tells his doing thus:

---

[21] *made on*] put on, tricked.

How Jemy Camber this Fat Fool, gave his Chain of Gold from his neck to warrant his life

When the King and Nobles of Scotland had welcomed Jemy Camber to the Court, who was their Countryman born in Sterling, but twenty miles from Edinburgh—this King's birth town as Greenwich was our late Queen's—they reasoned with him to understand his wit, which indeed was just none at all, yet merry and pleasing, whereat the King rejoiced and, seeing he was so fat, caused his Doctors and Physicians to minister to him.

But Physic could not alter nature, and he would never be but a Saint Vincent's Turnip, thick and round, wherefore the Doctors persuaded his grace that the purging of the Sea was good for him. Well, nothing was undone that might be done to make Jemy Camber a tall, little slender man when yet he looked like a Norfolk dumpling, thick and short. Well, to Leith was he sent, which is the harbor town of such ships as arrive at Edinburgh (nearer they cannot come) which is some miles from the city.

To sea they put in a ship, at whose departure they discharged Ordnance, as one that departed from the land with the King's favor. The Earl Huntly was sent with him to sea, to accompany him, so high he was esteemed with the King. He, hearing the Ordnance go off, would ask, "What they do now?"

"Marry," says the Earl, "they shoot at our enemies."

"O," says he, "hit, I pray God."

Again they discharge. "What they do now?" quoth he.

"Marry, now the enemy shoots at us."

"O miss, I pray God," says Jemy Camber.

So ever after, it was a jest in the Scottish Court, "'Hit or miss,' quoth Jemy Camber"—that if a maid had a Bairn and did penance at the Cross in the High Town of Edinburgh: "What hath she done? Did she hit or miss?"

"She hath hit," says the other.

"Better she had missed," says the first. And so, long time after, this Jest was in memory—yea, I have heard it myself, and some will talk of it at this day.

Well, to sea they put on a fair Sunshine day, where Jemy stood fearful of every calm billow, where it was no boot to bid him tell what the ship was made of, for he did it devoutly. But see the chance: A sudden flaw or gust rose, the wind held strong East and by West, and the ship was in great danger, insomuch as the Earl, Master, and all began to fear the weather. By and by, a stronger gale blew and split their main Mast and gave their ship a mighty leak, insomuch as the crack made them all screak out—which Jemy hearing was almost dead with fear. Some fell to pumping, others on their knees to praying. But the fat Fool seeing themselves in this danger thought there was no way but one with them, and was half dead with fear.

In the end, the wind turned and the raging of the Sea began to cease. "I warrant thee now," quoth the Master, "Jemy, we shall not be drowned."

"Aye, will ye warrant us?" says the Fool.

"Aye," says the Master, "I'll give thee my ship for thy Chain if we be drowned."

"Bear witness, my Lord," says he, "a plain bargain"—and with that threw the Master his Chain, who would have given it to the Earl, but joy of their escape made him delight in the Jest and therefore the Master enjoyed his bargain.

With much ado they attained thither again, where the King, fearful before, awaited their landing now, and seeing Jemy not a jot less of body than he was (only lightened of his Chain), "How now," quoth he, "how dost thou, man?"

"O," says Jemy, "well now, King, but ill had not the Master been—who warranted our lives for my Chain—the best bargain that ever I made, for no way could I have been a loser."

"How?" says the King.

"Marry, I'll tell thee, King," quoth he. "Say we had been drowned, his ship was forfeit to me for my Chain. Earl Huntly was a witness to the bargain. And now we are not drowned, for my chain did warrant our lives of the Master."

"Nay," says the Earl, "not our lives, none but yours, Jemy. Our lives were as safe unwarranted without a chain."

With this, the Fool had some feeling of sense and on a sudden cried out mainly for his Chain again, which was restored to him by the Master. But he lost nothing by that, for he attained to a suit, as the story says, that he had been three years about. Thus the King and Nobles went to Edinburgh merrily talking of their fear and welfare.

How Jemy Camber gave five French Crowns for a Salad of an atchison price, which in our money was three farthings

Jemy, this fat Fool, used every day to go from the Abbey in the Low Town up the hill into the City of Edinburgh, and one evening above the rest he met with a broken Virgin, one that had had a bairn (as there they are known by their attire, wearing a loose kerchief hanging down backward). She, I say, cried Salads as thus: "Buy any *Cibus Salletea*."

Jemy, desirous of Salads, calls her to him. "Lass," says he, "what shall I give thee for a good Salad?"

"Fair sir," says the Wench (for she knew him for the King's Fool and she could not please him better than to call him "fair sir"), "you must give me an atchison."

Now he having nothing but six French Crowns about him, "Canst thou change me a crown?" says he.

"Yea, sir," says she. He gives her a French Crown and she gave him a Salad for it, and she went her way.

Jemy thinks it was much to give a crown for that for which she did demand but an atchison—which in our money is but three farthings. He runs after and says she had his fairest crown—"But," says he, "give me that and take your choice of these"—thinking by that device to get the first Crown again.

"Will ye change?" says the lass.

"Aye," says the Fool. So she takes all the five and gives him one again and so, laughing at his folly, goes her way.

It was in vain to exclaim, for they will hold fast what they get. But my fat Fool goes home to eat his Salad and invites the King to a dear dish, and made him laugh heartily at the jest. The King calls for Vinegar to his Salad because his sweet meat should have sour sauce, and persuaded him it was well bought. Otherwise, if the Fool had repented his bargain, it was his manner to cry for his money again—yet with it, all the Court could not quiet him.

How Jemy this fat Fool sweat almost to death and never knew the reason

Betwixt Edinburgh Abbey, the King's place, and Leith there stands an even, plain, green Meadow in which the King used most of his sports, amongst which he rode thither one day to run at the Glove, or the Ring, as his Grace should please. With him rides Jemy Camber on a trotting mule. It was then a marvelous hot day. "O," says Jemy, "how cold the weather is" (so wise he was that he scarce knew hot from cold).

"No," says the King, "it is hot. Look how I sweat."

"No," says Jemy, "the Sun blows very cold."

"No," says the King, "the wind shines very hot."

The Fool was almost angry to be crossed and said he would be hanged at night if he did sweat that day. With this merry talk they rode on. But one of the King's Footmen, hearing this, told the King at their return he would make his Grace laugh heartily.

So the King very gallantly ran that time and never missed the Glove, and so did the Lords—which Jemy seeing said it was nothing to do. The King bade him run. He did so, but the Glove lay still, and Jemy could not do it. The King's Footman, that watched to do him a good turn, said, "Jemy could do it better blindfolded."

"What, can he?" quoth the King. "I will never believe it."

"You shall see else," quoth he. Whereat Jemy marveled much that without sight a man could do that which with all his might and sight he could not do, was desirous to make trial, so was blinded with a scarf, while another took up the Glove, and was ready for the jest.

Jemy runs. "Now for my Mistress!" says he. They all shout aloud and cry, "Rarely well done!" And one unblinds him, while another puts the Glove on the spear. So simple he was, that he thought it was strange and bragged all that day not a little.

The King did alight and went to drink wine at the Lord Hume's house, and Jemy went with him, while the Footman had time to work his will. And mingling a conceit[22] with butter (which I will not name lest someone should practice the like), clapped it under the saddle. And as they rode to Edinburgh, says the King, "What say you to the weather now, Jemy? Methinks it is hotter than it was."

"Nay, it is colder," says he, "for I begin to sweat."

The trotting of this Mule made the mingled confection lather so that it got into his breeches and wrought up to the crown of his head and to the sole of his foot, and so he sweat profoundly. Still he wiped and he wiped, sweating more and more. They laughed a-good to see him in that taking.

"Now you must be hanged," quoth the King, "as your bargain was, for you sweat very much."

"What remedy?" says he. "I am content to be hanged, but while I live after, I'll never believe cold weather will make one sweat."

"No more will I," says the King. "But hot weather will."

"Hot or cold," says Jemy, "I am warm now, I am sure. I would I were over head and ears in some river to cool me." So simple he was that he knew not whether it was the sun or the wind made him sweat. At night the King caused him to be washed and perfumed, yet he was scarce sweet twenty days after. Thus this fat Fool chafed, but not in his own grease.

How this fat Fool Jemy Camber ran with the King's best Footman for a wager and won it

Jemy, who was, as you have heard, a tall low man and was swift of foot, on a time challenged the King's best Footman for a

---

[22] *conceit*] concoction.

wager to run with him from the Abbey up the hill to Canongate (which stood entering to Edinburgh as Ludgate doth to London and the King's place about Temple Bar). The King, being told of this challenge, thought it would be good sport to see it performed, still persuaded Jemy to dare his Footman who before denied him and knew Fools would talk anything though far unfit to perform anything.

Still the King would say he was made nimble to run, and asked every Nobleman's judgment, who likewise soothed the King. It was so that they made him believe he was swift of foot that I think Jemy in the end persuaded himself that none but fat men could run well, and nimble men being light would fall soonest, considering that light things being of small substance, not feeling themselves, would surely fall. But here is the sport:

The Footman, seeing it was the King's pleasure to see the wager tried, dared him, which made Jemy mad, that he would run with him from Edinburgh to Berwick (which was forty miles) in one day, a thing as unpossible as to pull down a Church in one hour and to build it again in another: For Jemy was lost in the King's company once of purpose but five miles from the City, at the Earl Morton's castle at Dalkeith, and they thought he would never have come home again when the King heard every hour he was coming (and still as he entreated every passenger to let him ride—by the King's watch in the highway they had warning given to the contrary), for he was seven days going five mile. Then judge how long he would be a-running forty.

(You will muse how he did for meat all the time. I'll tell you. He fasted all day and went supperless to bed, but being in his first sound sleep, meat was brought and laid by him and a Choppin[23] of Wine—for so they call it there—which made him at his coming to court tell the King, heaven was gentler then. Earthly men would show him no favor, neither to ride nor feed him. When he was every night cast into a sound sleep, then when he waked, he was sure of meat from heaven to feed on—when the meat came from the King's kitchen at Edinburgh Abbey.)

But to go forward with our challenge: The King said the first

[23] *Choppin*] quart.

word should stand, and on Jemy's head he laid a thousand marks. The Lady Carmichell, that laughed to hear all this, wagered as much on the Footman's head. The day was appointed the next morning, being Thursday, to begin at five o'clock in the afternoon in the cool of the evening, and everyone to his race must make him ready. Jemy, as he had seen the King's Footmen do, washed his feet with Beer, and soaked them in Butter, so all that night and the next day there was nothing but Jemy and his provision to that great journey.

The time came. Jemy was stripped to his shirt, trussed round for the purpose. The Footman and he begins to run. The Footman makes show of great labor, and the Fool made the substance, for he was quickly in a sweat. They puffed and they blowed, they ran as swift as a pudding would creep. Jemy thought himself no small fool to outrun the Footman, and did in his mind assure himself to win. The King laughs to see the toil he made, and the Footman made great show and little pains.

By and by Jemy calls for drink, and the King, loathe he should have any harm with labor, caused him to have a mixed drink to cast him into a sleep—who, when he had drunk, as he ran on his wager he dropped down in the street as heavy as if a leaden plummet that makes a Jack turn the spit had fallen on the earth dab. There he slept, and was carried by command to the top of the hill and laid down again. There he slept half an hour, and when he waked he remembered his journey. Seeing people still about him, up he gets, away he jogs and never looks behind him—and seeing Canongate so near him, had not the wit to wonder how he came there, but laid hold on the ring of the gate and stayed to be seen.

By and by the Footman comes sweating, with water poured on his face and head. "O, my heart!" says he.

"O, my legs!" says Jemy. "I will not do so much for all Scotland again." Well, Jemy cries, "Victory, victory" and there was the King's Coach at hand to carry him home, for of himself he could never have gone had his life lain on it.

But when he came home, the brags he made, the glory he got, how he outran the Footman (and ran so easily as if he had been asleep) was wonderful. Aye, it was sport enough for the King a month after, to hear him tell it. Well, the King won the wager, he thought, and that was honor sufficient for him. Not three days after, he bade the King put away all his Footmen and he would serve his turn to any place. The King thanked him for his good will, and said when his need was great, he would make bold to use him. So Jemy this fat Fool ever bragged of this wager.

How this fat Fool Jemy was stung with nettles, and how after, unknown to himself, helped to make his own grave

There was a Laundress of the Town whose daughter used often to the Court, to bring home shirts and bands, which Jemy had long time loved and solicited, but to no end. She would not yield him an inch of her maidenhead. Now Jemy vowed he would have it all. Well, she consented at last and, to be short, soon at night at nine o'clock, being in the winter, when she knew her mother to be gone to watch with a sick body, he should come and all that night lie with her. Jemy, though witless, wanted no Knavish meaning in this, thought long till it was night. But in the afternoon this maid goes up to the castle and gathers a great basket of Nettles, and, coming home, strews them under the bed.

Night comes, nine o'clock strikes, Jemy on his horse comes riding forward, sets him up and knocks at the door. She lets him in and bids him, "Welcome, bonny man." To bed he goes—and Jemy ever used to lie naked, as is the use of a number, amongst which number she knew Jemy was one—who no sooner was in bed but she herself knocked at the door and herself asked who was there, which Jemy hearing was afraid of her mother.

"Alas, sir," says she, "creep under the bed—my mother comes." Jemy bustled not a little. Under he creeps, stark naked, where he was stung with nettles. Judge you that have feeling of such matters: There he lay turning this way and that way. Here he stung his leg, here his shoulder, there his buttocks. But the Maid, having locked the door to him, went to bed and there lay he in durance (as they say) till morning.

When the day broke, up gets the Maid, to Court she goes and tells the King's Chamberlain of the matter, and he told the King, who laughed thereat right heartily. The Chamberlain was sent to see him there, who when he came found him fast asleep under the bed stark naked, bathing in nettles, whose skin, when he wakened him, was all blistered grievously. The King's Chamberlain bid him arise and come to the King. "I will not," quoth he. "I will go make my grave."

See how things chanced: He spake truer than he was aware, for the Chamberlain, going home without him, told the King his answer. Jemy rose, made him ready, takes his horse and rides to the Churchyard in the High Town where he found the Sexton (as the custom is there) making nine graves—three for men, three for women, and three for children, and whoso dies next, first comes first served. "Lend me thy spade," says Jemy, and with that digs a hole, which hole he bids him make for his grave, and doth give him a French Crown. The man, willing to please him (more for his gold than his pleasure), did so, and the Fool gets upon his horse and rides to a Gentleman of the town, and on the sudden, within two hours after, died—of whom the Sexton telling, he was buried there indeed.

Thus you see fools have a guess at wit sometimes, and the wisest could have done no more nor so much. But thus this fat Fool fills a lean grave with his carcass, upon which grave the King caused a stone of Marble to be put, on which the Poets writ these lines in remembrance of him:

> He that gard all men till jeare,[24]
> Jemy a Camber he ligges here:
> Pray for his sale, for he is geane,
> And here a ligges beneath this steane.

"Is this possible," says the World, "that I should be so served?"

"Nay, thou art worse served hereafter," says he, "for thou knowest not the following scene—but attend it:

"By the Fool is meant all fatness; by the King, nature that

---

[24] *He . . . jeare*] He that caused all men to jeer.

nursed him; by the Nobles, such as soothe him; and by the Ship, thee, in which so many dangers are floating through the sense of sin. And so, if life were a-warranted, Fools—fat ones, rich ones—would give the Chain of their souls that is linked to salvation only to inherit this earth in thy company—when earth, though it be heaven to hell by reason of the pains, yet the comparison averts, it is hell to heaven in respect of pleasures.

"By the second is meant the surfeits of soul and body that Fools buy with their gold, not sparing any price to please appetite, though the edge of it slice from the bosom of good old Abraham, very heaven itself. By the third, how the fat Fools of this age will grunt and sweat under this massy burden, and purge to the crown from the foot, though their brain perish through the prevailing practice of busy endeavor. The Mule morally signifies the Devil, upon whose trot their fatness takes ease and rides a-gallop to destruction.

"By the fourth tale is prefigured the presumption of greatness, who are willing to outrun speed itself through greedy desire. In this is shown how flattery feeds them, placing before them, as in a sleep, work and wonder when, to say sooth, all is not worth the wonder. Their desire is more than ability to perform, and their practice above all, yet the nimble overshoot them in act, leaving them a quickness in will.

"In the fifth, answer is made to the fourth when often such forward deeds meet with backward lurches, and they are stung with their own follies, nettling very lust with shame and disgrace. It signifies Adultery in fat ones who (above their own), whoring after strange Gods, make their Religion ride hackney to hell. And when shame takes them from the horse, they make their own graves and are buried in their own shame, with this Motto above written:

> Fat fools gather to their woe
> Sorrow, shame, and care;
> Here they lie that galloped so,
> In Death's engraved snare."

This moral motion gave the World such a buffet that she scringed her face as though she were pinched home; yet seeing no remedy but that the flat and fat Fools should draw in her Coach together, she sits in the boot and rides on. The Critic reacheth his glass to her view and presents the third: O, this was an humorous Sir indeed—lean Leonard they call him—a Fool of strange and preposterous breeding, begat of envy and out of doubt his base Son. His description hath a strain of more wonder, long like a lath and of proportion little better—but give his report hearing.

> Curled locks on idiot's head
> Yellow as the amber,
> Plays on thoughts as girls with beads
> When their mass they stamber;
> Thick of hearing yet thin eared,
> Long of neck and visage;
> Hooky-nosed and thick of beard,
> Sullen in his usage;
> Clutter-fisted,[25] long of arm,
> Body straight and slendered,
> Boistrous hipped, motley warm,
> Ever went lean Leonard;
> Gouty leg'd, footed long,
> Subtle in his folly,
> Showing right but apt to wrong,
> When a 'peared most holy;
> Understand him as he is,
> For his marks you cannot miss.

"You hear, Madam," says our Cynic, "how he is marked. If ye meet him in your pottage-dish, yet know him."

The World, though she loved not the description, yet she coveted his condition and began to woo his report—which, making no bones of the sweet youth, gave his doings thus:

How Leonard, a lean Fool, played at slide-groat[26] by himself after dinner, when his belly was full

In the merry Forest of Sherwood dwells a kind Gentleman whose name I omit, fearing I too much offend in meddling with his Fool. But I trust he will pardon me for sithence he is so well known thereabouts I think it not amiss to tell it at London, that people

[25] *Clutter-fisted*] clumsy-handed.
[26] *slide-groat*] push penny.

seeing the strange works of God in his differing creatures, we that
have perfect resemblance of God, both in sense and similitude, may
the better praise his name that we differ from them whose humors
we read, see, and hear are not so strange as true.

I say again, this Gentleman had a Fool, Leonard they call him,
lean of body, looking like envy, whose conditions agree with his
countenance. One time above all others, he locked himself into a
Parlor where all alone he played at slide-groat, as his manner was.
Pieces or counters he had none, yet casting his hand empty from
him, "Fly!" says he. "Short! with a vengeance!" Then "Play,"
says he to his fellow, when indeed there is none but himself.

But thus with supposes he plays alone, swaggers with his game
fellow, outswears him with a thousand oaths, challenges him the
field to answer him if he be a man, appoint the place and all, that,
if any not knowing his conditions should stand without and hear
him, would think two swaggerers were fighting in the room. To
his play again he falls, seven up for twelve pence, for that is his game
still. Well, they fall out, they go together by the ears, and such a
hurly-burly is in the room that passes—at the last the stools they
fly about, the Pots they walk, the glasses they go together, nay the
Prayer books they fly into the fire—that such a noise there was that
the whole house wondered at his folly.

Persuasions were to no purpose. Doors he would open none
till they violently broke them open, though they were of gold—and
so they did and entered the Parlor, found all this level-coil[27] and
his pate broken, his face scratched, and leg out of joint, as (a
number say to this hour) that he is a playfellow for the devil and
in game they cannot agree. But that is otherwise, for in the great
hall, at the Servingmen's request he will play by himself if they
will not play with him. And whoso plays with him, though they
play for nothing and with nothing, all is one they must fall out.
And if others be not by to part them, mischief may be done, for he
will lay it on, take it off who will—so that at his first coming he
endangered many and now "take heed" is a fair thing, for few will
come near him. Thus you may see fools that want wit to govern
themselves well have a wilful will to go forward in folly.

[27] *level-coil*] a rough, noisy game.

How this lean Fool Leonard, eating his belly full, was revenged of one that clapped cozier's[28] *wax to his head*

This lean, greedy Fool having a stomach and seeing the butler out of the way, his appetite was such as, loathe to tarry, breaks open the Dairy house, eats and spoils new cheese curds, cheesecakes, overthrows cream bowls, and having filled his belly and knew he had done evil, gets him gone to Mansfield in Sherwood, as one fearful to be at home.

The Maids came home that morning from milking and finding such a massacre of their Dairy, almost mad, thought a year's wages could not make amends. But "O, the Fool! lean Leonard," they cried, "he did this mischief!" They complained to their Master but to no purpose—Leonard was far enough off. Search was made for the Fool, but he was gone none knew whither. And it was his property, having done mischief, never to come home of himself. But if anyone entreated him, he would easily be won.

All this while, the Fool was at Mansfield in Sherwood and stood gaping at a shoemaker's stall, who not knowing him, asked him what he was. "Go look," says he. "I know not myself."

They asked him where he was born. "At my mother's back," says he.

"In what country?" quoth they.

"In the country," quoth he, "where God is a good man."

At last one of the three journeymen imagined he was not very wise and flouted him very merrily, asking him if he would have a stitch where there was a hole (meaning his mouth). "Aye," quoth the Fool, "if your nose be the needle."

The Shoemaker could have found in his heart to have took measure on his pate with a Last instead of his foot, but let him go as he was. A Country Plow-jogger being by, noting all this, secretly stole a piece of Shoemaker's wax off the stall, and coming behind him, clapped him on the head and asked him how he did. The Fool, seeing the pitch ball, pulled to have it off but could not but with much pain—in an envious spleen, smarting ripe, runs after him, falls at fisty cuffs with him.

[28] *cozier's*] shoemaker's.

But the fellow belabored the Fool cunningly, and got the Fool's head under his arm and bobbed his nose. The Fool, remembering how his head was, strikes it up and hits the fellow's mouth with the pitched place so that the hair of his head and the hair of the Clown's beard were glued together. The fellow cried, the Fool exclaimed, and could not suddenly part. In the end, the people, after much laughing at the Jest, let them part fair. The one went to pick his beard, the other his head.

The Constable came, asked the cause of their falling out, and knowing one to be Leonard the lean Fool whom he had a warrant from the Gentleman to search for, demands of the Fellow how it happened. The Fellow he could answer nothing but "um um," for his mouth was sealed up with wax. "Dost thou scorn to speak?" says he. "I am the King's Officer, knave."

"Um um," quoth he again, meaning he would tell him all when his mouth was clean. But the Constable, thinking he was mocked, clapped him in the stocks, where the fellow sat a long hour farming his mouth. And when he had done and might tell his grief, the Constable was gone to carry home Leonard to his Master, who, not at home, he was enforced to stay Supper time, where he told the Gentleman the Jest—who was very merry to hear the story, contented the Officer, and bade him to set the Fellow at liberty—who betimes in the morning was found fast asleep in the stocks. The fellow, knowing himself faulty, put up his wrongs, quickly departed, and went to work betimes that morning with a flea in his ear.

How Lean Leonard eat up his Master's Hawk and was almost choked with the Feathers

The Gentleman with whom this Leonard dwelt, having bought a goodly fair Hawk, brought her home, being not a little proud of his pennyworth, and at Supper to other Gentlemen fell a-praising of her who, smoothing up his humor, likewise, failed not to add a torch of fire to increase more flame, for indeed the Bird was worthy of commendations and therefore did merit praises.

Leonard, standing by with his finger in his mouth as it was his custom, often hearing them praise the goodness of the Hawk thought indeed they had meant for goodness being far better meat than a Turkey or a Swan, was very desirous to eat of the same; and unknown goes down and suddenly from the perch snatched the Hawk and, having wrung off her neck, begins to besiege that good morsel but with so good a courage that the feathers had almost choked him. But there lay my friend Leonard in a lamentable taking.

Well, the Hawk was missed and the deed was found. The Master was fetched and all men might see the Hawk, feathers and all, not very well digested. There was no boot to bid run for drams to drive down this undigested modicum. The Gentleman of the one side cried, "Hang the Fool!" The Fool on the other side cried not, but made signs that his Hawk was not so good as he did praise her for. And though the Gentleman loved his Hawk, yet he loved the Fool above, being enforced rather to laugh at his simplicity than to vex at his losses suddenly, being glad to make himself merry, jested on it ever after—upon whose Hawk a Gentleman of his very wisely writ these lines and gave unto his master:

> Fools feed without heed, unhappy be their feeding,
> Whose heed being in such speed, attempted without heeding;
> May they choke that provoke, appetite by pleasure,
> When they eat forbidden meat and feed so out of measure.

The Gentleman laughed at this rhyme, yet knew not whether was the more Fool, he for writing, the other for eating, or he for losing. Well, putting the Hare to the Goose-giblets,[29] seeing there was no remedy, made himself pastime, pleased himself, and did rest contented.

How the Lean Fool set fire on the Wheelbarrow that he loved so, unknown to himself

He that mischiefs many, sometimes wrongs himself—as harken to this Jest: Leonard of all things loved his Wheelbarrow, and

[29] *putting . . . Goose-giblets*] setting off one thing against another.

would work all day and carry dung in it, yet would sleep in it at night. He would set up meat for his belly in it. Aye, what did he without it? Once at a Christmas time, when the fire in the Hall was full, Leonard was sore a-cold. He got coals out of the Scullery and put them into his Barrow and set them on fire—and so sat him down to warm him, quite forgetting it was made of Wood and Wood would burn. So in the end, being warm, goes for a Jack of Beer, brings it, and sets it on the fire to warm, so that the inside melted and he drank the drink notwithstanding.

But on a sudden, he seeing the Wheelbarrow flame that he so loved, aloud he cries, "O me, O me, O me," and takes it up flaming and trundles it into the Hall among the people to show. The young men and maids tumbled over one another for fear. Some had their faces burned, others their legs. The maids their smocks, yea, one set fire on another for their Aprons burned, and, being many people, the flame increased rather than decreased.

Leonard, seeing none would help him, runs (for fear lest the Gentleman should know it) and thrusts it into the Barn to hide it—which some seeing runs after. And had they not come at that time the Hay and Straw had been all burnt, for it was already of a light fire. But being quenched out, all was well. Such is the envy of Fools who, seeing none would help him, thought to do them mischief—which he did, but not much.

The World laughing a-good at these jests, though to say sooth she could hardly afford it, for fear of writhing her sweet savor,[30] yet straining courtesy in this kind, did as our wantons do at a feast—spare for manners in company, but alone, cram most greedily. So she, forgetting modesty, gaped out a laughter and, like women hardly won, cried, "More, more!"

The currish Critic said she should, and gave her the third penn' orth of the moral, and said, "You laugh at lean envy in a long Fool, but you have cause to weep at long envy in a lean age as you live in. This Fool cries not, 'All mine,' but distributes like a kind companion, being a superficial glass to gaze in. There be lean fools as well as fat. Such are they whose noses drop necessity and they

[30] *savor*] reputation.

smell out for Church lands, many tenements, unthrifts, surfeits; looking leanly in all this, but feeding[31] fatly in hope.

"This fatness goes to the heart, not seen in the visage. These seem simple, but like Leonard hit home at advantage. They can stop men's mouths and seal them up in advantage, and give the stocks to the simple deserver when themselves are not blameless. O, beware when you see a long, meager look—search him, he hath also reaching fingers and can slide a groat by himself as Leonard did, fall out, curse, swear, and batter heaven itself with humor of folly. Such was the lean-necked Crane who had the fat Fox to dinner, making him lick the outside of the glass while his leanness fed within. You understand me, Madam. Such are your landlords to the poor, your lean lords to the fat tenant, or by a figure one for the other. Thus they batten here, but the Devil will gnaw their bones for it.

"By the third jest we observe a greediness in lean folly that so good report come in their way. These eat up hawk—feathers and all—to put it by, though they choke in the deed. Hereupon comes it lean envy swallows fat bits, I mean honest manners, and makes them sterile of all good means—as the Lawyer the poor client's plow pence, the city the country commodities—that under show of leanness they fat themselves to the ribs, good hold for flesh hooks at the general waste.

"By the fourth and last (I would it were least), it bewrays a curious and common leanness in lewd livers who, to revenge on others, will fire their own wheelbarrow. Like the lean tenant who, fallen out with his landlord and seeing his neighbor's house on fire, desired his neighbors to pull down his first, for fear of more danger—not that he loved his neighbor's safety and his own, but that he hated his landlord. Or the contrary—covetous of their own commodity, fire themselves and, because they will not burn alone, endanger their friends and say 'tis kind to have company. These are Fools, indeed lean ones. These are fat at soul and make thick doings for the devil's diet. World, I name them not—thou knowest them well enough."

[31] *feeding*] text reads "feed."

At this she bit her lip, knowing some that were lean Leonards in this, but "kay me I'll kay thee,"[32] give me an inch today I'll give thee an ell tomorrow and we'll to hell together. The World, dimpling her chin with mere modesty, as it were throwing off variety of squeamish nicety, began to say, "Sooth, thou sayest true, there are such tricks in me, but I know not how to mend. I am willing but flesh is weak. Prithee be more sparing, carp but confound not, hope the best amendment may come. Prithee go in, furnish thy salad—these herbs already are savory and I pick out to my appetite—and though I be not altogether pleased, yet am I not quite past patience. I will endure. For that disease that festers so must receive cure gladly. Though it come with exceeding pain, yet so much the profit by how much the perplexities cries *ave* to the danger."

"Mistress," says Sotto, "I am glad to sit so near you, and to be thought a kind neighbor too is more than the world affords. But look who is here—we have fellowed one with our Flat and Fat Fool, disturbed by the lean. Now as in a history we mingle mirth with matter to make a please-plaster for melancholy, so in our glass we present to the Lean a Clean—one that was more beloved among Ladies than thought can hatch or opinion produce. His name is Jack Miller. He lives yet and hath been in this city within few days. And give me leave to describe him thus:

> You that folly comprehend,
> Listen to my story;
> This description well attend,
> I have writ it for ye;
> This clean nigit[33] was a fool,
> Shaped in mean of all,[34]
> And of order fit to rule
> Anger in her loudest brawl;
> Fat and thick, neat and clean,
> And delights in pleasure,
> Save a nasty ugly strain
> Of another measure
> From his nostrils rheumatic.

[32] *kay me I'll kay thee*] You scratch my back, I'll scratch yours.
[33] *nigit*] simpleton.
[34] *Shaped . . . all*] of average proportions.

Grief it was to see
Such a neatness spring
From imbecility;
Creatures of the better sort,
For the Fool was clean,
Gave him love with good report
Had not this ill been;
But let slip it was no fault,
Men as sluggish be,
Since the wisest jump as short
In all cleanliness as he."

"Alas," quoth the World, "I am sorry, trust me, that one so outwardly well should be so inwardly ill, and have that appearance in nasty defect which of itself is neat. But go on with the repetition since we are mended in[35] the condition. We will wink at small faults, though we yield it great in nature. *Nemo sine crimine*[36] and so forth."

"Aye," quoth Sotto, "say ye me so? Have at him then—out it goes—but mark it well."

How Jack Miller simply burned the hair of his head and face

In a Gentleman's house where Jack Miller resorted, as he was welcome to all, it chanced so there was a Play. The Players dressed them in the Gentleman's Kitchen and so entered through the Entry into the Hall. It was after dinner when Pies stood in the Oven to cool for Supper. Jack had not dined, and seeing the Oven stand open and so many Pies there untold (he thought because they seemed numberless), "O," says Jack, "for one of them p-p-pies"—for so he stammered in speaking.

The Player's Boy, being by and in his Lady's Gown, could have found in his heart to creep in, clothes and all, but he persuaded Jack to do so; to which he was willing and very nimbly thrusts in his head into the hot Oven—which being but newly opened, on the

---

[35] *mended in*] i.e., aware of.
[36] *Nemo sine crimine*] nobody's perfect.

sudden he was singed both of head and face and almost not a hair left on his eyebrows or beard. Jack cries, "O, I burn!" and had not the wit to come back, but lay still. The Gentlewoman Boy took him by the heels and pulled him out, but how he looked I pray you judge that can discern favors.

Jack was in a bad taking with his face, poor soul, and looked so ugly and so strangely that the Lady of the Play being ready to enter before the Gentles to play her part, no sooner began but, remembering Jack, laughed out and could go no further. The Gentleman mused at what he laughed. But such a Jest, being easily seen, was told the Gentleman, who sent in for Jack Miller—who came like bald Time to tell them time was past of his hair. But he so strangely looked as his countenance was better than the Play.

But against night, the Players dressed them in another place, and at Supper Jack Miller sung his song of "Derry's Fair" with a barmy[37] face to take out the fire and looked like the *Pater* of the Ale vat. It was no boot to bid him stut and stammer. Poor Fool, as clean as he was, he was now but beastly faced, for he looked like a man that, being ashamed to show his face, had hid it in a dry loam wall and, pulling it out again, left all the hair behind him.

How the clean Fool was loathe to foul his shoes or foul his band

Jack on New Year's day in the morning was to carry a New Year's gift to a gentleman a mile off and—as he stayed to have it delivered to him to bear—asked which was the cleanest way thither. A fellow, knowing his cleanliness, sends him over a dirty marsh and so he folded up his band (then clean) for fouling, that at the gentleman's door he might put it on. The present came, which Jack seeing, made legs to the Gentlewoman, forgetting his band was in his hose, carried a stiff neck to and fro to the Gentlewoman—and whate'er she spake, or where'er she stood, Jack would look but one way, as though his neck had been starched.

[37] *barmy*] yeasty.

"And remember," says the Gentlewoman, "you abuse not my message nor my gift."

"No, fo-fo-forsooth," says Jack, and away he goes and thought he would see what it was. And as he went he lift up the basket lid and looked. "Ah ha," quoth Jack, "I see now it is Almond bu-bu-butter."

Along he goes and, seeing the marsh wet and dirty, thought to leap a little ditch and so to go a clean highway. But (O poor Jack) he, basket and all, lay in the midst of the ditch up to the armpits in mud—which Jack, seeing, got out and goes to a river by and washes himself first, his band next—where if it had been about his neck as it should, it had been labor well saved. [But last his basket of Almond butter, he washed the dirt off] so long that the butter was washed away—which he, perceiving, in that woeful taking comes back and called for more "bu-bu-butter."

The gentlewoman, seeing how things went, rather laughed than vexed because she was so simple to trust a fool with matters of trust, and bade him get him to the fire and dry him—and said next time she would stay her servants' leisure (who then were abroad) rather than trust to a rotten staff. [Jack stood singing "Derry's Fair" by the fire with a Jack of good beer, and while he dried himself without, wet himself within—and there is all the thought he takes.] Thus clean fools light still on beastly bargains.

How Jack Miller the clean fool ventured over the Avon on foot in great danger

In the town of Evesham in Worcestershire (Jack Miller, being there born, was much made of in every place) it happened that the Lord Chandos' Players came to town and played there—which Jack not a little loved, especially the Clown, whom he would embrace with a joyful spirit and call him Grumball—for so he called himself in Gentlemen's houses where he would imitate plays, doing all himself, King, Gentleman, Clown, and all. Having spoken for one, he would suddenly go in and again return for the other and, stammering

as he did, made much mirth. To conclude, he was a right innocent without any villainy at all.

When these Players I speak of had done in the town, they went
to Pershore and Jack swore he would go all the world over with
Grumball[, that he would]. It was then a great frost new begun and
the Avon was frozen over thinly. But here is the wonder: The
Gentleman that kept that Hart (an Inn in the town) whose backside
looked to the way that led to the riverside to Pershore, locked
up Jack in a chamber next the Avon where he might see the players
pass by. And they of the town, loath to lose his company, desired
to have it so.

But he, I say, seeing them go by, creeps through the window
and said, "I come to thee, Grumball!" The Players stood all still
to see further. He got down very dangerously and makes no more
ado but ventures over the Avon which is, by the long bridge, as I
guess, some forty yards over. Yet he made nothing of it. But my
heart ached [to see it, and] my ears heard the ice crack all the way.
When he was come unto me I was amazed and took up a brickbat
which lay thereby and threw it, which no sooner fell upon the ice
but it burst. Was not this strange, that a Fool of thirty years was
borne of that ice which would not endure the fall of a brickbat?

[Yes, it was wonderful, methought,] but everyone rated him for
the deed, telling him the danger. He considered his fault, and
knowing faults should be punished, he entreated Grumball the
Clown, who he so dearly loved, to whip him—but with Rosemary,
for that, he thought, would not smart. But the Players in jest
breeched him till the blood came, which he took laughing, for it
was his manner ever to weep in kindness and laugh in extremes.
That this is true, mine eyes were witnesses, being then by.

*How Jack the clean Fool sung his song of "Derry's Fair" in divers places,
where he made good sport*

Jack Miller, welcomed to all places and barred of none, came
to a Gentleman who, being at dinner, requested him for mirth to

make him a play, which he did, and to sing "Derry's Fair," which was in this manner: First, it is to be noted he stuttered hugely and could neither pronounce b nor p—and thus he began,

> As I went to Derry's Fair, there was I ware of a jolly beggar,
> Mistress Annis, Master Thomas under a tree mending of shoon,
> Mistress Annis, Master Thomas hight brave beggars every one.

And so forward. But the jest was to hear him pronounce "brave Beggars." And his quality was, after he began his song, no laughing could put him out of it.

One standing by, noting his humor—that b and p plagued him—bade him say this after him, which Jack said he would do: "Buy any flawn,[38] pasties, pudding pies, plum pottage, or peascods." O, it was death to Jack to do it, but like a willing Fool he fell to it.

"Buy any, buy any fla flaw p-p-p-pasties and p-p-p-pudding p-p-p-pies p-p-p- etc." And ever as he hit on the word, he would pat[39] with his finger on his other hand, that more and more it would make a man burst with laughing almost, to see his action. Sometime he would be pronouncing one word while one might go to the door and come again. But ever after, Gentles would request him to speak that, where before "Derry's Fair" was all his Song.

He came not long after (to this I am witness because my ears heard it) to a Gentleman's not far from Upton-upon-Severn in Gloucestershire, where at the Table, amongst many Gallants and Gentlewomen, almost the 'state of the Country, he was to jest and sing. Especially they entreated him for his new speech of the Pees—which he began in such manner to speak, with driveling and stuttering, that they began mightily to laugh, insomuch that one proper Gentlewoman among the rest, because she would not seem too immodest with laughing (for such is the humor of many that think to make all, when God knows they mar all) so she straining herself, though inwardly she laughed heartily, gave out such an earnest of her modesty that all the Table rung of it.

"Who is that!" says one.

"Not I," says another.

38 *flawn*] pancake.
39 *pat*] stab.

But by her cheeks you might find guilty Gilbert, where he had hid the brush. This Jest made them laugh more and the rather that she stood upon her marriage and disdained all the Gallants there, who so heartily laughed that an old Gentlewoman at the Table took such a conceit at it with laughing that, had not the Fool been which stood (by fortune) at her back and was her supporter, being in a great swound, she had fallen to the ground backward. But down they burst the windows for air, and there was no little boot to bid run. She was nine or ten days ere she recovered that fit on my knowledge. Thus simple Jack made mirth to all, made the wisest laugh, but to this day gathered little wit to himself.

"This," quoth the World, "is mere mirth without mischief and I allow of it. Folly without faults is as radish without salt, may pass in digestion one without the other and do better, where both together engenders but rheum, and mirth does well in any."

"Aye," says Sotto, "so weigh you not the true weight. As it is sufferable to be whole so it is salvable to be hurt, and one to the other gives aim, but to be neither is monstrous. I would fain Moral of it, if you please."

Leave was granted, for the World knew it would else be commanded, and Sotto thus points at the Parable: "By the first merry emblem I reach at stars, how they fire themselves in the firmament, whether it be with sitting too near the Sun in the day or couching too near the Moon in the night I know not, but the hair of their happiness often falls off and shoots from a blazing Comet to a fallen star, and carries no more light than is to be seen in the bottom of Plato's inkhorn. And where they should study in private with Diogenes in his Cell they are with Cornelius in his tub.

"By the second the clean Fools of this world are patterned, who so neatly stand upon their ruffs and scutes[40] that the brain is now lodged in the foot, and thereupon comes it that many make their head their foot—and employment is the drudge to prodigality, made saucy through the mud of their own minds where they so oft stick fast that Banks his horse with all his strength and cunning

---

[40] *scutes*] metal tips on toes and heels of shoes.

cannot draw them out. By the third is figured saucy adventure in folly, for wisdom puts forward no further than warrant, and for pleasure the wisest make themselves fools.

"To conclude this foolish description: Of the fourth, many sing out their times and, like idiots true born, confound with folly what was created more holy, shutting out trifles that out-method matter of more weight, where nicety herself will let go in laughter, though she spoil her marriage."

The World liked not this well, but bit the lip again—but as rich men suffer wrongs for advantage, took her penn'orths together, casts her eye aside, and sees a comely fool indeed passing more stately. And who was this? Forsooth Will Sommers, one not meanly esteemed by the King for his merriment. His melody was of a higher strain, and he looked as the noon broad waking. His description was writ in his forehead and ye might read it thus:

> Will Sommers, born in Shropshire, as some say,
> Was brought to Greenwich on a holy day,
> Presented to the King, which Fool disdained
> To shake him by the hand—or else asham'd;
> Howe'er it was, as ancient people say,
> With much ado was won to it that day;
> Lean he was, hollow eyed, as all report,
> And stoop he did too; yet in all the Court
> Few men were more belov'd than was this Fool,
> Whose merry prate kept with the King much rule;
> When he was sad, the King and he would rhyme;
> Thus Will exiled sadness many a time;
> I could describe him, as I did the rest,
> But in my mind I do not think it best;
> My reason this: howe'er I do descry him
> So many knew him that I may belie him;
> Therefore to please all people one by one
> I hold it best to let that pains alone;
> Only thus much—he was a poor man's friend,
> And helped the widow often in the end;
> The King would ever grant what he did crave,
> For well he knew Will no exacting knave;
> But wished the King to do good deeds, great store,
> Which caus'd the Court to love him more and more.

The World was in love with this merry Fool and said he was

fit to the time indeed; therefore deserved to be well regarded insomuch as she longed to hear his frescoes[41] moralized and his gambols set down. And Sotto as willingly goes forward thus:

How the merry Fool Will Sommers brought his uncle to the King and got him twenty pound a year

Will Sommers, in no little credit in the King's Court, walking in the Park at Greenwich, fell asleep on the stile that leads into the walk, and many that would have gone that way so much loved him that they were loath to disease him but went another way— aye, the better sort, for nowadays beggars are gallants while gentles of right blood seem tame ruffians. But note the love that Will Sommers got: A poor woman seeing him sleep so dangerously, either to fall backward or to hurt his head, leaning so against a post, fetched him a cushion and a rope—the one for his head and the other to bind him to the post from falling backward. And thus he slept and the woman stood by, attending as groom of his chamber.

It chanced so that upon great occasion, as you shall after hear, Will Sommers' uncle came out of Shropshire to seek him in the Court, a plain old man of threescore years with a buttoned cap; a lockram falling band,[42] coarse but clean; a russet coat; a white belt of a horse hide, right horse-collar, white leather; a close round breech of russet sheep's wool, with a long stock of white kersey; a high shoe with yellow buckles, all white with dust—for that day the good old man had come three and twenty miles on foot.

This kind old man coming up in his Country's behalf and coming into Greenwich, asked the way to the court. Everyone directs him, but one villain Page directs him by the Court gate to cross in a Boat over to Blackwall, and told him that was the Court. The silly old man willingly paid his penny beforehand and was going over but some that overheard their talk hindered his journey and laughed at the Jest, yet pitied his simplicity and set him the right way.

[41] *frescoes*] friskings.
[42] *lockram falling band*] linen collar.

When he came in and saw such a place, he was amazed and stood gazing—which the Guard and Gentlewomen in their windows had much sport to see. At last one asked him what he was. The old man answers, "A poor Shropshire man," and demands if there were not a Gentleman in the Court dwelling, called by the name of Master William Sommers (for the Country, hearing him in favor in the Court, said he was so at least).

The Courtier answered, "Here is such a one indeed."

"For fault of a worse," says he, "I am his uncle," and wept with joy that he should see him.

"Marry," says the man, "I'll help you to him straight"—for, I tell you, not any in the Court durst but have sought him, which this man did. And it was told them he was walked into the Park while the King slept that hot day. Thither went they to seek him.

All this while my friend William was in counsel with the post, and the cushion stood as arbitrator betwixt them, and the woman by as a witness what was said and done. At last came these two and wakened him. William, seeing his head soft, "What soft post is this?" quoth he.

"A post of mine own making," says the woman. But she lost nothing by her good will, for ere she left Will Sommers she got him to get her son's pardon of the King, who was to be hanged three days after for piracy—but by Will Sommers' means he deceived the hangman. This and many good deeds he did to divers.[43]

The Fool, being wakened, looks about him. When he had thanked the woman, asked, "What news?"

Says the man, "Sir, here is your uncle come out of the Country to see you."

"God-a-mercy, cousin," says Will Sommers, "I thank thee for thy labor, you cannot uncle me so."

"Yes truly, Sir, I am your own dear uncle, Master William," and with that wept.

"Are you my uncle?" says Will.

"Aye, sir," says he.

"Are you my uncle?" says he again.

"Aye, sure and verily too."

[43] *divers*] sundry people.

"But are you my uncle indeed?"

"By my vuss[44] I am," says the old man.

"Then, uncle, by my vuss, welcome to Court," says Will Sommers. "But what makes you here, uncle?"

He up and tells his coming to him. Will takes him by the hand. "Come," says he, "thou shalt see Harry, uncle, the only Harry in England." So he led him to the Chamber of Presence, and ever and anon cries, "Aware! room for me and my uncle!" and "Knaves, bid him welcome."

"You are welcome, sir," said they. The old man thought himself no earthly man they honored him so much. But Will, ready to enter the Presence, looks on his uncle and seeing him not fine enough to look on the King, "Come, uncle," says he, "we will have your gear mended"; leads him to his chamber and attires him in his best fool's coat, simply, God wot, meaning well to him—and the simple old man as simply put it on, cap and all.

Out they come and up they came and to the King they go who, being with the Lord Treasurer alone merry, seeing them two how Will had got another fool, knew there was sport at hand. "How now," says the King, "what news with you?"

"O Harry," says he, "this is my own uncle, bid him welcome."

"Well," said the King, "he is welcome."

"Harry," says he, "hear me tell thee a tale and I will make thee rich and my uncle shall be made rich by thee."

Will tells the King how Terrill's Frith was enclosed. "Terrill's Frith?" says the King. "What is that?"

"Why, the Heath where I was born, called by the name of Terrill's Frith. Now a gentleman of that name takes it all in and makes all the people believe it is his, for it took the name from him, so that, Harry, the poor pine and their cattle are all undone without thy help."

"And what should I do?" says the King.

"Marry," says Will, "send to the Bishop of Hereford. He is a great man with Terrill. Command him to set the Frith at liberty again, who is now imprisoned by his means."

"And how shall I be rich by that?" says the King.

[44] *vuss*] vows.

"The poor will pray for thee," says Will, "and thou shalt be rich in heaven, for on earth thou art rich already."

All this was done and Will's uncle went home, who, while he lived, for that deed was allowed Bailiff of the Common, which place was worth twenty pound a year.

How this merry Fool Will Sommers, to make the King merry asked him three questions

Howsoever these three things came in memory and are for mirth inserted into stage plays I know not, but that Will Sommers asked them of the King, it is certain. There are some will affirm it now living in Greenwich.

The King upon a time being extreme melancholy and full of passion, all that Will could do will not make him merry. "Ah," says he, "this [cloud] must have a good shower to cleanse it," and with that goes behind the Arras.

"Harry," says he, "I'll go behind the Arras and study three questions and come again. See therefore you lay aside this melancholy muse and study to answer me."

"Aye," quoth the King, "they will be wise ones no doubt."

At last out comes William with his wit, as the fool of the play doth with an antic look to please the beholders. "Harry," says he, "what is that the lesser it is, the more it is to be feared?"

The King mused at it, but to grace the jest the better he answered he knew not. Will made answer it was a little bridge over a deep river—at which he smiled, [knowing it was fearful indeed].

"What is the next, William?" says the King.

"Marry, this is next: What is the cleanliest trade in the world?"

"Marry," says the King, "I think a Comfitmaker, for he deals with nothing but pure ware and is attired clean in white linen when he sells it."

"No, Harry," says Will, "you are wide."

"What say you then?" quoth the King.

"Marry," says Will, "I say a dirt-dauber."[45]

"Out on it," says the King, "that is the foulest, for he is dirty up to the elbows."

"Aye," says Will, "but then he washes him clean again and eats his meat cleanly enough."

"I promise thee, Will," says the King, "thou hast a pretty foolish wit."

"Aye, Harry," says he, "it will serve to make a wiser man than you a fool methinks." At this the King laughed and demands the third question.

"Now tell me," says Will, "if you can, what it is that, being born without life, head, lip, or eye yet doth run roaring through the world till it die?"

"This is a wonder," quoth the King. "No question, I know it not."

"Why," quoth Will, "it is a fart." At this the King laughed heartily and was exceeding merry, and bids Will ask any reasonable thing and he would grant it.

"Thanks, Harry," says he. "Now against I want, I know where to find. For yet I need nothing, but one day I shall, for every man sees his latter end but knows not his beginning." The King understood his meaning, and so pleasantly departed for that season, and Will laid him down amongst the Spaniels to sleep.

How Will Sommers the merry Fool borrowed ten pounds of Cardinal Wolsey to pay where the Cardinal owed it

On a time appointed, the King dined at Windsor in the Chapel yard at Cardinal Wolsey's (at the same time when he was building that admirable work of his tomb), at whose gate stood a number of poor people to be served of alms. When dinner was done within, and as Will passed by, they saluted him, taking him for a worthy personage, which pleased him. In he comes, and finding the King

[45] *dirt-dauber*] plasterer of mud walls.

at dinner, and the Cardinal by, attending—to disgrace him that he never loved, "Harry," says he, "lend me ten pound."

"What to do?" says the King.

"To pay three or four of the Cardinal's creditors," quoth he, "to whom my word is past[46] and they are come now for their money."

"That thou shalt, Will," quoth he.

"Creditors of mine!" says the Cardinal. "I'll give your Grace my head if any man can justly ask me a penny."

"No?" says Will. "Lend me ten pounds. If I pay it not where thou owest it, I'll give thee twenty for it."

"Do so," says the King.

"That I will, my Liege," says the Cardinal, "though I know I owe none." With that, he lends Will ten pounds. Will goes to the gate and distributes it to the poor and brought the empty bag.

"There is thy bag again," says he. "Thy creditors are satisfied and my word out of danger."

"Who received it," says the King, "the Brewer or the Baker?"

"Neither, Harry," says Will Sommers. "But, Cardinal, answer me in one thing: To whom dost thou owe thy soul?"

"To God," quoth he.

"To whom thy wealth?"

"To the poor," says he.

"Take thy forfeit, Harry," says the Fool. "Open confession [is] open penance. His head is thine, for to the poor at the gate I paid his debt, which he yields is due. Or if thy stony heart will not yield it so, save thy head by denying thy word and lend it me. Thou knowest I am poor and have neither wealth nor wit, and what thou lendest to the poor, God will pay thee tenfold. He is my surety, arrest Him—for by my troth, hang me when I pay thee."

The King laughed at the jest and so did the Cardinal for a show, but it grieved him to jest away ten pound so. Yet worse tricks than this Will Sommers served him after, for indeed he could never abide him, and the forfeiture of his head had like to have been paid had he not poisoned himself.

[46] *word is past*] debt is due.

How this merry Fool Will Sommers eat a mess of Milk without a spoon

There was in the time of Will Sommers another artificial Fool or Jester in the Court, whose subtlety heaped up wealth by gifts given him, for which Will Sommers could never abide him. But indeed lightly one fool cannot endure the sight of another, as Jack Oates the Minstrel in the flat Fool's story, and one beggar is woe that another by the door should go.

This Jester was a big man, of a great voice, long black locks, and a very big round beard. On a time (of purpose) Will Sommers watched to disgrace him when he was juggling and jesting before the King. Will Sommers brings up a mess of milk and a manchet.[47] "Harry," says he, "lend me a spoon."

"Fool," says the Jester, "use thy hands—'help hands, for I have no lands'" and meant that saying would warrant his gross feeding.

"Aye," says Will Sommers, "Beasts will do so and Beasts will bid others do as they do themselves."

"Will," said the King, "thou knowest I have none."

"True, Harry," says he, "I know that, therefore I asked thee. And I would (but for doing thee harm) thou hadst no tongue to grant that Fool his next suit. But I must eat my cream some way."

The King, the Jester and all gathers about him to see him eat it. Will begins thus to rhyme over his milk:

> This bit, Harry, I give to thee,
> And this next bit must serve for me,
> Both which I'll eat apace;
> This bit, Madame, unto you,
> And this bit I myself eat now,
> And all the rest upon thy face—

meaning the Fool, in whose beard and head the bread and milk was thick sown and his eyes almost put out.

Will Sommers he gets him gone for fear. This lusty Jester, forgetting himself, in fury draws his dagger and begins to protest. "Nay," says the King, "are ye so hot?" claps him fast and "though he draws his dagger here yet let him put it up in another place."

47 *manchet*] roll of fine wheat bread.

The poor abused Jester was jested out of countenance and lay in durance a great while, till Will Sommers was fain (after he had broken his head to give him a plaister) to get him out again. But never after came my Juggler in the Court more, so near the King, being such a dangerous man to draw in the presence of the King.

"Now, Lady World," says Sotto, "you wonder at this first jest. Do not, 'tis common, for who so simple that being gorged with broth themselves will not give their friends one spoonful, especially our kin. O we'll, to make them great, make ourselves, and politically rise again by their greatness. But he was simple in that, for though he raised many, himself stood at one stay. But the deed is not common, therefore may fitly be termed a Fool's deed since the wise meddle not with it, unless to plunge further in and wind from poverty, but leave it to the greatest power of all to remedy and revenge, while earthly Majesty grows great by adding liberty to their afflictions, as in our Commons of late, God preserve him for it.

"By the second, morally signification gives this, that Fool's questions reach to mirth, leading wisdom by the hand as age leads children by one finger; and though it holds not fast in wisdom, yet it points at it. Better so than the wise to put questions to Fools, for that's to put the money out of the bag and leave the money behind to bad use, while themselves beg with the bag. Such, like Will Sommers, sleep 'mongst dogs.

"The third bids us charitably learn of simplicity to pay our debts, when the poor creditor calls for it, but 'tis a general fault and such who have doors shut whereat the poor stand, shall find gates fast where themselves may not enter—but especially we of the laity, for while the Pastor cherishes the soul, we seek to starve the body, but let's be mindful lest decaying one we lose both."

O, the World could not endure this but offered to fling away. "Nay, nay," says the Cynic, "soft and fair, a word or two more" —and half angry, looking into his glass, sees one all in blue carrying his neck on the one side, looking sharply, drawing the leg after him in a strange manner, described in meter thus:

> Something tall, dribbling ever,
> Body small, merry never;

Splay footed, visage black,
Little beard, it was his lack;
Flat capped still in view,
The city's charge many knew;
Long coated, at his side
Muckender and inkhorn tied;
Preaching still unto boys,
Aiming well, but reaching toys;
Loving all, hating none,
Less such as let him not alone;
As 'a lived, so 'a died,
Was death's scorn, though life's pride.

"This is singular indeed," says the World. "I long to hear of this dry poor John."

"His name is John indeed," says the Cynic, "but neither John-a-nods nor John-a-dreams yet either, as you take it, for he is simply without tricks, not sophisticated like your Tobacco to taste strong, but as Nature allowed him he had his talent." Whereat the World so tickled her spleen that she was agog, claps her hands for joy and says she was deeply satisfied and cried, "More!"

The crooked stick of licorice that gave this sweet relish, being to set his teeth to it, wipes his rheumy beard and snites his philosophical nose, snapping his fingers Barber-like after a dry shaving, jogs on thus:

How John of the Hospital, the very Fool, walked and preached in Paul's Church and was bidden to dinner

This innocent Idiot that never harmed any—before I enter any further, I will let you understand in two words how he came to be of the Hospital of Christ's Church: Some certain years since (but not a few years) there dwelt a poor blind woman in Bow Lane in London called by the name of Blind Alice, who had this fool of a child to lead her, in whose house he would sit, either on the stairs or in a corner, and sing Psalms or preach to himself of Peter and Paul—because he delighted to go to Sermons with Blind Alice and heard the Preacher talk of them. It chanced the Worshipful of the City, good Benefactors to the poor, to take her into Christ's Hospital, with whom John went as a guide to lead her, who being old, after she died he was to be turned out of doors. But the City, more desirous to pity than to be cruel, placed him as a fostered fatherless child—and they did well in it too, seeing he was one of God's Creatures, though some difference in persons.

Well, to go forward in what I promised you: John went to Saint Paul's Church in London to meet with Mr. Nowell, the Dean, whose bounty to him was great—and the Fool knew it well enough, whom he would duly attend after his preaching, for ever he gave him at their meeting a groat, and he would bring it to his Nurse. Well, Mr. Dean preached not that day, whereupon John stands in a corner with boys flocking about him and begins to preach himself, holding up his muckender for his book, and reads his Text.

"It is written," says he, "in the Third Chapter of Paul to the Corinthians—'Brethren, you must not swear'" (for that was lightly all his text), then thus he begins: "Whereas or whereunto it is written, for because you must believe it, for surely else we are no Christians. Write the sermon, Boy," says he (as the Hospital Boys do) and then one must write on his hand with his finger, and then he would go forward thus: "The world is proud and God is angry if we do not repent. Good friend, give me a pin, or good friend give me a point—" as it came in his mind, and so sucking up his drivel and breath together, would pray and make an end; which being done, "Who bids me home to dinner now?" says John.

The Boys that knew his qualities answers, "That do I, John."

"Thank ye, friend," says he and goes home to his own dwelling at Christ's Church.

But at this time, one wealthy Merchant's son, to make his father merry, bade him [come] home to dinner indeed, and (will he or nill he) he must go with him. With much ado John went, and coming into the house simply sits him down (as his use was) in the chimney corner. It was in Lent, when peas pottage bare great sway and when every peas must have his ease. John, beholding peas pottage on the fire, thought on his Nurse, for he was all saving for her, seeing nobody by, stepped to the pot and put a great ladle of pottage into his pocket and piteously burned his thigh. And but that the leather was thick, it had been worse.

John, feeling something burn, leaped and cried. They ran in to see the matter why he cried, but more and more he exclaimed, "I burn! I burn!" and got out of doors and never leaves till he came to his Nurse, who quickly shifted him and mended what was amiss. But the jest was to see the folk of the house who, wondering what he ailed, could not devise what the matter was. But a beggar in the entry who beheld all, told the truth of the matter, who lost a good alms for his labor. But thus simple John, by his own folly, dyed the inside of his pocket peas-pottage tawny and set a good scarlet red upon his thigh.

How John tolled the Bell for Nurse's Chicken

Gaffer Homes, being Sexton of Christ's Church, would often set John a-work to toll the Bell to prayers or burials, wherein he delighted much. It chanced so that coming through the Church, and having nothing to do, seeing the Bell so easily come by, tolls it. The people (as the custom is) repairs to Church (as they used) to know for whom it was. John answers them still, for his Nurse's chicken.

They said, "Wherefore tolls the bell, John?"

"I know not."

"When died he?"

"Even now."

"Who, John? Who?"

"My Nurse's chicken," quoth he and laughs.

This jest was known to every neighbor thereabouts who sent to bid him leave tolling. But it was not his custom, till Goodman Homes took the rope from him that gave the rope to him. Well, there stood Jack tolling from four o'clock to six, Goodman Homes being from home, who was not a little vexed at John's diligence. But [he] laid the rope ever after where John could not reach it.

How this very Fool John of the Hospital sold a Gentleman's pair of boots for a groat that cost the Cobbler five shillings

John was of this humor—ask him what his coat cost him, he would say a groat; what his cap, band, or shirt cost, all was a groat; ask what his beard cost, and still a groat. So one Friday morning there was a Gentleman to ride down into Warwickshire about payment of an hundred pound upon a bond's forfeiture. The time was next day by Sunset. It was no boot to bid him pull on his boots and be gone. Well, he made haste and went to do it without bidding. And yet, for all his haste, his boots were seam-rent and must have a stitch or two needs. He sends them to a cobbler next to Christ's Church gate in Newgate market, who was diligent to mend them straight. And as he had done, comes John of the Hospital to him (as his use was) to carry home his work, and he sends John home with the boots.

As John was going through Ivy Lane a Country Fellow that knew him not meets him and seeing the boots, "What shall I give thee for them?" says he. John, who sold everything for a groat, asked a groat. The Fellow, seeing it was a good pennyworth, gives him a groat and departs with the boots.

John, as his use was, gave it to his Nurse. She asked him where he had it. He said, "For boots." But she, not knowing his mind, fell to work again as he found her.

The forfeiture of the bond so hammered in this Gentleman's head that he thought every hour two till he had his boots, and mused they came not from mending, sends for them presently. One comes sweating, "Zoons, Cobbler, the boots!" And being at work very busy, "Aye," says he, "they are mended and carried home."

Another comes, "Boots, boots!"

"Would the boots were in your belly," quoth the Cobbler. "Once again, they are gone home."

By and by comes the Gentleman in his white linen boot-hose ready to the purpose. "A pox of lazy cobblers," says he. "My boots! Shall I forfeit a bond for your pleasure?"

The Cobbler puts off his considering cap. "Why, sir," says he, "I sent them home but now."

"By whom?" says he.

"By John, blue[48] John," says the Cobbler.

The Gentleman he runs home one way, the Cobbler another. Well, no boots were to be had. The Gentleman he stayed and the Cobbler he prayed, but all this while the boots delayed and came not.

The Cobbler seeks John at his nurse's where he was, and found the boots were sold for a groat. The Cobbler seeing no remedy, because the Gentleman was in haste gives him five shillings (with a heavy "hey ho") towards a new pair and lost four shillings eight pence by the bargain. But the Cobbler would never let John carry home his ware more. "Nay," says the Cobbler, "if my money can be booted and ride post so by five shillings at a time, it is no boot for me to say Utinam.[49] But the next boots, I'll make a page of my own age and carry home myself, for I see fools will afford good pennyworths."

How this very Fool John lost himself on Easter Monday at the Spittal[50] Sermon amongst all the people

On Easter Monday the ancient custom is that all the children of the Hospital go before my Lord Mayor to the Spittal, that the world may witness the works of God and man in maintenance of so many poor people, the better to stir up living men's minds to the like good. Before which the children of the Hospital like a captain goes John, whom to behold the people flock apace. And the weather being hot, their thrusting made John extreme dry.

John considered he was like to fast while dinner, yet kept his rank to the Spittal, where the Cans[51] did walk apace by his nose but never came at him, which made him more eager of drink. Well, while the children were placing, John stood making of water

---

[48] *blue*] traditional color of Christ's Hospital scholar's coats.
[49] *Utinam*] i.e., I wish it were otherwise.
[50] *Spittal*] Hospital.
[51] *Cans*] i.e., the beer cans.

and, seeing a Gentleman's door open, slips in—and the household without, standing to see my Lord Mayor pass by, not regarded him. But he, whose nose had wit to smell good beer, got down into the Cellar and fell to it tipple square[52] till he was lost and quite drunk, and laid himself to sleep behind two barrels, and unseen slept all that day.

In the Sermon time he was missed, sought and not found. The afternoon came. The Gentleman's Butler with other good fellows fell to carouse soundly, till the Butler was laid up too. Here was a Cellar well fraught with fools. But all this while, the Beadles failed not to search up and down the City. The Crier cried a man child of the age of two-and-thirty years, for at least he was so old.

But return we to the Cellar. The two drunkards waked both together. John calls, "Nurse! Nurse!" which the Butler (half awake) hearing, thought the Devil had been playing bo-peep with him. But when he looked and beheld him, imagining how it was, he secretly sent him to the Hospital lest he were blamed for his negligence in looking to the door no better.

A number of things more John did, which I omit fearing to be tedious. Not long after, he died—and was old, for his beard was full of white hairs, as his picture in Christ's Hospital (now to be seen) can witness. Buried he is, but with no Epitaph. Methinks those that in his lifetime could afford him his picture might with his grave yield so much as four lines, that people may see where he lies whom they so well knew. And if I might persuade, his Motto should be to this effect:

> Here sleeps blue John that gives
> Food to feed worms and yet not lives;
> You that pass by look on his grave
> And say, yourselves the like must have;
> Wise men and fools all one end makes;
> God's will be done Who gives and takes.

"Surely," says Mistress Nicety, "this pleases well to see one so naturally silly to be simply subtle. It is strange, but I hear it and—like a tale out of a poor man's mouth—hardly credit it."

"This Fool," says Sotto, "signifies many who come to Church to

[52] *tipple square*] i.e., full-heartedly.

meet acquaintance more than for piety, and will sooner sell the
Church for money than pay aught to underprop it. At these the
boys and children of this world wonder, while manly age sees and
will not see. For these, as the second tale says, Folly tolls the bell,
and a number longs to hear it ring out, when the loss of John's
Chicken is of more want than theirs. But, a rope on't, it will one day
be better. There are, as Hamlet says, things called whips in store.[53]

"The third jest of John shows morally many things, amongst
which things I mean works are so cobbled that, to rid it with quickness, folly may bear it up and down to the owner while work-
manship and time is merely abused. But it boots not to meddle
in this lest some say, *ne sutra, etc.*[54] But let me tell ye this by the way,
World. There are knaves in thy seams that must be ripped out."

"Aye," says the World, "and such I fear was your father."

"O no," says the Critic, "he was the silly Gentleman that
stayed while the Fool brought home his boots and so forfeited his
bond, that his good conditions[55] lay at gage for it."

"Marry, yes," says the World, "and was after canceled at the
gallows, for such as he lies in wait to cozen simplicity, and for
a groat buy that which well got deserves a portague."[56]

At this the Cynic fretted, and here they begin to challenge the
combat, but a parley sounded, summoned them to the last tale
with John to the Cellar in the Spittal. Where if they please they
may carouse freely, though they dye deep in scarlet[57] as many do,
till they lose themselves in the open streets. Such Diogenes sought at
noondays with a lanthorn and a candle.

Well, the World so buffeted the Cynic at his own weapon that
he plays with her as weak fencers that carries flesh up and down
for others to dress. Such was the Cynic, unskilful in quips and
worldly flaunts, rather to play with short rods and give venies[58]
till all smart again—not in the brains, as the World did, but in

[53] *whips in store*] cf. *Hamlet*, III.i.70.
[54] *ne sutra*] a shoemaker should stick to his last.
[55] *good conditions*] prosperity.
[56] *groat . . . portague*] i.e., buy for four pence what should cost four pounds.
[57] *dye deep in scarlet*] ?indulge in deep sin; or, disguise themselves in ceremonial
costume or soldier's uniform.
[58] *venies*] a fencing bout ending in a thrust or stroke.

the buttocks—as such do, having their hoses displayed, making them expert till they cry it up in the top of the question.

Our sullen Cynic sets by his glass in malice, knits a beetle brow till the room grew dark again, which the wanton World seeing flings out of his Cell like a girl at barley-break.[59] Leaving the last couple in hell, away she gads and never looks behind her.

"A whirlwind," says the Cynic, "go after. Is this all my thanks, the old payment still? Doth the World still reward mortality thus? Is virtue thus bedridden? Can she not help herself?"— and looks up to heaven as he should say, "Some power assist." But there he sat fretting in his own grease, and for aught I know nobody came to help him.

Conclusio.

Thus, Gentlemen, as the kind hostess salutes her guests, saying, "You see your cheer and you are welcome," so say I. It may be you like it not. I am sorrier. You will say these salads were ill dressed —like enough, but good stomachs digest anything—and that it was a dry feast. The Cynic had not the World so much as drink. True, a worldling right, who, as the word is "Drink before you go," sets the cart before the horse and says, "Go before you drink," why may he not in his cell? His betters will. I have seen it in Gentleman's Cellars. But I cry you mercy, there I think it is drink till you cannot go. Bounce is the world's motto there, till they discharge the brain of all good a-bearing, making the body break the peace in every corner. But blame me not. I am tedious. Pardon my folly, writing of folly. If you knew, you would say, *nec mirum.*[60] Wherefore if my pardon may be purchased, then so. If not, you may bid me keep my fool's company.

FINIS

[59] *barley-break*] old country game in which whoever is "it" tries to find the other players, who hide in pairs, and "imprison" them in a ring called "hell."
[60] *nec mirum*] no wonder.

Selections from
GEORGE WILKINS and T. D.

JESTS TO MAKE
YOU MERRY
(1607)

The title page of this book lists as authors " T. D. and George Wilkins."
T. D. was probably Thomas Dekker (1572?–?1632), the most successful
hackwriter of his day, still well known for his Shoemaker's Holiday *and*
Gull's Hornbook. *George Wilkins, a fellow hackwriter, collaborated on*
plays with such better known figures as William Shakespeare, and under his
own name wrote The Miseries of Enforced Marriage. *Otherwise, little is*
known about him. As professional collaborators, it was natural for Dekker and
Wilkins to join in a jestbook.

Although the jests themselves seem generally familiar, they are all made to
appear drawn from contemporary life. At least one, number 16, is a dramati-
zation of an actual event recorded in 1606: " Will Forde fined for using evil
speeches to the Constable saying 'Blurt, Mr. Constable'" (North Riding
Records [*1883*], I, *37*). *Even when jests are patently derived from earlier*
jestbooks (such as number 57) they are given similar, contemporary treatment:
the actor is introduced, the setting is succinctly outlined, and the ensuing action
is worked out in dialogue. This dramatic technique is an obvious carryover
from Dekker's and Wilkins' playhouse experience. Their collection is thus
innovative in applying such art to a kind of literature previously thought not
worth the effort. Their sixty jests are remarkable also for their language, cap-
turing the rhythms as well as the diction of actual speech.

(STC 6541)

What a Jest is

A Jest is the bubbling-up of wit. It is a Bavin[1] which being well
kindled maintains for a short time the heat of laughter. It is a weapon
wherewith a fool does oftentimes fight and a wise man defends himself by. It is the food of good company if it be seasoned with judgment; but if with too much tartness, it is hardly digested but turns
to quarrel. A jest is tried as powder is—the most sudden is the best.
It is a merry Gentleman and hath a brother so like him that many
take them for Twins, for the one is a Jest spoken, the other is a Jest

[1] *Bavin*] bundle of brushwood.

done. Stay but the reading of this book some half an hour and you shall be brought acquainted with both.

The 1st Jest

A Fellow that (to be a fool in print) had spent the stock of his wits upon ink and paper, and made it into a book, offered it to sell at divers Stationers' stalls, but none would buy it. At the length, he came to one of the Company and swore to him he should not need to fear to venture money upon it, for it would be to him an everlasting book. "O," says the other, "then I will not meddle with it. Everlasting books are ill commodities in our trade. Bring me a book that will go away, and I am for you."

The 2nd Jest

A Justice of Peace found his man laying his mistress on the lips, at which the Justice in a rage and rapping out a great oath, called him Rascal and asked him what he did. "Why," says the fellow and swore as deep as he, "I was kissing your wife."

The Justice told him if he took him kissing there again, he would make him kiss in another place. "Truth, sir," says the Servingman, "had not you come in, I had kissed in another place indeed."

The 5th Jest

A mad country Parson inviting certain of his friends to the eating of a tithe pig and some other good cheer, one of the guests brought along with him a Precisian,[2] which sect the Parson never could abide.

[2] *Precisian*] Puritan.

And, having carved once or twice to the rest, at length he called aloud in Latin to the Precisian (for he took him to be a scholar because he went all in black), "*Heus domine, vis tu comedere Turdum, vis tu comedere Fartum, vis tu comedere pistum Fartum.*" At which the other, blessing himself to think that a Churchman should utter such filthy words (as he construed them), rose from the board and departed, reproving the Parson for a beastly and unmannerly Christian, whereas by *Turdum* he meant a black bird that stood on the board, by *Fartum* a pudding, and by *pistum fartum* a pan-pudding that's baked.

The 7th Jest

"Sirrah," says a Justice to a bailiff that had brought a cutpurse before him, "keep that knave till I call for him anon when I am at more leisure."

"Yes," quoth the bailiff, "I will keep the knave for your worship."

The 8th Jest

A Woman, seeing a tumult in the open street about a man and a woman, asked one of the standers-by what the matter was. Says he, "Thou art a whore."

"Thou art an arrant knave," says the Woman, "to call me whore."

"Why, about this," quoth the party that was asked the question, "did those two fall out."

The 9th Jest

One called a Captain coward and said he had no heart. "It's no matter," quoth the Captain, "I have legs."

The 11*th Jest*

A Tailor in this Town maintained a whore besides his wife, who afterwards came to the knowledge of it; whereupon one wondering how it should be discovered, because the Tailor was a close fellow, asked one of his neighbors how the devil his wife could smell out his wench. "O, easily," replied the other, "for he kept her under his wife's nose."

The 12*th Jest*

An ancient Gentlewoman, making her brags that she was descended from John of Gaunt, one that stood by said he thought she was rather descended from William the Conqueror because her face was so old.

The 14*th Jest*

A couple of Servingmen, having drunk hard in Southwark, came to take water about ten or eleven of the clock at night at Saint Mary-ovary's stairs. But the moon shining, and a puddle of water lying before them which they could not perfectly discern (without better eyes) by reason that their shadows hid it, one of them stumbled and fell in, laboring with his hands and feet as if he had been a-swimming.

His fellow stood (so well as a man in his case could stand) looking upon him and said, "Art thou gone? Art thou gone? Jesus receive thy soul. Yet if thou canst but get the Temple stairs, there's some hope thou shalt do well enough."

"Tush," says the other that was down, "I look not to *get*. So I may save myself, I care for no more."

The 16th Jest

A Player, riding with his fellows in a year of Peregrination up and down the countries, resolved to be merry, though they got little money. And being to pass through a Town, he gets a good way before the rest, crying with his drawn Rapier in his hand, "Which is the Constable's house? Where is the Constable?" The dogs of the parish at the noise fell to barking, the Threshers came running out with their flails, the Clowns with rakes and pitchforks, asking without what the matter was. [He] cried still, "And you be men, bring me to the Constable!"

At last, the wise Gentleman appeared in his likeness. "Are you the Constable?" says the Player.

"Yes, that I am, for fault of a better," quoth he.

"Why, then, blurt! Master Constable," says the other and, clapping spurs to his horse, galloped away amain—some of the companions laughing, others railing, the Constable swearing. And the rest of the Players that came behind post through the thickest of them and laughing the whole Town to scorn as if it had been the fool in a Comedy, which made the hobnail-wearers stamp ten times worse than they did before.

The 19th Jest

A Servingman bringing a Capon and white broth to the table stumbled and let all fall to the ground, for which his Master reviled him and said, "I could have done so much myself."

"I think so," quoth the fellow. "Any fool may do it, now 'tis done before him."

The 21st Jest

"I think," says one to his friend, "I am the arrantest coxcomb living."

"Truth, so think I," says the other.

"Why should you think so?" replied the first, and grew half angry.

"Marry," said the second, "because you say so, and I hope none should know that better than yourself."

The 22nd Jest

A pair of Players, growing into emulous contention of one another's worth, refused to put themselves to a day of hearing (as any Players would have done) but stood only upon their good parts. "Why," says the one, "since thou wouldst fain be taken for so rare a piece, report before all these," for they had a small audience about them, you must note, "what excellent parts thou hast discharged."

"Marry," says the other, "I have so naturally played the Puritan that many took me to be one."

"True," says the first again, "thou playedst the Puritan so naturally that thou couldst never play the honest man afterwards. But I," quoth he, "have played the Sophy."

"The Sophy?" replied the second. "What, a murrain, was he?"

"What was he?" says the other. "Why, he was a Turk."

"Right," quoth his adversary. "Get to play as many Turks' parts as thou canst, for I'll be hanged if ever thou playst a good Christian."

The 23rd Jest

A Gentlewoman, coming to one that stood at a window reading a book, "Sir," said she, "I would I were your book" (because she loved the Gentleman).

"So would I," quoth he. "I wish you were."

"But what book would you have me to be," said the other, "if I were to be so?"

"Marry, an Almanac," quoth the Gentleman, "because I would change every year."

The 26th Jest

"What reason," says one to his friend, "has your Lord to keep a fool?"

"He hath no reason at all," answered the other.

The 27th Jest

"Thou art an arrant Beggar," says a Merchant to a Scholar.

"True, sir," answered the Scholar, "for I am an honest man. But you can be no Beggar, for all the City knows you play the Merchant."

The 28th Jest

A woman, finding her husband reeling in the streets till he was unable to stand, railed upon him and said, "Art not thou ashamed to lie like a drunken beast thus in the open streets?"

"Thou liest like a sober whore as thou art," quoth he. "If I were a beast, I would not lie drunk."

The 29th Jest

One that had been knighted but lately, riding through Paul's churchyard, his wife, his chambermaid, the nurse, and two young children sitting in the Coach with him, his son and heir leading the way before, the creatures[3] in blue trotting two-and-two behind: "O," says a 'prentice that stood in his shop to his fellow, "by Jove, me-thinks it's a brave thing to be a Knight!"

"A brave thing?" quoth his fellow. "What an ass art thou! A man may have anything for money."

---

[3] *creatures*] i.e., footmen.

The 30th Jest

An old man, talking with his son and comparing this Age with that which he lived in when he was a boy, said that now the world was clean found upside down. "Nay, that's not true, father," replied the other, "for if it were so, women should go with their heels upwards."

The 31st Jest

A lady that, by sitting to see a play at Court, came home late, called for victuals and swore she was as hungry as a dog. "It may be as a bitch, Madam," said her page standing by, "else the comparison will not hold."

The 36th Jest

A Country Gentleman, coming down Westward by water to London upon the day when my Lord Mayor's Galley Foist was in all her holiday attire, and seeing such triumphing on the Thames but not knowing the cause, demanded of his Waterman why there was such drumming and piping and trumpeting and wherefore all those Barges (like so many Water-pageants) were carried up and down so gaily with Flags and Streamers? It was told him the Lord Mayor went that day to be sworn, to Westminster.

"What need your Lord Mayor," quoth he, "go so far to be sworn? I have heard there is as good swearing in London as in any place in England. But go all these in black gowns to be sworn there, too?"

"No, sir," said his Waterman. "These swear fast enough in the city."

The 37th Jest

A Company of Gallants having supped in a Tavern and being (as the fashion is) extremely over-reckoned in their bill of Items, yet paying all, departed in as extreme a chafe, swearing never to hold up their hands again at that unmerciful bar. One of the rest, as he went along, demanded in mockery what was to pay. "Nothing," said one of the pewter-pot-clinkers. "All is paid, sir, I'll take my oath upon a book."

"All is paid," answered the other, "for we paid you well and you have paid us soundly."

The 40th Jest

A Clerk of the Guild Hall, being requested by his Client, at the end of a Trial, to draw him out a bill of charges: "Yes," said the Clerk, "I will draw it out presently," and did so. The Client running it over knew to himself that he was at more cost with him than was needful, yet said nothing because he was to use his help in other matters, but paid it all and then requested my young Lawyer to go drink a cup of Muscadine with him at the Tavern, which he did— the Client at the end of the shot paying all too.

"Nay then," quoth the Clerk, "by the Lord, I have done you wrong to put you to so much charges."

"In good troth," answered the Client, "so I thought before though I said nothing. But since you swear it, now I dare verily believe it."

The 43rd Jest

A young wanton wench that had married an old man (being a Forester whom she had so transformed that, coming amongst the herd of deer, he went for a stag) fell suddenly sick for the love of a Gallant that had a good while together gone a-hunting with her, but upon some dislike of his game gave it over. The kind old fellow, her husband that suspected nothing, brought her to a Doctor. But the cause of her disease being love, she proved him a Dunce. He could neither by her water nor by feeling her pulse find what sickness bred within her, whereupon the old Ranger, her husband, persuaded her to show all how it came first upon her. "For," said he, "we must hide nothing from our Physician."

"Why, then," quoth she, "good husband, show your forehead to him, which methinks is all broken out."

"Alas," said he, "that's only the weakness of thy sight."

"Nay, husband," said the sick lover, "if your brows grieve not you, they shall never hurt me."

The 44th Jest

A country Hobbinoll,[4] having seen the mad folk in Bedlam, fell so in love with their tricks that he swore he could find in his heart to live in the Summertime amongst them, and demanded of him that carried him thither to see them how he might soonest be made to run mad. "If one had such a mind, easily," said the other. "For do but marry with a whore, or else have to do with players, and thou shalt quickly run mad."

The 45th Jest

A Wench, having a good face, a good body, and good clothes on, but of bad conditions, sitting one day in the two-penny room of a playhouse, a number of young Gentlemen about her against all whom she maintained talk: One that sat over the stage said to his friend, "Do you not think that yonder flesh will stink anon, having so many flies blowing upon it?"

4 *Hobbinoll*] a rustic.

"O," quoth his friend, "I think it stinks already, for I never saw so many crows together but there was some carrion not far off."

The 46th Jest

"Look," said one, "is it not strange? Yonder is a fellow that the last day went for a Lieutenant and now he is a Pander."

"Alas," said one that stood next him. "Soldiers, you know, if they cannot get it by fair means, they will have it out of the flesh."

The 50th Jest

A notable scolding Quean railing hand-to-hand with three men that were her neighbors and beating them all three at it because it was her own weapon, her husband standing by and taking part with neither: At last she began to revile him and told those that flocked about her how her husband thought to have every rascal atop on her. "And reason good," quoth one that stood by. "What serve Jades for but to be made hackneys?"

The 52nd Jest

A Waterbearer complained before a Justice of his wife's misusing and overmastering him. "'Tis strange," quoth the Justice, "that you two should jar, for I am told that you, Sirrah, are never seen to go into an Alehouse but your wife is seen there too. You are never drunk, but she is drunk too. You never quarrel with your neighbors but she quarrels too. I wonder that having qualities so alike, you should no better agree."

"So do I, and it please your Worship," said the Waterbearer. "For my own part, I could agree with her if she were worse so she would be but better. I pray therefore let me have her bound either to her good behavior or else to the peace."

"Seek but out a Scrivener," quoth the Justice, "that can make such a bond and thou shalt have my furtherance."

The 55th Jest

A young bride that had married a stale old bachelor sat at the wedding dinner with a very sad and discontented look, to think what a bad market she had been at. But an ancient, merry Gentlewoman sitting next to her cheered her up in her ear thus: "Daughter," quoth she, "never repent the bargain thou hast this day made, for an old horse will hold out a long journey, as well as a nag of four years old."

"It may be so," quoth the bride, "but as little skill as I have in riding, I doubt whether he can hold out in some highways that I could name."

The 56th Jest

An impudent fellow meeting a civil Gentlewoman upon a narrow causey, that she could not pass him without striving, in courtesy, to give way, rudely broke out into this question: "Gentlewoman, are not you a whore?"

She being nothing daunted at his blunt behavior, but having more wit about her than he had civility, answered him thus: "Trust me, sir, I am none now nor ever was I any but once, and that was when your father, being no better than a Chimney sweeper, lay with me all night whilst she whom you now call mother kept the door."

The 57th Jest

A company of thieves broke one night into a country school-master's house, but he, hearing them, never stirred out of his bed for the matter, but cried out aloud, "You mistake your mark, my masters. Go to the next house, that's a rich Farmer's. I wonder you will lose time to seek anything here by night when I myself can find nothing by day."

The 58th Jest

Three Waiting Gentlewomen sitting up late one evening began to shrive one another, and to know what manner of Lovers each other had. Says the first, "I love one of our Servingmen."

"And I," quoth the second, "love the Tutor."

"Nay," says the third, "then I like my choice best, for I love my lady's Gentleman Usher."

"Out upon him," cried one of the other. "I had rather ten other men should lie with me night by night than one gentleman usher."

Selections from

TARLTON'S JESTS
(1611)

Principal comedian in the company of actors given Queen Elizabeth's patronage as " The Queen's Men," Richard Tarlton (d. 1588) is supposed to have served as her jester also, but this supposition is supported only by tales such as those in Tarlton's Jests. *There is no doubt, however, about his having been the foremost comic actor of his day, setting the pattern for the clown in russet suit and button-down cap who specialized in antic gestures, extempore rhyming, funny faces, and jigs—dance routines accompanied by metrical patter to the beat of the tabor or the drum. According to legend, he was a natural clown, a farmer's boy whose "happy unhappy" monologue attracted the notice of a passing courtier who took him to the Queen, and so forth. He was instead city bred, an apprentice water-bearer turned actor, whose clowning was the product of art rather than nature.*

Tarlton's Jests *was compiled by someone bent on perpetuating the memory of this paragon clown. Though the book may have been issued in 1609, the earliest surviving edition dates from 1611. It was reprinted in 1638. The seventy-three jests relate Tarlton's antics in court (seventeen jests), city (twenty-five), and country (thirty-one). Of the total, one-quarter seem based on "fact" drawn from such sources as Stow's* Annals *(1592) or from contemporaries who had known Tarlton. The remainder are familiar from conventional jest-books. The humor of the "factual" jests is lost without the physical antics and the spontaneity that must have accompanied them. We know that all Tarlton had to do to raise a laugh was to show his face through the curtain, and, as Stow says, "For a wondrous plentifull pleasant extemporall wit he was the wonder of his time."*

(STC 23684)

2. *How Tarlton Deceived the Watch in Fleet Street*

Tarlton having been late at Court and coming homewards through Fleet Street, he espied the Watch and not knowing how to pass them, he went very fast, thinking by that means to go unexamined. But the Watchmen, perceiving that he shunned them, stepped to him and commanded him in the Queen's name to stand. "Stand!" quoth Tarlton. "Let them stand that can, for I cannot."

So falling down as though he had been drunk, they helped him up and so let him pass.

22. *How Tarlton and One in the Gallery Fell Out*

It chanced that in the midst of a Play, after long expectation for Tarlton, being much desired of the people, at length he came forth, where (at his entrance) one in the Gallery pointed his finger at him, saying to a friend that had never seen him, "That is he."

Tarlton, to make sport at the least occasion given him, and seeing the man point with the finger, he in love again held up two fingers. The captious fellow, jealous of his wife (for he was married) and because a Player did it, took the matter more heinously and asked him why he made horns at him. "No," quoth Tarlton, "they be fingers:

> For there is no man which in love to me
> Lends me one finger but he shall have three."

"No, no," says the fellow, "you gave me the horns."

"True," says Tarlton, "for my fingers are tipped with nails which are like horns, and I must make a show of that which you are sure of."

This matter grew so, that the more he meddled, the more it was for his disgrace; wherefore the standers-by counseled him to depart, both he and his horns, lest his cause grew desperate. So the poor fellow, plucking his hat over his eyes, went his ways.

23. *How Fiddlers Fiddled Away Tarlton's Apparel*

It chanced that one Fancy and Nancy, two Musicians in London, used often with their boys to visit Tarlton when he dwelt in Gracious Street at the sign of the Saba, a Tavern, he being one of their best friends or benefactors by reason of old acquaintance—to requite which they came one Summer's morning to play him "The Hunt's Up" with such Music as they had.

Tarlton, to requite them, would open his chamber door, and for their pains would give them Muscadine, which a Cony-catcher noting and seeing Tarlton came forth in his shirt and nightgown to drink with these Musicians the while, this nimble fellow stepped in and took Tarlton's apparel, which every day he wore, thinking that if he were espied to turn it to a jest. But it passed for current and he goes his ways.

Not long after, Tarlton returned to his chamber and looked for his clothes. But they were safe enough from him. The next day this was noised abroad, and one in mockage threw him in this theme, he playing then at the Curtain:

> Tarlton, I will tell thee a jest
> Which after turned to earnest:
> One there was, as I heard say,
> Who in his shirt heard Music play
> While all his clothes were stolen away.

Tarlton, smiling at this, answered on the sudden thus:

> That's certain, Sir, it is no lie,
> That same one in truth was I;
> When that the thief shall pine and lack,
> Then shall I have clothes to my back,
> And I, together with my fellows,
> May see them ride to Tyburn gallows.

27. How Tarlton was Deceived by His Wife in London

Tarlton, being merrily disposed as his Wife and he sat together, he said unto her, "Kate, answer me to one question without a lie and take this crown of gold"—which she took on condition that if she lost, to restore it back again. Quoth Tarlton, "Am I a Cuckold or no, Kate?" Whereat she answered not a word, but stood silent, notwithstanding he urged her many ways.

Tarlton, seeing she would not speak, asked his gold again. "Why?" quoth she. "Have I made any lie?"

"No," says Tarlton.

"Why, then, goodman fool, I have won the wager."

Tarlton, mad with anger, made this rhyme:

> As women in speech can revile a man,
> So can they in silence beguile a man.

31. *How Tarlton Gave Away His Dinner*

As Tarlton and his wife sat at dinner, his wife being displeased with him and thinking to cross him, she gave away half his meat unto a poor Beggar, saying, "Take this for my other husband's sake." Whereupon Tarlton took all that was left and likewise bade the poor fellow to pray for his other wife's soul.

35. *How Tarlton Jested at His Wife*

Tarlton and his wife, keeping an Ordinary in Paternoster Row, were bidden out to Supper, and because he was a man noted, she would not go with him in the street but entreats him to keep one side and she another, which he consented to. But as he went he would cry out to her and say, "Turn that way, wife!" and anon, "On this side, wife!" so the people flocked the more to laugh at them. But his wife, more than mad angry, goes back again and almost forswore his company.

37. *How Tarlton Made Armin His Adopted Son to Succeed Him*

Tarlton keeping a Tavern in Gracious Street, he let it to another who was indebted to Armin's Master, a Goldsmith in Lombard Street, yet he himself had a chamber in the same house. And this Armin, being then a wag, came often thither to demand his Master's money, which he sometimes had and sometimes had not. In the end, the man, growing poor, told the boy he had no money for his Master and he must bear with him. The man's name being Charles, Armin made this verse, writing it with Chalk on a Wainscot:

> O world, why wilt thou lie?
> Is this Charles the great? That I deny.
> Indeed Charles the great before,
> But now Charles the less, being poor.

Tarlton, coming into the room, reading it and partly acquainted with the boy's humor—coming often thither for his Master's money, took a piece of Chalk and wrote this Rhyme by it:

> A wag thou art, none can prevent thee,
> And thy desert shall content thee;
> Let me divine: As I am, so in time thou'lt be the same,
> My adopted son therefore be,
> To enjoy my Clown's suit after me.

And see how it fell out. The boy reading this so loved Tarlton after, that, regarding him with more respect, he used to his Plays and fell in a league with his humor. And private practice brought him to present playing, and at this hour performs the same where, at the Globe on the Bankside, men may see him.

38. *Tarlton's Greeting with Banks His Horse*

There was one Banks, in the time of Tarlton, who served the Earl of Essex and had a Horse of strange qualities, and being at the Cross Keys in Gracious Street, getting money with him as he was mightily resorted to, Tarlton (then with his fellows playing at the Bell by) came into the Cross Keys amongst many people to see fashions—which Banks perceiving, to make the people laugh says, "Signior," to his horse, "go fetch me the veriest fool in the company." The Jade comes immediately, and with his mouth draws Tarlton forth. Tarlton, with merry words, said nothing but, "God-a-mercy, Horse."

In the end, Tarlton, seeing the people laugh so, was angry inwardly and said, "Sir, had I power of your horse, as you have, I would do more than that."

"Whate'er it be," said Banks to please him, "I will charge him to do it."

"Then," says Tarlton, "charge him to bring me the veriest whoremaster in this company."

"He shall," says Banks. "Signior," says he, "bring Master Tarlton here the veriest whoremaster in the company."

The Horse leads his Master to him, then "God-a-mercy, Horse, indeed," says Tarlton. The people had much ado to keep peace, but Banks and Tarlton had like to have squared and the horse by to give aim.[1] But ever after, it was a byword through London, "God-a-mercy, Horse," and is to this day.

39. *An Excellent Jest of Tarlton Suddenly Spoken*

At the Bull at Bishopsgate was a Play of Henry the Fifth wherein the Judge was to take a box on the ear. And because he was absent that should take the blow, Tarlton himself (ever forward to please) took upon him to play the same Judge, besides his own part of the Clown. And Knell, then playing Henry the Fifth, hit Tarlton a sound box indeed, which made the people laugh the more because it was he. But anon the Judge goes in, and immediately Tarlton, in his Clown's clothes, comes out and asks the Actors what news. "O," saith one, "hadst thou been here thou shouldst have seen Prince Henry hit the Judge a terrible box on the ear."

"What, man!" said Tarlton. "Strike a Judge?"

"It is true, i'faith," said the other.

"No other like," said Tarlton, "and it could not be but terrible to the Judge, when the report so terrifies me that methinks the blow remains still on my cheek that it burns again." The people laughed at this mightily, and to this day I have heard it commended for rare

[1] *to give aim*] encourage them.

but no marvel, for he had many of these. But I would see our Clowns in these days do the like. No, I warrant ye, and yet they think well of themselves, too.

42. *How Tarlton Took Tobacco at the First Coming Up of It*

Tarlton, as other Gentlemen used, at the first coming up of Tobacco did take it more for fashion's sake than otherwise. And being in a room set between two men overcome with Wine, and they never seeing the like, wondered at it, and seeing the vapor come out of Tarlton's nose cried out, "Fire! Fire!" and threw a cup of wine in Tarlton's face.

"Make no more stir," quoth Tarlton. "The fire is quenched. If the Sheriffs come, it will turn to a fine, as the custom is." And drinking[2] that again—"Fie," says the other, "what a stink it makes. I am almost poisoned."

"If it offend," says Tarlton, "let's every one take a little of the smell, and so the savor will quickly go." But Tobacco whiffs made them leave him to pay all.

44. *Tarlton's Jest of a Gridiron*

While the Queen's Players lay in Worcester City to get money, it was his custom for to sing *extempore* of Themes given him, amongst which they were appointed to play the next day. Now, one fellow of the City amongst the rest, that seemed quaint of conceit, to lead other youths with his fine wit gave out that the next day he would give him a Theme to put him to a *non plus*. Divers of his friends, acquainted with the same, expected some rare conceit.

Well, the next day came and my Gallant gave him his invention in two lines, which was this:

> Methinks it is a thing unfit
> To see a Gridiron turn the Spit.

[2] *drinking*] smoking.

The people laughed at this, thinking his wit knew no answer there-
unto, which angered Tarlton exceedingly. And presently, with a
smile looking about, when they expected wonders he put it off thus:

> Methinks it is a thing unfit
> To see an Ass have any wit.

The people hooted for joy to see the Theme-giver dashed, who,
like a dog with his tail between his legs, left the place. But such
commendations Tarlton got that he supped with the Bailiff that
night where my Themer durst not come, although he were sent for,
so much he vexed at that unlooked-for answer.

46. *Tarlton's Jest of a Bristol Man*

When the Queen's Players were restrained in summer, they traveled down to Saint James his Fair at Bristol, where they were wor-
thily entertained both of Londoners and those Citizens. It happened
that a wealthy Citizen called Master Sunbanke one morning secretly
married his maid, but not so secret but it was blown abroad. That
morning, Tarlton and others walking in the Fair to visit his familiar
friends of London and being in company of Bristol men, they did
see Master Sunbanke coming—who had this property with his neck,
not to stir it any way but to turn body and all.

It chanced at the Fair end he stood to piss against a wall, to whom
Tarlton came and, clapping him on the shoulder, "God give you joy
of your marriage," says he.

Master Sunbanke, being taken pissing against the wall, would
have looked back to thank him, and suddenly turns about body and
all in the view of many, and showed all—which so abashed him
that, ashamed, he took into a Tavern, protesting that he had rather
have spent ten pound.

"Sure," said the Vintner, "the fault is in your neck, which will
not turn without the body's assistance, and not in Master Tarlton."

"Call you him Master Tarlton?" says Master Sunbanke.

"Yea, Sir," says the Vintner. "He is the Queen's Jester."

"He may be whose Jester he will be, but this jest agrees not with me at this time," says Master Sunbanke.

48. *How Tarlton Made One of His Company Utterly Forswear Drunkeness*

At Salisbury, Tarlton and his fellows were to play before the Mayor and his brethren, but one of his company, a young man, was so drunk that he could not. Whereat Tarlton, as mad angry as he was mad drunk, claps me on his legs a huge pair of bolts. The fellow, dead asleep, felt nothing. When all was done, they conveyed him to the Jail on a man's back, and entreated the Jailer to do God good service and let him lie there till he waked.

While they were about their sport, the fellow waked and, finding himself in durance and the Jail, hung round with bolts and shackles, he began to bless himself and thought sure in his drunkeness he had done some mischief. With that, he called to know, but none came to him. Then he thought verily his fault was capital, and that he was close prisoner.

By and by comes the Keeper and moaned him that one so young should come to so shameful a death as hanging. Anon another comes, and another with the like, which further put him in a puzzle. But at last comes Tarlton and others, entreating the Keeper yet if it might be that they might see their fellow ere they went. But he very hardly was entreated. But at length the poor drunken Signior called out for them. In they come.

"O, Tom," says Tarlton, "hard was thy hap in drunkeness to murder this honest man, and our hard hap too, to have it reported, any of our company is hanged for it."

"O God, O God," says the fellow, "is my fault so great? Then commend me to all my friends."

Well, short tale to make, the fellow forswore drunkenness if he could escape, and by as cunning a wile (to his thinking) they got him out of prison by an escape and sent him to London before, who was not a little glad to be gone. But see how this jest wrought: By little and little the fellow left his excessive drinking, and in time altered his desire of drunkenness.

50. *How Tarlton Saved His Head from Cutting Off*

Tarlton, upon a time being in the Country and lodging in an homely Inn, during which time there was a Gentleman dwelling in the same town somewhat frantic and distraught of his wits—which madman on a sudden rushed into Tarlton's bedchamber with his sword drawn and, finding him there in bed, would have slain him, saying, "Villain, were it not valiantly done to strike off thy knave's head at one blow?"

Tarlton answered, "Tut, Sir, that's nothing with your Worship to do. You can as easily strike off two heads at one blow as one, wherefore, if you please, I'll go down and call up another, and so you may strike off both our heads at once." The madman believed him and so let him slip away.

56. *How Tarlton Would Have Drowned His Wife*

Upon a time, as Tarlton and his Wife, as passengers, came sailing from Southampton towards London, a mighty storm arose and endangered the Ship, whereupon the Captain thereof charged every man to throw into the Seas the heaviest thing he could best spare, to the end to lighten somewhat the Ship. Tarlton, that had his Wife there, offered to throw her overboard, but the company rescued her. And being asked wherefore he meant so to do, he answered, "She is the heaviest thing I have, and I can best spare her."

57. *Tarlton's Jest of a Country Wench*

Tarlton, going towards Hogsdon, met a country maid coming to market. Her Mare stumbling, down she fell over and over, showing all that ever God sent her. And then rising up again, she turned her round about unto Master Tarlton, and said, "God's body, Sir, did you ever see the like before?"

"No, in good sooth," quoth Tarlton, "never but once in London."

61. *Of Tarlton's Wrongful Accusation*

Upon a time, Tarlton was wrongfully accused for getting of a Gentleman's Maid with child, and for the same brought before a Justice in Kent, which Justice said as followeth: "It is a marvel, Master Tarlton, that you being a Gentleman of good quality and one of her Majesty's servants, would venture thus to get Maids with child."

"Nay, rather," quoth Tarlton, "were it a marvel if a maid had gotten me with child."

62. *Tarlton Deceived by a Country Wench*

Tarlton, traveling to play abroad, was in a Town where in the Inn was a pretty maid whose favor was placed in a corner of Tarlton's affection. And talking with her, she appointed to meet him at the bottom of a pair of stairs. Night and the hour came, and the maid subtly sent down her Mistress, whom Tarlton catching in his arms, "Art come, wench?" says he.

"Out, alas," says the Mistress, not knowing who it was.

Tarlton, hearing it was the Mistress, start aside, and the maid came down with a candle and she espied a glimpse of Tarlton in the dark, who stepped into another room.

"How now, Mistress?" said the maid.

"Something," said she, "affrighted me, some man sure, for I heard him speak."

"No, no, Mistress," said the Maid. "It is no man. It was a Bull calf that I shut into a room till John our Pounder came to have pounded him for a stray."

"Had I thought that," saith she, "I would have hit him such a knock on his forehead that his horns should never have graced his Coxcomb," and so she departs up again afraid. But how Tarlton took this jest, think you.

73. *Tarlton's Jest to a Maid in the Dark*

Tarlton, going in the dark, groping out his way, hears the tread of someone to meet him. "Who goes there?" says he. "A man or a monster?"

Said the maid, "A monster!"

Said Tarlton, "A candle, ho!" And seeing who it was, "Indeed," said he, "a monster, I'll be sworn, for thy teeth are longer than thy beard."

"O, Sir," said the maid, "speak no more than you see, for women go invisible nowadays."

Selections from

SCOGIN'S JESTS
(Ca. 1680)

There is no evidence outside of this jestbook that John Scogin ever lived. The little we can gather about him from the book itself is that he flourished in the time of Edward IV, but some of the jests allude to events in the reigns of Richard III and Henry VII also. Nor are we quite sure about the date of the book itself. It may have appeared as early as 1565, although the earliest surviving complete edition dates from 1626. That edition attributes authorship to Dr. Andrew Board (Borde or Boord), a physician better known for another jestbook, Merry Tales of the Mad Men of Gotham *(ca. 1565). The prologue alludes to his* Dietary of Health *(1542).*

Our text is from the edition of about 1680, entitled The Merry Jests and Witty Shifts of Scogin, *an abridgment of the 1626 edition, one that was being reprinted as late as 1796. The abridgment omits nineteen of the original seventy-seven jests. Ten of those omitted were concerned with the buffoonish antics of Scogin's pupil, introduced in Jest 7. In omitting this sequence, the printer or bookseller obscures the fact that the earlier book had consisted of four distinct story lines. One featured fools, rogues, and knaves associated with Scogin. The others emphasized Scogin in three distinctly different roles—fool, rogue, and knave—roles which in the earlier edition had been distributed equally. In the abridgment, most weight is thrown on Scogin as fool and as rogue. Very likely, the original edition was a mixture of four different jestbooks, cohering only through the name Scogin.*

(Wing B3750)

The Prologue

There is nothing, beside the goodness of God, that preserves health so much as honest mirth used at dinner and supper, and mirth towards bed, as it doth plainly appear in the *Directions for Health:* Therefore considering this matter, that mirth is so necessary for man, I published this Book, named *The Jests of Scogin*, to make men merry: for amongst divers other Books of grave matters I have made, my delight had been to recreate my mind in making something merry, wherefore I do advertise every man in avoiding pensiveness, or too much study or melancholy, to be merry with honesty in God, and for God, whom I humbly beseech to send us the mirth of Heaven, Amen.

I have heard say that Scogin did come of an honest stock, no kindred, and his friends did set him to school at Oxford, where he did continue until the time he was made Master of Art, where he made this jest:

> A Master of Art is not worth a fart,
>   Except he be in Schools,
> A Bachelor of Law is not worth a straw,
>   Except he be among fools.

Jest 1. *What shift Scogin and his Chamber fellow made to fare well in Lent*

On a time in Lent Scogin consulted with a Chamber fellow of his, a Collegianer, and said, "How shall we do to fare well this Lent?"

The Scholar replied, "I cannot tell, for I lack money."

"Nay," said Scogin, "if you will be ruled by me, we will fare well."

The Scholar answered, "I will do as you shall counsel me."

Then Scogin said, "Feign yourself sick, and go to bed, groan and cry out for help, and call me to come unto you"—which was done. And when Scogin came to his Chamber fellow, he feigned himself sore sick. Scogin asked how he did.

"I am so sick," quoth he, "that I think I shall die."

Then said Scogin, "Be of good comfort. I see no peril of death in you."

"O, Sir," said the Scholar, "you do not feel the pains that I feel. I pray you, Sir, as my trust is in you, keep me and go not from me until I am amended. For every Lent is unto me very evil, unless that I have some good cherishing. As you see, this little sickness hath made me so faint and weak that I cannot stand on my legs, and I fear I shall pine away."

"Not so," said Scogin. "Be of good cheer and pluck up your heart. Here be of your fellows, which will take the pains to go to the Bowsers[1] of your place to entreat them to take care of you."

When it was known in the College that Scogin's Chamber fellow was so sore sick, some were afraid that it had been the Pestilence, or else some other infectious sickness, wherefore Scogin was put in trust both for the keeping and to do other necessary things for his Chamber fellow, and had every night the Keys of the Bowsery and Buttery delivered—whereby he provided for bread and drink, good salt Eels, salt Salmon, and other salt Fishes. So they did lack no good cheer, besides fresh fish which came out of the Kitchen.

This done, the fellows of the place would that the Patient's Urine should be had to the Physician, to know what manner of sickness the Patient had. Scogin, being afraid then that the Physician would know that his fellow was not sick, said to him, "We shall be both ashamed and shent,[2] except thou wilt suffer me to burn thy Lips and singe thy Nose with a Candle, and then let me alone with the Physician, for I must have your Water to him."

Scogin did burn his Chamber fellow's Nose and Lips and had his Water to the Physician. The Physician said, "He that doth own this Water, or Urine, is a whole man."

"Nay," said Scogin, "that is not so. That man is a sore sick man and doth break out about the Lips and Nose."

"Ah," said the Physician, "a water, or urine, is but a Strumpet. A man may be deceived in a water. And if he be as you do say," said the Physician to Scogin, "then hath he a great heat in the Liver and in the Stomach."

"Yea, Sir," said Scogin, "he doth complain of his stomach."

"Then," said the Physician, "you shall have a bill of the Apothecary, and let him take such Medicines as shall be there made."

"Sir," said Scogin, "it is but a poor Scholar, and he hath little to spend."

"Then," said the Physician, "for your sake it shall be but a groat matter"—which when he had bought and brought home, he cast

[1] *Bowsers*] bursars.
[2] *shent*] disgraced.

the medicine into the fire, saying to his fellow, "I have deceived the Physician, and now let us make merry, and fill all the pots in the house."

After this, Scogin showed the Bowsers and the fellows how he was with the Physician, and that he had sent the Patient medicines. "But for all that," Scogin said, "the Physician cannot tell as yet unto what infirmity this matter will turn. But," said Scogin, "I fear much the Pestilence"—which he said because none should visit the Patient.

This continued until that Lent was ended, and on Maundy Thursday, Scogin said to his Chamber fellow, "We will make our Maundy, and eat and drink with advantage."

"Be it," said the Scholar.

On Maundy Thursday at night they made such cheer that the Scholar was drunk. Scogin then pulled off all the Scholar's clothes and laid him stark naked on the Rushes, and set a form[3] over him and spread a Coverlet over it, and set up two tallow candles in candlesticks over him, one at his head, the other at his feet, and ran from Chamber to Chamber and told the fellows of that place that his Chamber fellow was dead. And they asked of Scogin if he died of the Pestilence. Scogin said, "No. I pray you go up and pray for his Soul." And so they did.

And when the Scholar had slept his first sleep, he began to turn himself and cast down the Form and the Candles. The fellows of the House seeing that Scogin did run first out of the Chamber, they and all that were in the Chamber (running and tumbling down one another's neck) were afraid. The Scholar seeing them run so fast out of the Chamber followed them stark naked. And the fellows, seeing him run after them like a Ghost, some ran into their Chambers and some ran into one corner and some into another. Scogin ran into the Chamber to see that the Candles should do no harm, and at last fetched up his Chamber fellow, which ran about naked like a mad-man, and brought him to bed—for which matter Scogin had rebuke.

3 *form*] frame.

Jest 2. What shift Scogin and his Fellow made when they lacked Money

After this, Scogin and his Chamber fellow lacked Money and Scogin said, "If thou wilt be ruled after me, we will go to Thame Market where we shall overtake, going or coming, some that drive Sheep. Now, do as I shall tell thee and we will get some Money."

And as they went to Thame, they did see a man drive Sheep. Then Scogin said to his fellow, "Go thou before and make a bargain with him that the Sheep þe no Sheep, but Hogs. And when that thou hast made a full bargain, ask him by whom the matter shall be tried, and say thou, 'By him that shall next overtake us.'"

The Scholar did overtake him that drove the Sheep and said, "Well overtaken, my friend. From whence hast thou brought these fair Hogs?"

"Hogs?" quoth the fellow. "They be Sheep."

Said the Scholar, "You begin to jest."

"Nay, Sir," said the fellow, "I speak in good earnest."

"Art thou in earnest?" said the Scholar. "Thou wilt lay no wager with me to the contrary?"

"Yes, by the bone of a Pudding, I will lay all the money in my purse."

"How much is that?" said the Scholar.

The fellow said, "I have two shillings."

"Two shillings?" said the Scholar. "That is nothing. Wilt thou lay half thy Hogs and two shillings, and I will lay as much against it? Strike hands, and he that loseth shall pay."

"Be it," said the fellow.

"Now," said the Scholar, "by whom shall we be tried?"

The fellow said, "We will be tried in the Town of Thame."

"Nay," said the Scholar. "Thame is out of my way. Let us be tried by him that shall next overtake us."

"Be it," said the fellow.

By and by, Scogin did overtake them, saying, "Well overtaken, good fellows."

"Welcome, Master," said the Scholar and the fellow.

"Master," said the fellow, "here is a Scholar of Oxford hath made a bargain with me of two shillings and the price of half my Sheep, that they be Hogs that I do drive before me."

Scogin did set up a-laughing, saying, "Alack, good fellow, dost thou think these be Sheep?"

"Yea, Sir," said the fellow.

"Alack, good fellow, thou hast lost thy bargain," said Scogin, "for they be fair Hogs."

Then said the Scholar, "Give me my money and divide these Hogs, for I must have half of them."

"Alack," said the fellow, "I bought these for Sheep and not for Hogs. I am undone."

"Nay," said Scogin, "I will be indifferent between both. Let the Scholar have the two shillings, and take thou the Hogs away with thee."

The fellow said, "Blessed be the time that ever you were born. Hold, Scholar—there is two shillings." The fellow was glad he lost not his Hogs, which were Sheep.

Jest 5. How Jack made his Master pay a penny for the Herring bones

On a time, Scogin did send Jack to Oxford to Market to buy a pennyworth of fresh Herrings. Scogin said, "Bring four Herrings for a penny or else bring none."

Jack could not get four Herrings but three for his penny, and when he came home Scogin said, "How many Herrings hast thou brought?"

And Jack said, "Three Herrings, for I could not get four for a penny."

Scogin said he would have none of them. "Sir," said Jack, "then will I and there is your penny again."

When Dinnertime was come, then Jack did set Bread and Butter before his Master, and roasted his Herrings, and sat down at the lower end of the Table, and did eat the Herrings. Scogin said, "Let me have one of thy Herrings, and thou shalt have another of me another time."

Jack said, "And if you will have one Herring, it shall cost you a penny."

"What!" said Scogin, "Thou wilt not take it on thy conscience?"

Jack said, "My conscience is such that you get not a morsel here except I have my penny again." Thus contending together, Jack had made an end of his Herrings.

A Master of Art of Oxford, one of Scogin's fellows, did come to see Scogin. And when Scogin had espied him, he said to Jack, "Set up the bones of the Herrings before me."

"Sir," said Jack, "they shall cost you a penny."

Then said Scogin, "What, Whoreson! wilt thou shame me?"

"No, Sir," said Jack. Give me my penny again and you shall have up the bones, or else I will tell all."

Scogin then cast down a penny to Jack, and Jack brought up to Scogin the Herring bones. And by this time the Master of Art did come in to Scogin, and Scogin bade him welcome, saying, "If you had come sooner, you should have had fresh Herrings to dinner."

Jest 7. How a Husbandman put his Son to School with Scogin

There was a Husbandman beside Oxford, and he would fain have his Son go to School with Master Scogin, and that Scogin should help to make him a Priest. And to obtain Scogin's favor and good will, the Husbandman gave Scogin a Horse. Scogin was pleased, so that he would pay for his Son's board. The Husbandman was contented and Scogin pleased.

The slovenly Boy, almost as big as a Knave, would begin to learn his A,B,C. Scogin did give him a lesson of nine of the first letters of A,B,C, and he was nine days learning them. And when he had learned the nine Christcross-row letters, the good Scholar said, "Am ich past the worst now?"

"Yea," said Scogin.

Then said the Scholar, "Would God ich were, for dis is able to cumber any man's wits alive." Scogin then thought his Scholar would never be but a fool, and did apply him as well as he could to learning.

But he that hath no wit can never have learning or wisdom.

Jest 8. How Scogin and his Scholar went to seek his Horse

On a time Scogin had lost his Horse, wherefore in the morning he called up his Scholar, saying, "Will, ho!" Will heard him call and would not speak. At last Scogin said, "What, Will! I say arise and let us go look [for] my Horse."

Will said, "Master, hold your peace, vor ich am vast asleep."

"What, old Lusk!" said Scogin. "Arise and meet me at Shot-over," which is a great Wood nigh St. Bartholomews beside Oxford.

Will followed his Master with ill will, they seeking one in one place and the other in another place for his Horse. At last Scogin did lower and whoop to him. Will said (as he was brought up with his Father), "What a devil will you have now?"

Scogin said, "Hast thou found my Horse?"

"No, I say, but I have found a better thing."

"What is that?" said Scogin.

"By my vay," said Will, "ich have found a bird's nest."

"Well, Will," said Scogin, "mark the place and look out for my horse."

"By my vay," said Will, "'chill mark the place, vor ich have shit under the tree, and now chould[4] ich could find another bird's nest, for all your horse."

Thus you see a fool will not leave his bauble for a thing of better worth.

Jest 11. How Scogin sold Powder to kill Fleas

Scogin divers times did lack money and could not tell what shift to make. At last he thought to play the Physician and did fill a box

4 *chould*] I wish.

full of the Powder of a rotten Post. And on a Sunday he went to a Parish Church and told the Wives that he had a Powder to kill up all the Fleas in the Country, and every wife bought a pennyworth and Scogin went his way ere Mass was done. The wives went home and cast the Powder into their beds and in the chambers, and the Fleas continued still.

On a time Scogin came to the same Church on a Sunday and when the wives had espied him, the one said to the other, "This is he that deceived us with the Powder to kill Fleas." "See," said the one to the other, "this is the selfsame person."

When Mass was done the wives gathered about Scogin and said, "You be no honest man to deceive us with the Powder to kill Fleas."

"Why," said Scogin, "are not your Fleas all dead?"

"We have more now," said they, "than ever we had."

"I marvel of that," said Scogin. "I am sure you did not use the Medicine as you should have done."

They said, "We did cast it in our beds and in our chambers."

"Ah," said he, "there be a sort of fools that will buy anything and will not ask what they shall do with it. I tell you all, that you should have taken every Flea by the neck, and then they would gape, and then you should have cast a little of the Powder into every Flea's mouth, and so you should have killed them."

"Then," said the wives, "we have not only lost our money, but we are mocked for our labor."

Jest 12. *How Scogin drew out an old Woman's Tooth*

There was an old woman that had but one Tooth in her head and that did ache very sore. She went to Master Scogin for remedy. "Come with me, Mother," said Scogin, "and you shall be healed by and by." He then got a pack-thread and went to the Smith's forge with the woman, and he said to the Smith, "I pray you heat me a Colter in your Forge."

"I will," said the Smith.

Then he went to the old woman and said, "Mother, let me see

your tooth." And she did. So he took his pack-thread and bound it fast about the Tooth, and tied the other end of the thread at the ring of the Forge door, whereat the Smith used to tie his Horses and Mares. And when the Colter was glowing hot, Scogin took the Colter and ran with it against the old woman, saying, "Ah, whore, dost thou stand like an old Mare? I will run thee through with this hot Colter!"

The woman being afraid gave a braid⁵ with her head and ran her way and left her tooth behind her. Scogin ran after the woman, and she cried out for help (for she was afraid that Scogin would have burnt her). The Smith ran after Scogin for his Colter, for he was afraid that Scogin would have run away with it.

Whereby you may see what a terrible thing fear is.

Jest 13. *How Scogin gave one a Medicine to make him go to it*

On a time there came a young man to Scogin to have a Medicine, saying, "Sir, I would have a Medicine to make me go to it lustily" (he meant of Venus's acts). Scogin did give him an extreme purgation. The young man went to be with his Leman. Within a while his belly began to rumble, and there was no remedy but he must needs go to it so long that he did defile both the chamber and the bed, so that he and his Leman bathed themselves that night in dirt.

Wherefore it is good for all men, when they ask counsel of any man, to be plain in his words and not to speak in parables.

Jest 14. *How Scogin gave one a Medicine to make him find his Horse*

There was a man that had lost his Horse and he came to Master Scogin and said, "Sir, I hear say that you be a good Physician, and I have lost my Horse and would fain know a remedy how I might

⁵ *braid*] jerk.

find out my Horse." Scogin gave that man such a purgation that he was constrained to run to every bush and hedge; and peeping so about here and there, at last he found his Horse. Then he reported that Scogin was the best Physician in the world.

Jest 15. *How Scogin was robbed as he went to London*

When Scogin did pretend to leave Oxford, he went to dwell at London. And as he went towards London he met with thieves and they robbed him. And when he came to London, he espied one of the thieves, and then he said to the Sergeants[6] of London, "Yonder man robbed me when I came from Oxford."

The thief had espied Scogin talking with the Sergeants and fled his way. The Sergeants followed the thief, the thief did run, and the Sergeants after. One came to Scogin and said, "Wherefore do yonder men run so fast?"

Scogin said, "For a wager, but the foremost man hath won, for lately he had all my money from me."

The Sergeants cried, "Hold the thief!"

The thief said, "Hold me not. I do run for a wager." And when he was within St. Martin's, he said, "I have run well now, or else I had been hanged."

Jest 16. *Scogin told his Wife he had parbraked[7] a Crow*

After a while that Scogin came to London, he married a young woman, taking her for a Maid as other men do. At last he thought to prove his wife and feigned himself sick. "O, good wife," says he, "I will show you a thing, if you will promise me to conceal it."

His wife said, "Sir, you may tell me what you will. I were worse than accursed if I should disclose your counsel."

[6] *Sergeants*] police officers.
[7] *parbraked*] vomited.

"O, wife," said Scogin, "I had a great pang today in my sickness, for I did parbrake and cast out a Crow."

"A Crow!" said she.

"Yea," said Scogin, "God help me."

"Be of good comfort," said she, "you shall recover and do well."

"Well, wife," said Scogin, "go to Church and pray for me."

She went to the Church, and by and by one of her Gossips met with her and asked how her Husband did. "Iwis," said she, "a sore sick man he is and like to die, for there is an evil sign and token in him."

"What is that, Gossip?" said she.

"Nay, by giss[8]," said Scogin's wife..., "if I wist that you would keep my counsel, I would tell you."

Then said the woman, "Whatsoever you do tell, I will lay it dead under my feet."

"O," said Scogin's wife, "my Husband parbraked two Crows."

"Jesus," said the woman, "I never heard of such a thing."

This woman as she did meet another Gossip of hers showed that Scogin had parbraked three Crows. So it went from one Gossip to another, that ere matters were finished, all the Parish knew that Scogin had parbraked twenty Crows. And when the Priest was ready to go into the Pulpit, one came to request him and all the Parish to pray for Scogin, for he had parbraked twenty Crows. The Priest blessed him and said to the Parishioners, "I pray you pray for Scogin, for he is in peril of his life and hath parbraked twenty-one Crows."

By and by, one went to Scogin and said, "Sir, is it as it is spoken in the Church of you?"

"What is that?" said Scogin.

"The Priest said in the Pulpit that you had parbraked twenty-one Crows."

Said Scogin, "What a lie is this!"

By and by, the Bells were tolled for sacring, and Scogin hied him to Church lustily and merry, and when the men and women did see him in the Church, they looked one upon another and marveled of this matter. After Mass, Scogin asked what were they that should

8 *by giss*] by Jesus!

bring up such a tale upon him. At last the matter was so bolted out that the original of the cause began at Scogin's wife.

Here a man may see that it is hard to trust a Woman with a man's Secrets; wherefore it is good to prove a friend ere one have need.

Jest 43. How Scogin told the Frenchmen he would fly into England

On a time, Scogin made the Frenchmen believe that he would fly into England, and did get him many Goosewings and tied them about his arms and legs, and went up on a high tower and spread his arms abroad as though he would fly, and came down again and said that all his feathers were not fit about him and that he would fly on the morrow.

On the morrow he got him up on the tower, and there was much people gathered together to see him fly. Scogin did shake his feathers and said, "All my feathers be not fit about me. Come tomorrow and I will fly." On the morrow Scogin got up on the tower and did shake his feathers, saying, "Go home, fools, go home. Trow you that I will break my neck for your pleasure? Nay, not so."

There was a Frenchman had indignation at Scogin and said, "Tomorrow you shall see me fly to Paris." And he got him wings and went up on the Tower, and spread his wings abroad, and would have flown, and fell down into the moat under the tower. Every man was diligent to get the man out of the water, and Scogin did take him by the hand and said, "Sir, you be welcome from Paris. I think you have been in a great rain."

Here a man may see that one cannot have a shrewd turn in playing the fool, but he shall have a mock for his labor.

Selections from

JOHN TAYLOR

WIT AND MIRTH

(1629)

John Taylor the Water Poet (*1580–1653*) was a household name throughout the nation. Son of a Gloucester surgeon and educated in the Gloucester grammar school, he went to London to become a waterman on the Thames, rowing a water taxi between the City and the theaters, entertaining his passengers with doggerel and merry tales. During summers when the theaters were closed, he would embark upon sculling or walking tours across the country or to the Continent, subsisting on the sale of subscriptions to books he promised to write after each tour. His tour books and other pamphlets were so successful that in *1630* a collected editon of his Works was issued in a sumptuous folio. A less expensive quarto edition went through nine editions in five years. At the same time, new editions of individual titles continued to appear, a testament to their popularity among the various social classes.

Wit and Mirth, *first published in 1629, was one of the books that continued to be issued independently. Though it took on an additional twenty-five jests in the* Works, *it was reissued in its original form in 1635 with 112 jests, while the jests added in the* Works *appeared in another of Taylor's jestbooks,* Bull, Beare, and Horse *the same year.*

There is no reason to doubt Taylor's claim in his dedication that his jests were drawn from "relation and hearsay" rather than books. Even a well-worn classical jest like number 16 is transplanted to Taylor's time in Taylor's style, a style consistently colloquial and direct, free from digression and superfluous ornament. The collection seems designed to show his versatility in various kinds of jests, and its variety made it a well-mined source for the rest of the century.

(STC 23814)

---

from The Dedication

I . . . entreat you that, when your more serious affairs will permit, you would bestow the looking upon these my poor and beggarly wardrobe of witty Jests whom I dare not call Apothegms. And because I had many of them by relation and hearsay, I am in doubt that some of them may be in print in some Authors, which I do assure you is more than I do know—which, if it be so, I pray you but to connive or tolerate and let the Authors make twice as bold with me at any time.

I.

Myself carried an old fellow by water that had wealth enough to be Deputy of the Ward and wit sufficient for a Scavenger. The water being somewhat rough, he was much afraid and, instead of saying his prayers, he threatened me that if I did drown him, he would see me hanged for it.

I desired him to be quiet and fear nothing, and so in little space I landed him at the Bear's College on the Bankside, alias Paris Garden. "Well," said he, "I am glad I am off the water, for if the Boat had miscarried I could have swum no more than a Goose."

2.

An old Painter, at the repairing of a Church, was writing sentences of Scripture upon the walls. By chance, a friend of mine came into the Church and reading them perceived much false English. "Old man," said my friend, "why do you not write true English?"

"Alas, Sir," quoth the Painter, "they are poor simple people in this Parish and they will not go to the cost of it."

3.

Two men being set at a Table, one against the other, the one of them having a cup in his hand drank to the other, saying, "Here, Opposite, I will drink to you."

"Opposite?" said the other, being angry. "What is that? I would not have thee put any of thy nicknames upon me, for thou shalt well know that I am no more opposite than thyself or the skin between thy brows."

4.

A Wealthy Monsieur in France, having profound revenues and shallow brain, was told by his man that he did continually gape in his sleep, at which he was angry with his man, saying he would not believe it. His man verified it to be true. His master said that he would never believe any that told him so, "except," quoth he, "I chance to see it with mine own eyes, and therefore I will have a great Looking glass hanged at my bed's feet for the purpose, to try whether thou art a lying knave or not."

5.

The said Monsieur commanded his man to buy him a gray hat with a button on the brim to button it up behind. His man bought him one and brought him. He put it on his head with the button before, which when he looked in the glass and saw, he was very angry, saying, "Thou cross untoward knave! Did I not bid thee buy a hat with the button to hold it up behind, and thou hast brought me one that turns up before! I command thee once more go thy ways and buy me such a one as I would have, whatsoever it cost me."

6.

The same Gallant ,as he traveled would have a Goose to his Supper, which when she was roasted and brought to the Table, he said she stank. "Not so, I hope," said the Host. "It cannot be, for I am sure she was alive since you came into the house."

"That may be," quoth the Monsieur, "but then I am sure that you killed her when she was shitting. She would never stink so else."

7.

An exceeding tall Gentlewoman was riding behind a very short little man, so that the man's head reached no higher than her breast, which the aforesaid Monsieur perceiving said, "Madam, you will ride a great deal better if you put your leg over that same pummel of your saddle."

Another time he chanced to meet a Lady of his acquaintance and asked her how she did, and how her good Husband fared—at which word she wept, saying that her Husband was in heaven. "In heaven?" quoth he. "It is the first time that I heard of it, and I am sorry for it with all my heart."

8.

Once the said Monsieur saw a fellow that had a Jack-Daw to sell. "Sirrah," quoth he, "what wilt thou take for thy daw?"

"Monsieur," said the fellow, "the price of my Daw is two French Crowns."

"Wherefore," said the other, "dost thou ask so much for him?"

The fellow replied that the Daw could speak French, Italian, Spanish, Dutch, and Latin, "all which tongues he will speak after he is a little acquainted in your Lordship's house."

"Well," quoth he, "bring thy Daw in and there is thy money."

In conclusion, Jack Daw, after a month or five weeks time, never spake otherwise than his father's speech, "Kaw, Kaw," whereat the Monsieur said that the knave had cozened him of his money. "But it is no matter. There is no great loss in it, for," quoth he "though my Daw do not speak, yet I am in good hope that he thinks the more."

9.

Another time, he commanded his man to buy some sweet thing to burn in his Chamber, "for," quoth he, "my Chamber stinks most odoriferously." His man brought Frankincense in a paper, and as he was going for fire, his master tasted of it and finding it stick in his teeth and relish very bitter, he called his man "cozening knave," that would bring him such bitter trash for his money, and straightway commanded him to buy a pound of the best sugar and burn it straight to sweeten and perfume his Chamber.

10.

This Gallant in his youth was much addicted to dicing, and many time when he had lost all his money then he would pawn his cloak and so go home without either cloak or coin, which grieved the Lady his mother very much. For remedy whereof, she caused all his doublets, of what stuff soever, to be made with canvas painted backs whereon was fashioned two fools, which caused the Gentleman ever after to keep his cloak on his back, for fear two of the three should be discovered.

11.

Will Backstead the Player cast his Chamber-lye out of his window in the night, which chanced to light upon the heads of the watch passing by, who angrily said, "Who is that offers us this abuse?"

"Why," quoth Will, "who is there?"

"Who is here?" said one of the pickled watchmen. "We are the Watch."

"The Watch!" quoth William. "Why, my friends, you know, 'Harm watch, harm catch.'"

12.

A Cardinal of Rome had a goodly fair house new built, but the broken bricks, tiles, sand, lime, stones, and such rubbish as are commonly the remnants of such buildings lay confusedly in heaps and scattered here and there. The Cardinal demanded of his Surveyor wherefore the rubbish was not conveyed away. The Surveyor said that he purposed to hire an hundred carts for the purpose. The Cardinal replied that the Charge of Carts might be saved, for a pit might be digged in the ground and bury it.

"My Lord," said the Surveyor, "I pray you, what shall we do with the earth which we dig out of the said pit?"

"Why, you whoreson Coxcomb," said the Cardinal, "canst thou not dig the pit deep enough and bury all together?"

13.

A poor Countryman praying devoutly superstitious before an old image of Saint Loy, the image suddenly fell down upon the poor man and bruised his bones sorely, that he could not stir abroad in a month after—in which space the cheating Priests had set up a new image. The countryman came to the Church again and kneeled afar off to the new image, saying, "Although thou smilest and lookest fair upon me, yet thy father played me such a knavish prank lately that I'll beware how I come too near thee, lest thou shouldst have any of thy father's unhappy qualities."

16.

A proper Gentlewoman went to speak with a rich Miser that had more gout than good manners. At her taking leave, he requested her to taste a cup of Canary. She, contrary to his expectation, took him at his word and thanked him. He commanded Jeffrey Starveling his man to wash a glass and fill it to the Gentlewoman. Honest Jeffrey filled a great glass about the bigness of two Tailor's thimbles and gave it to his Master, who kissed it to save cost and gave it to the Gentlewoman, saying that it was good Canary of six years old at the least. To whom she answered, seeing the quantity so small, "Sir, as you requested me, I have tasted your wine, but I wonder that it should be so little being of such a great age."

18.

One being in a Chamber with his friend, looking out at the window he saw one riding on a horse in the street. Said he, "Do you see that horse?" "Yea," quoth the other. "Then," said he, "you may swear you have seen the best horse in England."

"How do you know that?" said the other.

"I know it well," said he, "for it is my horse and I am sure that he is the best, and yet I dare swear that I have one in my stable worth ten of him."

19.

An unhappy boy that kept his father's Sheep in the country did use to carry a pair of Cards in his pocket, and meeting with boys as good as himself would fall to Cards at the Cambrian game of Whip-her-ginny, or English one-and-thirty, at which sport he would some days lose a sheep or two. For which, if his father corrected him, he, in revenge, would drive the sheep home at night over a narrow bridge where some of them, falling besides the bridge, were drowned in the swift brook.

The old man, being wearied with his ungracious dealing, complained to a Justice, thinking to affright him from doing any more the like. In brief, before the Justice the youth was brought, where (using small reverence and less manners) the Justice said to him, "Sirrah, you are a notable villain. You play at Cards and lose your father's sheep at one-and-thirty."

The boy replied that it was a lie. "A lie!" quoth the Justice. "You saucy knave, dost thou give me the lie?"

"No," quoth the boy. "I gave not you the lie, but you told me the lie, for I never lost sheep at one-and-thirty, for when my game was one-and-thirty I always won."

"Indeed," said the Justice, "thou sayest true. But I have another accusation against thee, which is that you drive your father's sheep over a narrow bridge, where some of them are oftentimes drowned."

"That's a lie too," quoth the boy, "for those that go over the bridge are well enough. It is only those that fall beside which are drowned."

Whereto the Justice said to the boy's father, "Old man, thou hast brought in false accusations against thy son, for he never lost sheep at one-and-thirty, nor were there ever any drowned that went over the bridge."

20.

A Captain passing through a room where a woman was drining[1] a buck of clothes, but he, thinking she had been brewing, saw a dish and dipped some small quantity of the Lye which he, supposing to be malt wort, drank up and presently began to swear, spit, spatter, and spawl. The woman asked him what he ailed. He told her, and called her some scurvy names, saying he had swallowed Lye.

"Nay, then, I cannot blame you to be angry, for you being a Soldier and Captain, it must needs trouble your stomach to swallow the Lye."

21.

A Country fellow, that had not walked much in streets that were paved, came to London, where a Dog came suddenly out of a house and furiously ran at him. The fellow stooped to take up a stone to cast at the Dog, and finding them all fast rammed or paved

[1] _drining_] drenching.

in the ground, quoth he, "What strange Country am I in, where the people tie up the stones and let the dogs loose!"

23.

A Justice of the Peace, being angry with a pilfering knave, said, "Sirrah, if thou dost not mend thy manners, thou wilt be shortly hanged or else I will be hanged for thee."

The bold knave replied, "I thank your worship for that kind offer, and I beseech your worship not to be out of the way when I shall have occasion to use you."

24.

Certain Justices of the Peace, being informed of the odious abuses daily committed by drunkenness in their Jurisdictions, did according to their places and duties meet at a market town and sat two days hearing informations and working reformations. At last they concluded that the Ale and Beer were too strong and therefore commanded that from thenceforth smaller drink should be brewed, whereby these unruly people might sometime go to bed sober.

But one mad tosspot fellow, being much grieved at this order, having made himself half pot-shaken,[2] without fear or wit came to the Justices and asked them if they had sat two days about the brewing of small drink. To whom one of the Justices replied, "Yes."

"Why, then," quoth the drunkard, "I pray you sit three days more to know who shall drink it, for I will none of it."

25.

There was a Scottish Gentleman that had sore eyes who was counseled by his Physicians to forbear drinking of wine. But he said he neither could nor would forbear it, maintaining it for the lesser evil to shut up the windows of his body than to suffer the house to fall down through want of reparations.

[2] *pot-shaken*] drunk.

26.

Upon the death of Queen Elizabeth there was a Mayor of a Country Town sitting in consultation with his brethren to whom he gravely said, "My Brethren and Neighbors, I do hear that the Queen is dead, wherefore I thought it exceeding fit we should despair to this place, that being dissembled together we might consult of our estates, for I doubt me we shall have another Queen or a King, and I stand in great fear that the people will be unrude, so that we shall be in danger of strange Resurrection."

27.

Another Mayor that was on hunting, by chance one asked him how he liked the Cry. "A pox take the Dogs," saith he. "They make such a bawling that I cannot hear the Cry."

28.

An old Justice was fast asleep on the Bench, when a poor Malefactor was judged to be hanged. At which word the Justice suddenly awaked and said to the Thief, "My friend, I pray let this be a warning to you. Look you do so no more, for we do not show every man the like favor."

29.

An old Recorder of a City in this land was busy with a Country Mayor. In the mean space, they were interrupted by a fellow that was brought before him for killing of a man. My Lord asked the fellow's name, who answered his name was Gilman. Said my Lord, "Take away G, and thy name is Ilman. Put K to it, thy name is Kilman. And put Sp and thy name is Spilman.[3] Thou art half hanged already, as the proverb says, for thou hast an ill name, let a man vary it how he can."

The Mayor all this while stood by musing at my Lord's canvassing the man's name and afterward being at home among his own good people, he had an offender brought before him for getting a

[3] *Spilman*] i.e., spoiler.

Wench with child. Master Mayor asked him his name. The fellow
said, "If it please your worship, my name is Johnson."

The Master Mayor, striving to imitate my Lord, said, "Take
away G and thy name is Ilman. Put K to it, it is Kilman. Put Sp to
it and thy name is Spilman. Thou art a knave, thou hast an ill name,
and thou shalt be hanged, etc."

30. *A Quiblet*

Master Field the Player, riding up Fleet Street a great pace,
a Gentleman called him and asked him what play was played that
day. He, being angry to be stayed upon so frivolous a demand,
answered that he might see what play was to be played upon every
Post. "I cry you mercy," said the Gentleman. "I took you for a
Post, you rode so fast."

31.

One, being long vexed with the spirit of jealousy, came suddenly
into his house and found a man, whom he suspected, somewhat
too busy with his wife, to whom he said, "Now, good fellow, I
thank thee, for thou hast cured me of a strange hellish torment.
My suspicion is cleared, and apparent knowledge hath given me
such ease of heart that I will be jealous no more."

32.

A skilful Painter was requested to paint out a fair Courtesan—
in plain English, a Whore. "I pray you spare that cost," said
the Painter, "for if she be a right whore, she daily paints herself."

33.

Seigneur Valdrino, paymaster to the Camp of Alphonsus, King of
Aragon, a man exquisite in courtship and compliment, as two or
three were at strife laying wagers what Countryman he was, a
blunt bold Captain asked what was the matter. "Why, Captain,"
said one, "we are laying a wager what Countryman my Lord
Treasurer Valdrino is."

"O," said the Captain, "I can tell you that. I am sure he was
born in the land of Promise, for I have served the King in his wars

these seven years without pay, and ever when I petition to my Lord, he pays me with no coin but promises, which makes me half assured that he is that Countryman."

34.

A Nobleman of France, as he was riding, met with a yeoman of the country to whom he said, "My friend, I should know thee. I do remember I have often seen thee."

"My good Lord," said the Countryman, "I am one of your Honor's poor tenants and my name is T. L."

"I remember thee better now," said my Lord. "There were two brothers of you, but one is dead. I pray, which of you doth remain alive?"

35.

The aforesaid Nobleman having had a Harper that was blind play to him after supper somewhat late, at last he arose and commanded one of his servants to light the Harper down the stairs; to whom the Servingman said, "My Lord, the Harper is blind."

"Thou ignorant knave," quoth my Lord, "he hath the more need of light."

36.

A Young fellow wished himself the richest Cuckold in England. To whom his Mother said very angrily, "You foolish covetous boy, why dost thou desire such a wish? Hath not thine own father enough in store for thee?"

37.

A Whore Rampant made her husband a Cuckold Dormant, with a front Crescent, surprised by the watch Guardant, brought to the Justice Passant, with her playfellow Pendant, after a course Couchant. The Justice told her that her offense was heinous, breaking the bonds of matrimony in that adulterate manner, and that she should consider that her husband was her Head.

"Good sir," quoth she, "I did ever acknowledge him so. And

I hope it is no such great fault in me, for I was but trimming,[4] dressing, or adhorning my Head."

38.

A Man being very sickly, one said to his wife, "I marvel your husband doth not wear a nightcap."

"Truly," quoth she, "within these six months that my husband hath been sick, although his legs be shrunk, yet he hath outgrown all his nightcaps."

39.

A Boy, whose mother was noted to be one not overladen with honesty, went to seek his Godfather, and enquiring for him, quoth one to him, "Who is thy Godfather?"

The boy replied, "His name is goodman Digland the Gardener."

"O," said the man, "if he be thy Godfather, he is at the next Alehouse. But I fear thou takest God's name in vain."

40.

A Scholar riding from Cambridge toward London, his horse being tired (a lazy disease often befalling such hackneys), met a Post on the way who notwithstanding he did what he could to make his horse give him place by spur, switch, and bridle, yet the Post was fain to give him the way. To whom, in anger, he said, "Thou paltry fellow, dost thou not see I am a Post?"

The Scholar straight replied, "And thou ignorant fellow, dost thou not see that I ride upon a Post?"

41.

A Fellow having more drink than wit, in a winter evening made a foolish vow to take the wall of as many as he met betwixt the Temple Bar and Charing Cross, and coming near the Savoy, where stood a Post a little distance from the wall, the drunkard took it for a man and would have the wall—beginning to quarrel and give the Post foul words. At which a man came by and asked the matter

4 *trimming*] pun on getting pregnant.

and whom he spoke to. He answered, he would have the wall of that fellow that stood so stiffly there.

"My friend," said the other, "that is a Post. You must give him the way."

"Is he so?" said the fellow. "A pox upon him, why did he not blow his horn?"

42.

A Sailor being on a tired horse, riding from Dover to London, his company prayed him to ride faster, to whom he answered, "I can come no faster. Do you not see that I am becalmed?"

43.

Two Gentlemen were jesting, and one of them cast away the other's hat. But the other catched his hat off and put it on his own head. "Now, fie, fie," quoth the other, "thou spoilest my hat."

"Wherewith?" said the other.

"Marry," said he that was bareheaded, "thou spoilest my hat with putting a Calf's head into it."

44. *The figure Conversion*

If a Vintner draw me good wine upon money or credit, then he is fitter to draw than hang. But if he draw me bad wine for good money, then he is much fitter to hang than to draw.

48.

A Gentlewoman cheapened a close stool in Paul's Churchyard, and the shopkeeper did ask her too much money for it, as she thought. "Why, mistress," said he, "I pray you consider what a good lock and key it hath."

She replied that she had small use for either lock or key, for she purposed to put nothing into it but what she cared not who stole out.

49.

A Countrywoman at an Assize was to take her oath against a party. The said party entreated the Judge that her oath might not be taken. The judge demanded why he excepted against her. "My Lord," quoth he, "she is a Recusant or Roman Catholic, and they hold it no matter of conscience to swear anything against us."

"Come hither, woman," said the Judge. "I do not think thou art a Recusant. I am persuaded that for forty shillings thou wilt swear the Pope is a knave."

"Good my Lord," said she, "the Pope is a stranger to me, but if I knew him as well as I know your Lordship, I would swear for half the money."

52.

A rich Grazier dwelling 150 miles from Oxford, having a son that had seven years been a student there, at last sent for him home, to whom he said, "Son, I do hear that you are well practiced in the rudiments of learning, but that withal you are addicted to an idle vein of the poor and threadbare art of Poetry—which I charge thee to leave and avoid, as thou tenderest my favor. For my mind is not to have thee live beggarly and die poorly. Yet I will ask thee one Poetical question, which is: Wherefore thinkest thou that so beautiful a creature as Venus was so besotted to match herself with so ill-favored a knave as Vulcan?"

"In truth, father," quoth the young man, "I can yield you no reason for it, but I wonder at it. And yet I do admire as much wherefore my mother married with you."

53.

A Man going with his Wife by a deep river's side began to talk of Cuckolds, and withal he wished that every Cuckold were cast into the river—to whom his wife replies, "Husband, I pray you learn to swim."

54.

A Man riding through a village with his dog running by him, which dog's name was called Cuckold, leaping and frisking into every house he passed by where the door was open—whereupon the man, being afraid his dog would be lost, calls and whistles, "Here, here, Cuckold!"—to whom an old woman said, "Whom dost thou miscall? I would have you know that no Cuckold dothd well in this house."

"Good woman," said the Man, "you mistake me. I do call nobody but my dog."

"Now out upon thee, thou misbelieving knave," said she. "Where learnest thou that manners, to call a dog by a Christian body's name?"

55.

A lusty Miller that in his younger days had been much given to the flesh and the devil, so that not one pretty maid or female servant did or could bring grist to his mill to be ground but the knave Miller would do his best to undermine and blow up her chastity. And withal he would bargain with as many as his temptations overcame that at his day of marriage every one of them should give him a Cake.

In process of time, the Miller was married and those foresaid free-hearted Wenches sent each one their cakes, to the number of ninety-nine. His wife the bride, who also went for a maid, did muse and ask what was the meaning of so many Cakes. The Miller told her the truth of all, without any dissembling, to whom his wife answered, "If I had been so wise in bargaining as you have been in your time, the young men of my acquaintance would have sent me a hundred cheeses to eat with your cakes."

> This bawdy Miller in a trap was catched,
> Nor only married but most fitly matched;
> In this the proverb is approved plain,
> What bread men break is broke to them again.

56.

There was a fair ship of two hundred tons lying at the Tower Wharf at London, where a Countryman passing by most earnestly looked on the said ship and demanded how old she was. One made answer that she was a year old. "Good Lord bless me!" said the Countryman. "Is she so big grown in one year? What a greatness will she be by that time she comes to my age!"

> This man's blind ignorance I may compare
> To Aqua vitae given to a Mare;
> Let each man his own calling then apply,
> *Ne sutor ultra crepidam*,[5] say I.

57.

Twelve Scholars riding together, one of them said, "My masters, let us ride faster!"

"Why?" quoth another. "Methinks we ride a good pace. I'll warrant it is four mile an hour."

"Alas," said the first, "what is four mile an hour amongst all us?"

> Let no man boast of wit or learning deep,
> For ignorance may out of knowledge creep;
> Amongst twelve men four mile an hour to ride,
> He that hath wit to each his share divide.

58.

An Apprentice in the market did ask the price of an hundred Oysters. His friend persuaded him not to buy them, for they were too small. "Too small?" replied the Apprentice. "There is not much loss in that, for I shall have the more to the hundred."

> If up the hill a measured mile it be,
> Then down the hill's another mile, I see;
> A groat to pay, fourpence will quit the cost;
> What's won in the hundred, in the shire is lost.

59.

Six Gentlemen riding together were in doubt that they were out of their way, wherefore they rode a flight-shot to an old shepherd, one of them inquiring of him if that were the way to such a town and how far it was thither. "Sir," quoth the Shepherd, "that is the right way, and you have six miles thither."

Quoth one of the Gentlemen, "What a lying old knave art thou! It cannot be above four miles."

The Shepherd replied, "Sir, you offer like a chapman. And you shall have it for four miles, but, I'll assure you, it shall cost every one of these Gentlemen six miles before they come thither."

---

[5] *Ne . . . crepidam*] A shoemaker should stick to his last.

> Here rashness did the Gallant's tongue o'erslip,
> To whom the Shepherd gave a pleasing nip;
> Thus softest fire doth make the sweetest Malt
> And mild reproofs make rashness see his fault.

60.

A Man was very angry with his Maid because his eggs were boiled too hard. "Truly," said she, "I have made them boil a long hour. But the next you have shall boil two hours, but they shall be tender enough."

> The boiling of this wench's eggs, I find,
> Much like unto a greedy miser's mind;
> The eggs the more they boil are harder still;
> The miser's full, too full, yet wants his fill.

61.

Two learned good fellows drinking a pipe of Tobacco, it being almost out—that he that drunk last did partly feel the ashes to come hot to his lips—giving the pipe to his friend, said, "Ashes to ashes."

The other, taking the pipe and being of a quick apprehension, threw it out to the dunghill saying, "Earth to earth."

> Thus wit with wit agrees, like cake and cheese
> Both sides are gainers, neither side doth leese;
> Conceit begets conceit, jest, jest doth father,
> And butter fallen to ground doth something gather.

62.

One said a Citizen was a man all in earnest and in no part like a jest, because the Citizen was never bad or the jest never good till they were both broke.

> What's one man's yea may be another's nay;
> The sun doth soften wax and harden clay;
> Some Citizens are like to jests—for why?
> They'll break in jest or bankrupt policy.

63.

A Gallant with a galloping wit was mounted upon a running horse toward a Town named Tame, within ten miles of Oxford, and riding at full speed, he met an old man and asked him, "Sirrah, is this the way to Tame?"

"Yes, sir," he replied, "—your Horse, I'll warrant you, if he were as wild as the devil."

> This is a riddle to a fool, methinks,
> And seems to want an Oedipus or Sphinx;
> But, Reader, in my book I hold it fit
> To find you lines, yourself must find you wit.

64.

A complimental Courtier that in his French, Italian, and Spanish cringes, congees, and curtsies would bend his body and bow every way like a tumbler—a Mercer's servant espying his marmositical Apishness said, "O, if my master could have bowed but half so much, I am certainly persuaded that he had never broke."

> Too much of one thing oft proves good for nothing
> And dainties in satiety breed loathing;
> The one's flattery mingled with the other's pride
> Had serv'd them both, both might live long unspied.

65.

I myself gave a book to King James once in the great Chamber at Whitehall as his Majesty came from the Chapel. The Duke of Richmond said merrily unto me, "Taylor, where did you learn the manners to give the King a book and not kneel?"

"My Lord," said I, "if it please your Grace, I do give now, but when I beg anything then I will kneel."

> Be it to all men by these presents known,
> Men need not kneel to give away their own;
> I'll stand upon my feet when as I give
> And kneel when I beg more means to live;
> But some by this may understand
> That Courtiers oftener kneel than stand.

68.

A country Fellow was much grieved that he had not gone seven miles to a market town to have seen the Baboons. "Why," said his wife, "it is too far to go and come in a day to see such babbles. Especially 'tis too great a journey on foot."

"O," quoth he, "I could have gone thither with my neighbor Hobson on foot, like a fool as I was, and I might have rid back upon my neighbor Jobson's mare, like an ass as I am."

> Thus in the preter tense a fool he was,
> And in the present tense he is an Ass,
> And in the future fool and ass shall be
> That goes or rides so far such sights to see.

69.

There was a lusty young Scholar preferred to a Benefice in the Country, and commonly on Sundays and holydays after evening prayer, he would have a dozen bouts at cudgels with the sturdiest youths in his parish. The Bishop of the Diocese, hearing of it, sent for the Parson, telling him that this beseemed not his profession and gravity, and that if he did not desist from that unmeet kind of exercise, he would unbenefice him.

"Good my Lord," said the Parson, "I beseech you to conceive rightly of me, and I doubt not but my playing at cudgels will be accounted tolerable, for I do it on purpose to edify the ruder sort of my people."

"How so?" said the Bishop.

"Marry, my Lord," quoth the Parson, "whatsoever I do teach them at morning and evening prayer, I do beat soundly into their heads at cudgels afterward for their better remembrance."

> I wish that all the Fencers in our nation
> Were only of this Parson's congregation;
> That he his life and doctrine should explain
> By beating them whilst they beat him again.

70.

A Judge upon the Bench did ask an old man how old he was. "My Lord," said he, "I am eight and fourscore."

"And why not fourscore and eight?" said the Judge.

The other replied: "Because I was eight before I was fourscore."

> Eight's before eighty, all men descry,
> Yet we name eighty first contrarily;
> Pull off my Boots and Spurs, I you beseech,
> When Spurs and Boots is rather proper speech.

71.

A Fellow made his boast that he rode 220 miles with one horse and never drew bit. "That may be," quoth another. "Perhaps you rid him with a halter."

> The proverb says, he that will swear will lie;
> He that will lie will steal by consequency;
> Swearers are liars, liars most are thieves,
> Or God help Jailors and true Undershrieves.[6]

72.

One saw a decayed Gentleman in a very threadbare cloak, said to him, "Sir, you have a very watchful cloak on."

"Why?" said the poor Gentleman.

"I do not think it had a good nap this seven years."

The Gentleman replied, "And truly, sir, methinks you want a nap as well as my cloak, for you talk idly for want of sleep."

> The prodigal at Poverty doth scoff,
> Though from his back the beggar's not far off;
> Here flout with flout and bob with bob is quitted,
> And proud vainglorious folly finely fitted.

78.

A Servingman going in haste in London, minding his business more than his way, a Gallant jostled him from the wall almost into the kennel. The fellow turned about and asked the Gentleman why he did jostle him so. The Gentleman said because he would not give the wall to a saucy knave. The Servingman replied, "Your worship is not of my mind, for I will."

> Here Pride that takes Humility in snuff
> Is well encountered with a counterbuff;
> One would not give the wall unto a knave,
> The other would and him the wall he gave.

80.

Divers Gentlemen being merry together, at last one of their acquaintance came to them whose name was Sampson. "Aha,"

---

[6] *Undershrieves*] undersheriffs.

said one of them, "now we may be securely merry. No Sergeant or Bailiff dare touch us. For if a thousand Philistines come, here is Sampson who is able to brain them all."

To whom Sampson replied, "Sir, I may boldly venture against so many as you speak of, provided that you will lend me one of your Jawbones."

81.

Two Plasterers being at work for me at my house in Southwark did many times patch and daub out part of their day's labor with prating, which I, being digging in my garden, did overhear that their chat was of their wives and how that "If I were able," quoth one, "my wife should ride in pomp through London as I saw a Countess ride yesterday."

"Why," quoth the other, "how did she ride, I pray?"

"Marry," said he, "in state, in her Horse-litter."

"O, base!" quoth the other. "Horse-litter! I protest as poor a man as I am, I would have allowed my wife a threepenny truss of clean straw."

82.

Sir Edward Dyer came to town on some business just at the time as the Gate was newly shut and the Warders going away with the keys. He, looking through the gate, called to one of them, saying, "Ho, fellow, I pray thee open the gate and let me in."

"None of your fellow, Sir, but a poor knave."

"Why, then," said Sir Edward, "I pray thee, poor knave, let me in."

"Nay, no knave neither," quoth the Warder.

"Why, then," said the knight, "he was a knave that told me so."

83.

One met his friend in the street and told him he was very sorry to see him look so ill, asking him what he ailed. He replied that he was now well amended, but he had been lately sick of the Pox.

"What pox? The small pox?" said his friend.

"Nay," quoth the other, "my mind was not so base. For I had the biggest pox that I could get for my money."

84.

An honest Hostess of mine at Oxford roasted an old shoulder of a Ram, which in the eating was as tough as a Buff Jerkin. I did ask her what the reason was that the mutton was so tough. She said she knew not, except the Butcher deceived her in the age of it, and she would tell him on both sides of his ears like a knave as he was.

"Nay," quoth I, "I think there is another fault in it which will excuse the Butcher, for perhaps you roasted it with old wood."

"In truth," quoth the hostess, "it is like enough, and my husband never doth otherways but buy old stumps and knots which makes all the meat we either roast or boil so exceeding tough that nobody can eat it."

85.

One hearing a clock strike three when he thought it was not two said, "This Clock is like an hypocritical Puritan, for though he will not swear, yet he will lie abominably."

86.

Dick Tarlton said that he could compare Queen Elizabeth to nothing more fitly than to a Sculler,[7] for, said he, "neither the Queen nor the Sculler hath a fellow."

88.

A poor laboring man was married and matched to a creature that so much used to scold waking that she had much ado to refrain it sleeping, so that the poor man was so batterfanged and belabored with tongue-mettle that he was weary of his life. At last, four or five women that were his neighbors, pitying his case, came in his absence to his house to admonish and counsel his wife to a quiet behavior towards her husband, telling her that she was a shame to all good women in her bad usage of so honest a painful man. The woman replied to her neighbors that she thought her husband

[7] *Sculler*] oarsman who rows alone.

did not love her, which was partly the cause that she was so froward towards him.

"Why," said an old woman, "I will show thee how thou shalt prove that he loves thee dearly. Do thou counterfeit thyself dead and lie under the table, and one of us will fetch thy husband and he shall find us heavy and grieving for thee, by which means thou shalt perceive his lamentation for thee how much he loves thee." This counsel was allowed and effected.

When the poor man came home, he hearing the matter, being much oppressed with grief, ran under the table bemoaning the happy loss of his most kind vexation, and making as though he would kiss her, with a most loving embrace (to make all sure) he broke her neck.

The neighbors pitying the man's extreme passion, in compassion told him that his wife was not dead, and that all this was done but to make a trial of his love towards her—whereupon they called her by her name, bidding her to rise, and that she had fooled it enough with her husband. But for all their calling, she lay still, which made one of the women to shake and jog her, at which the woman cried, "Alas, she is dead indeed!"

"Why this it is," quoth her husband, "to dissemble and counterfeit with God and the world."

91.

A miserable fellow in the country did once a year use to invite his neighbors to dinner, and as they were one time sat he bade them welcome, saying that there was a sirloin of beef, that the ox it came from cost twenty pound, and that there was a Capon that he paid two shillings sixpence for in the market. At which a country yeoman sitting against the Capon fell to and cut off a leg of it (the rest of the guests being not yet past their roast beef), to whom the man of the house said, "My friend, I pray thee, eat some of this same Sirloin."

"O, sir, God forbid," quoth the fellow. "I am but a poor man. An ox of twenty pound price is too dear meat. A Capon of half a crown will serve my turn well enough, I thank you."

93.

A fellow having been married but five weeks, perceived his wife to be great with child, wherefore she desired him to buy a cradle. Shortly after, he went to a Fair and bought ten cradles. And being demanded why he bought so many, he answered that his wife would have use for them all in one year.

97.

One said that Bias the Philosopher was the first Bowler and that, ever since, the most part of Bowls do in memory of their original wear his badge of remembrance and very dutifully hold Bias.[8] Now, to tell you, this Bias was one of the Seven Sages or wise men of Greece. My authors to prove him the inventor of Bowling are Shamrook, a famous Scythian Gymnosophist in his Nine Books of Rubbing and Running, of which opinion Balductus the Theban Orator seems to be in his third treatise of court performances.

The likeliest conjecture is that it was devised as an emblem, to figure out the world's folly and inconstancy. For though a child will ride a stick or staff with an imagination that he is on horseback, or make pies of dirt or houses of Cards, feed with two spoons and cry for three pieces of bread and butter—which childish actions are ridiculous to a man—yet this wise game of Bowling doth make the Fathers surpass their children in apish toys and most delicate dog-tricks.

As first, for the postures: (1) Handle your Bowl; (2) Advance your Bowl; (3) Charge your Bowl; (4) Aim your Bowl; (5) Discharge your Bowl; (6) Ply your Bowl—in which last posture of plying your Bowl you shall perceive many varieties and divisions, as wringing of the neck, lifting up of the shoulders, clapping of the hands, lying down of one side, running after the Bowl, making long dutiful scrapes and legs (sometimes bareheaded), entreating him to "flee, flee, flee" (with "pox on't" when 'tis too short). And though the bowler be a Gentleman, yet there he may meet with attendant rooks that sometimes will be his betters six-to-four or two-to-one.

I do not know anything fitter to be compared to Bowling than

[8] *Bias*] The path of a ball is controlled by the way the bowler grasps its lopsided shape, or bias.

wooing, or lovers, for if they do not see one another in two days, they will say, "Good Lord! it is seven years since we saw each other." For Lovers do think that in absence time sleepeth, and in their presence that he is in a wild gallop. So a Bowler, although the alley or mark be but thirty or forty paces, yet sometimes I have heard the Bowler cry "rub, rub" and swear and lie that he was gone an hundred miles when the Bowl hath been short of the block two yards, or that he was too short a thousand foot when he is up on the head of the Jack, or ten or twelve foot beyond. In a word, there are many more several postures at Bowl than there are ridiculous idle tales or jests in my book.

Yet are the Bowlers very weak stomached, for they are ever casting. Sometimes they give the stab at the alley head, but, God be thanked, no blood shed. And sometimes they bestow a pippin one upon the other, but no good apple, I'll assure you. The mark which they aim at hath sundry names and epithets—as a Block, a Jack, and a Mistress: a Block because of his birth and breeding, showing by his mettle of what house he came; a Jack because he, being smoothed and gotten into handsome shape, forgets the house he came of, suffering his betters to give him the often salute whilst he like Jack Sauce neither knows himself nor will know his superiors.

But I hold a Mistress to be the fittest name for it, for there are some that are commonly termed mistresses which are not much better than mine aunts. And a mistress is oftentimes a mark for every knave to have a fling at—everyone strives to come so near her that he would kiss her. And yet some are short, some wide, and some over. And whoso doth kiss, it may perhaps sweeten his lips, but I assure him it shall never fill his belly, but rather empty his purse.

So much for Bowling—that I fear me I have bowled beyond the mark.

98.

A Minister riding into the west parts of England happened to stay at a village on a Sunday, where he offered kindly to bestow a Sermon upon them—which the Constable hearing did ask the Minister if he were licensed to preach. "Yes," quoth he, "that I am." And with that he drew out of a box his License, which was in Latin.

"Truly," said the Constable, "I understand no Latin, yet I pray you let me see it. I perhaps shall pick out here and there a word."

"No, good sir," quoth the Minister, "I will have no words picked out of it, for spoiling my License."

99.

A countryman being demanded how such a River was called that ran through their Country, he answered that they never had need to call the River, for it always came without calling.

102. *This Tale I writ on purpose to stick in the teeth of my proud, squeamish, nice critical Reader*

A countryman brought his wife's water to a Physician, saying, "Good morrow to your Worship, Master Confusion."

"'Physician,' thou wouldst say," said the other.

"Truly," said the fellow, "I am no Scholar but altogether unrude and very ingrum,[9] and I have here my wife's water in a pottle pot, beseeching your mastership to cast[10] it."

So the Physician took the water, which having put into an urinal and viewed it, he said, "My friend, thy wife is very weak."

"Truly," quoth he, "I think she be in a presumption."

"A 'consumption' thou wouldst say," said the Physician.

"[I told you before," the fellow replied, "that] I do not understand your allegant speeches."

"Well," quoth the Doctor, "doth thy wife keep her bed?"

"No, truly, sir," said he. "She sold her bed a fortnight since."

"Verily," quoth the Doctor, "she is very costive."

"Costly?" said the man. "Your Worship says true, for I have spent all that I have upon her almost."

Said the Doctor, "I do not say 'costly' but 'costive.' And I pray thee tell me, is she loose or bound?"

9 *ingrum*] ignorant.
10 *cast*] analyze.

"Indeed, sir," said the man, "she is bound to me during her life, and I am bound to her."

"Yea, but I pray thee," said the Doctor, "tell me in plain terms how she goes to stool."

"Truly," said the fellow, "in plain terms, she goes to stool very strangely. For in the morning, it is so hard that your Worship can scarce bite it with your teeth, and at night it is so thin that you might eat it with a spoon."

103.

Good fellows having well washed their wits in wine at a Tavern, one of them was very importunate to be gone—to whom another of them said, "I pray thee, be patient. Talk no more of going, for if thou wilt sit still but a little, thou shalt find that we shall all be gone, though we stay here."

105.

A fellow being scolded at by his wife would make her believe he would drown himself. And as he went toward the river, his wife followed him, desiring him to forbear, or at the least to let her speak with him. "Well," quoth he, "speak briefly, for I am in haste."

"Then, husband," said she, "seeing you will drown yourself, let me entreat you to take my counsel, which is that you cast [not] yourself into this shallow place here, for it will grieve my heart to see how long you will be a-dying. But go with me a little way and I will show you a deep place where you shall be dispatched presently."

106.

A woman in Scotland lay dying, to whom her husband said, "Wife, now thou art about to leave me alone I pray thee tell me with whom shall I marry?"

She replied, "Are you in haste to marry before the breath be out of my body? Then marry the devil's dam!"

"Not so, wife," said he. "I have had his daughter already, and if I should match with his mother, too, then I should be guilty of incest."

109.

One borrowed a cloak of a gentleman and met one that knew him, who said, "I think I know that cloak."

"It may be so," said the other. "I borrowed it of such a gentleman."

The other told him that it was too short. "Yea, but," quoth he that had the cloak, "I will have it long enough before I bring it home again."

110.

A poor woman's husband was to be hanged at the town of Lancaster, and on the execution day she entreated the Shrieve to be good to her and stand her friend. The Shrieve said that he could do her no hurt, for her husband was condemned and judged by the Law and therefore he must suffer. "Ah, good master Shrieve," said the woman, "it is not his life that I ask. But because I have far home and my mare is old and stiff, therefore I would entreat you to do me the favor to let my husband be hanged first."

111.

One came into a College in an University and asked how many Fellows belonged to the house. Another replied that there were more good fellows than good Scholars two to one.

112.

A fellow being drunk was brought before a Justice, who committed him to prison. And the next day, when he was to be discharged, he was to come to the Justice again, who said to him, "Sirrah, you were not drunk the last night?"

"Your Worship says true," said the fellow.

"Yea, but you were drunk," said the Justice, "and you did abuse me, and said I was a wise Justice."

The fellow replied, "If I said so, I think I was drunk indeed, and I cry your Worship mercy, for I will never do you that wrong when I am sober."

113.

A Spaniard having but one eye chanced to meet a man in the field where, drawing both their Rapiers, the other man with an unfortunate thrust struck out the other eye of the Spaniard— whereat the blind man suddenly cast down his Rapier, saying, "*Buenas noches*," which in the Spanish tongue is "Goodnight."

FINIS

Selections from

ROBERT CHAMBERLAIN

CONCEITS, CLINCHES,
FLASHES, AND WHIMZIES
(1639)

This book is attributed to Robert Chamberlain (1607–ca. 1660). We know very little about him other than that he was a lawyer's clerk who so impressed his employer that he sent him to Exeter College when Chamberlain was thirty years old. He attended Oxford around 1637 without taking a degree but while there he established a reputation as a witty poet, playwright, and jester. He was long thought to be responsible for the New Book of Mistakes *(1637) because some of its puns are characteristic of work we know to have been Chamberlain's, but even more consistently characteristic are those in* Conceits, Clinches, Flashes, and Whimzies. *Of the 287 jests in that book, half are one- and two-line epitomes of the kind reprinted below, earning Chamberlain the honor of being known today as the first to specialize in puns. The book was issued in an expanded version,* Jocabella, or a Cabinet of Conceits, *in 1640.*

(STC 4942)

1.

An idle Justice of Peace is like the picture of Saint George upon a signpost with his sword drawn to no purpose.

4.

Lovers' oaths are like mariners' prayers: when once the heat is over, they are not the same men.

14.

One asked why a Knight took place of a Gentleman. It was answered, because they were Knights nowadays before they were Gentlemen.

16.

One said a good Client was like a study gown that sits in the cold himself to keep his Lawyer warm.

17.

One said the fees of a pander and a puny clerk are much alike, for the pander had but twopence next morning for making the bed, and that was a penny a sheet.

19.

One compared a domineering fellow to a walking Spur that keeps a great jingling noise but never pricks.

26.

Those that say gallants put all upon their backs abuse them, for they spend a great deal more upon their bellies.

28.

One persuaded another to marry a whore because she was rich, telling him that perhaps she might turn. "Turn?" said the other. "She hath been so much worn that she is past turning."

29.

One put a jest upon his friend. "O," said his friend, "that I could but see your brains! I would even hug them for this jest."

30.

One asked why Sextons did use to wear black. It was answered that in regard of their office they were to meddle with grave matters and did therefore wear black.

33.

One wondered much what great Scholar this same Finis was, because his name was almost to every book.

40.

One said a jealous wife was like an Irish trouse, always close to a man's tail.

42.

One said a Physician was natural brother to the worms, because he was engendered out of man's corruption.

43.

One gave a fellow a box on the ear. The fellow gave him another.

"What do you mean?" said he that gave the first box. "I did not lend you a box, I freely gave it you."

The other answered he was a gamester and had been always us'd to pay the box.

60.

A simple fellow in gay clothes, says one, is like a Cinnamon tree: the bark is of more worth than the body.

63.

A gentleman riding on the way would needs turn back to kiss his wife that was behind him. He was therefore commended for a kind husband in regard he was before, to kiss his wife behind.

64.

One asked whether such a man were wise or no. It was answered that he was otherwise.

66.

One said poetry and plain dealing were a couple of handsome wenches. Another answered, "Yes, but he that weds himself to either of them shall die a beggar."

74.

One asked why Ladies called their husbands Master such-a-one and Master such-a-one and not by their titles of knighthood, as Sir Thomas, Sir Richard, Sir William, etc. It was answered that, though others called them by their right titles, as Sir William, Sir Thomas, etc., yet it was fit their wives should master them.

83.

A vainglorious man was bragging that his Father and his Uncle had founded such a Hospital. One answered, "'Tis true, but yet know that your Father and your Uncle were the mere confounders of that Hospital you speak of."

85.

One asked why he that drew beer was not called a drawer as well as he that drew wine. It was answered that beer made a man to piss but it was wine made him draw.

90.

One being asked what countryman he was, he answered, a Middle-sex man. The other told him, being he was neither of the male sex nor of the female sex but of a middlesex, he must then be a Hermaph-rodite.

92.

"Why do Ladies so affect slender waists?" said one.

"'Tis," replied another, "because their expenses may not be too great."

96.

"The severest stoics," said one, "are the greatest Students, be-cause their contracted brows are always bent to study."

98.

"Tapsters," said one, "should be men of esteem, because they are men not only of a high calling but also of great reckoning."

102.

"A Smith," said one, "is the most pragmatical fellow under the Sun, for he hath always many irons in the fire."

106.

One said that tall men of all others were most happy, because they were nearer heaven than all other men.

108.

One said that tall men should be great politicians, because they have an extraordinary reach.

109.

One said hangmen were very happy, because those men they do most hurt will never be able to render them *quid pro quo.*

115.

"Carpenters," said one, "are the civilest men in a Commonwealth, for they never do their business without a rule."

117.

Bricklayers are notable wanton fellows, for they have always to do with one trull[1] or other.

133.

Smiths of all handicraftsmen are the most irregular, for they never think themselves better employed than when they are addicted to their vices.

140.

Horse-keepers and hostlers (let the world go which way it will, though there be never so much alteration in times and persons) are still stable men.

145.

One asked what the reason was that few women loved to eat eggs. It was answered, "Because they cannot endure to bear the yoke."

194.

One asked another what Shakespeare's works were worth, all being bound together. He answered, "Not a farthing."
"Not worth a farthing!" said he. "Why so?"
He answered that his plays were worth a great deal of money, but he never heard that his works were worth anything at all.

214.

A Scholar that had his study hung round with brown paper was

[1] *trull*] trowel.

used (when any came in to visit him in his study) to say he did love
sometimes to sit in a brown study.

229.

A Dyer who was an idle drunken fellow was complaining to a
Scholar that he had very ill fortune in his business, and that commonly those things that he undertook to dye were spoiled. The
Scholar told him that the only way to have this amended was to
reform himself, for he that lived ill could never dye well.

240.

An Upholsterer was chiding his Apprentice because he was not
nimble enough at his work, and had not his nails and hammer in
readiness when he should use them, telling him that when he was an
Apprentice, he was taught to have his nails at his fingers' ends.

247.

One questioned which were the greatest wonders in the world.
'Twas answered, women's and Lawyers' tongues, for that they did
always lie yet never lay still.

263.

Two Gentlemen were in a deep dispute whether the man in the
Moon were a gentleman or a citizen. It was determined by a Scholar
that, when she was at full there was a gentleman in her, but when
she appeared like a horn, there was a citizen in her.

286.

A maid told her Mistress she must entreat her to keep more maids
because she was much overlaid.

Selections from

A BANQUET OF JESTS
(1633–1660)

Popularly known as "Archee's Jests," this was the favorite jestbook of mid-seventeenth-century England. It was attached to the name of Archee Armstrong (d. 1672), the official jester to both James I and Charles I until 1637 when he was dismissed for insulting Archbishop Laud. In 1633 the dedication of the first edition was signed "Anonymos." In 1640, while still signed "Anonymos," it was now subtitled "The King's Jester to the Reader," and in 1657 it was signed "Archee." In 1660, its imitator A Choice Banquet of Jests *boasted that it contained many jests of Archee's never published in his lifetime—as though he were then dead. But Archee was alive and prosperous in his native Cumberland. As court jester, he had accumulated a fortune, with guaranteed annual income from pensions, annuities, and the monopoly on the sale of tobacco pipes. Though an energetic litigant in civil law courts, he did nothing to injoin booksellers from using his name. At the same time, however, there is no evidence that he had anything to do with any of the nine editions of the jestbook. In fact, his own jesting was antithetical to the spirit of the book, and consisted of vitriolic raillery and acerbic insult. He was a devious politician and arch confidence man, a personality reflected in the few jests about him that appear below.*

Over twenty-five years, the Banquet of Jests *grew from 198 to 316 jests, and we can see how different kinds and styles of jests rose and fell in popularity. The pattern of change favors the epitome, the two-line dialogue, and the one-line pun, with the resulting loss of a long line of fine fabling.*

(STC 1372; Wing A3705, A3706)

from A BANQUET OF JESTS (1633)

6. *Of one that had a curst shrew to his wife*

One that had a notorious shrew to his wife, in a great jangling that did happen between them could not contain himself, but, taking up a flagon pot which stood near him, gave her a very deep wound in the head, which cost his purse soundly.

This woman, sitting on a time among her gossips, said openly, "My husband doth not dare to break my head anymore, because he paid so dearly for the last cure." This being told to her husband, he considered with himself and the next day sent for the Apothecary and Surgeon home to his house, who when they were come, he called for his wife and in her presence did pay them all to a farthing, and also gave to either of them a piece, and said, "I deliver you this money in earnest of the next cure."

13. *Of gray hairs*

One being asked the reason why his head was so intermixed with white hairs insomuch that it was grown gray, but not one white hair did appear in his beard, he answered, "It is no wonder. The hair of my head is elder than that of my beard by twenty years."

16. *The answer of a plain farmer to a great man of the Country*

The Lord of a Manor, preparing to build, had occasion to use many carts in his work, and therefore had sent as well unto his neighbors as his tenants and employed their Teams and Wains to their no small charge and trouble. At length, in close of business, he invited them all to supper, having two tables in the Hall but something unequally furnished.

The meat being set on the board, the Lord of the house came into the Hall and bade them welcome after this manner: "Neighbors and Friends, I do thank you all. Such of you as have helped me in my work for love, take their places at that board, for that other table is provided for them that expect money," and withal willed them likewise to take their places, which they did accordingly as they were disposed.

Only, one plain fellow did walk between the two tables, which the master of the house, perceiving, demanded why he did not do as the rest did. He answered, because that there was no place belonging unto him. He, desirous to know the reason, urged the plain fellow to tell it him.

"You have provided a table for them that come for love, another for them that come for money, but, to deal plainly with your Lordship, I came hither only for fear."

19. *A pretty, accidental Jest of a prating Parrot*

A Wine Merchant having a prating Parrot—when the price of French wine was fallen, it was cried in the streets for a groat a quart, which note the bird had got and had it perfect. But soon after, the price was risen again to sixpence. The Parrot still kept her old tone and cried, "A groat a quart, a groat a quart," being then caged in an inner room. Nevertheless, she spake so loud that divers came and knocked at the Merchant's door and desired to have wine at the same rate that he had caused it to be cried in the house. But he, ignorant of the error and not being able to afford it at that low rate, told them that they had abused him, for he never made any such outcry.

While they were arguing about this business, the Parrot fell again into her old note, "Wine a groat a quart," whereby the mistake was found on both sides. But the Merchant, being extremely angry that the bird had so fooled him, did fling her in a great rage into the kennel—from whence she crawled forth, being nothing all over but dirt—and then thinking them satisfied and himself fully revenged, went about his business into the Exchange, the poor Parrot climbing up to the top of one of the posts, there to dry herself.

By chance, came by a Sow which had been wallowing in the mire and was in a most beastly pickle, which the Parrot spying, and looking upon herself and afterwards viewed the Sow and said, "Alas, poor Sow, hast thou cried wine for a groat a quart, too?"

36. *Of a Countryman and his Landlord*

Asses are very rare in some parts of this land. Now, a Country Farmer, being none of the wisest, at the renewing of his lease was bound to present his Landlord with a handsome Colt, which might prove of sufficient stature, and seeking for one, the fittest as he thought for his turn, he came to a place where he found a young Ass's Colt, bargained with the owner and came and presented it to his Landlord, who, being much offended, said, "Friend, thou dost owe me by Covenant such a young beast as may in time become a large and fair horse for my use, and what a little small tit hast thou brought me!"

To whom the other replied, "Nay, good Landlord, I pray you find no fault with his stature, for if the rest of his body grow but according to the length of his ears, I make no question but he will prove the tallest Gelding in the Country."

51. *Of a Controversy decided betwixt a Lawyer and a Physician*

In the University of Leyden, where anyone may take a degree for money, there happened a great controversy, whether the Doctors of Law or Physic should have the precedence. A pleasant fellow took upon him to decide the controversy and demanded of them a question, whether the thief or the hangman used to go before. It was answered that the thief went before. "Why, then," saith he, "you Lawyers go before as the thieves, and Physicians follow after as the hangmen."

53. *Of a scholar that was persuaded to steal Conies*

A Young Scholar, being persuaded one night to go along with others to steal Conies (who never had been at the sport before), being come to the place and the moon shining clear, he no sooner spied them feeding but as one overjoyed with the sight of them, cried out aloud, "*Ecce cuniculi multi!*"[1] the noise of which voice drove them all into their burrows.

Being reproved by the rest that he had spoiled their sport, he replied, "Why, who would ever have imagined that the Conies could have understood Latin?"

59. *Of a Gentleman and a Barber*

A Gentleman whose face was full of pimples came rudely into a Barber's shop to be trimmed, but before he would sit down he entered into this discourse with the Barber: "Friend," saith he, "view me well. Thou seest my complexion, and how well my nose and cheeks are beset with rubies, which I prize the dearer because they cost me much in purchasing them. If you will undertake to trim me, you must do it without bloodshed, and I will give thee a crown. If otherwise, I will stab thee."

The Barber accepted of these conditions, though never so hard, and performed his task so well that no fault could be found therewith. The Gentleman paid the Barber according to his promise, and being ready to depart demanded of the Barber how he durst undertake such a task considering that his life was in hazard if his razor had slipt awry.

The Barber answered that he did it with ease and with little danger or difficulty. "For," saith he, "if I had perceived that I had drawn the least drop of blood from you, I would have first cut your throat."

74. *The King of Sweden's Goose*

The King of Sweden coming to a town of his Enemies with very little company, his Enemies to slight his force did hang out a Goose for him to shoot at. But, perceiving before night that these few

[1] "*Ecce cuniculi multi!*"] Look at all the rabbits!

Soldiers had invaded and set their chief holds on fire, they demanded of him what his intent was. To whom he answered, "To roast your Goose."

105. *Horses to Let*

A Country Fellow riding to London, by chance casting his eyes upon a sign, read there these words: "Here are horses to be let 1633" —which was the year when the sign was first set up; who, turning to his companion, said unto him, "So many horses in one place to be hired! I much marvel what shift they make for stable room."

115. *Of a young Bridegroom and his Bride*

A Young Gentleman, being greatly enamored on a Farmer's daughter, had so far insinuated into her favor that opportunity furthering him, he had vitiated her upon faithful promise of marriage, and got her with child. In the interim, the Parents of the Young Gentleman, jealous of their son's affection and fearing that he might hinder his better fortunes by matching below his degree, they carefully provided him of another wife, a Gentleman's daughter of their own rank, and suddenly clapped up the match betwixt them —which was not so closely done but it came to the hearing of the Farmer's daughter, who upon this necessity was enforced to discover how far all things had passed betwixt the Gentleman and her to her Father, who, perceiving his daughter not only to be fooled but utterly disgraced, and being much grieved thereat, got certain notice of the marriage day and place, and closely waylaid them in their passage to Church and so cunningly ordered the business that upon private conference betwixt the young man and him, he forced him to make composition for the injury done unto his daughter.

The Bride and her Parents and friends stay at the Church wondering at this delay, but at length commeth the Bridegroom, and the marriage without any suspicion is instantly dispatched. The day is spent in feasting, music, and dancing, and much joy. Supper is past, and bedtime come, where the new married couple with no small content embraced each other.

At length, the Bride, after some discourse, was very importunate to know of him the reason of his long stay from Church, and what the business was between him and the Farmer's daughter. Loathe he was to tell her, but she urged it so far, and he thinking it unnatural in himself to deny her anything, especially the first night, began to discourse all the passage of the business from the beginning, saying the sum of all was that he had gotten the Girl's Maidenhead and she had told it to her Father.

To whom the Bride, lovingly clasping him in her arms, replied, "Now, fie upon her for a foolish wench that could not keep her own counsel. One of my Father's Servingmen hath kept me company in the like kind for the space of this twelve month and upward, and my Father knoweth it not to this hour. For you I protest are the first that ever I revealed it to."

140. *A fat Man and a lean Horse*

A fat man riding on a lean horse, one would needs know of him the reason why his horse was so lean, himself being so fat. His answer was: "Because I look to myself and my servants to my horse."

154. *A Soldier begging of a Scholar*

A Soldier came to beg of a poor Scholar. The Scholar asked him by what authority he went thus a-begging. "Sir," said the Soldier, "I have a License."

The Scholar replied, "Well thou mayst have Lice, but thou hast no sense to beg of a poor Scholar."

159. *A Welshman's strange News*

A Welshman having been at London, his friend, according to the common custom, at his return demanded of him what news—who answered that he knew little news, only one strange thing he observed there, that every little Boy of five or six years old could speak English perfectly, which he thought very strange, because in his Country they learn to speak it as in England they learn to speak French, Italian, and the like.

164. *A Drunken Man's Mistake*

A Waterman being very drunk sat down in frosty weather on the shore near the Tower Wharf at a low water in a Moonshine night, and fell fast asleep, and slept so long until the tide came in and flowed by degrees even up to his mouth, the Moon shining in his face.

Whereupon, suddenly awakening, he said, "No more drink, I thank you heartily, but a few more clothes if you please and then put out the candle."

166. *The Beard White before the Head*

One being demanded why his beard was white and his head black, considering that his head was so much the elder, answered, "Because I have taken more care for the employment of my chops than for anything else."

169. *A Jest more Witty than Modest*

A Gentleman by chance espying a Gentlewoman's leg, said unto her, "Indeed, Lady, there is a very good leg!"

"Nay, truly, Sir," saith she, "here are two."

"Then," said he, "they are twins."

"Not so, neither," said she, "for there was one borne between them."

186. *Hard of Belief*

I have heard of a great Magistrate that, being often deceived by false rumors of Queen Elizabeth's death, protested that he would never believe she was dead until he saw it under her own hand.

from A BANQUET OF JESTS (1657)

Ad Populum, or A short Lecture by way of Preface to the People whom I desire to be as Courteous as Conceited

To you (of all sorts) that shall vouchsafe the perusal of these few sheets bound up in a small volume, I prepare you to expect no more in this collection of Jests than the Title Page promiseth, wherein is nothing earnest saving a pledge of my good meaning toward you. If you look that I should feast your Senses, or banquet your particular Palates, these papers will much deceive you. For instead of Dainties, you shall find *Dicteria;* for Junkets, *joci;* and for curious Sallets, *sales.*[2] Only they are passages of mirth, fit to entertain time and employ leisured hours, when they cannot be more seriously and profitably employed. So mild and gentle they are in their condition, that as they bark at none, so they bite not any. And therefore you may sport with them freely and safely.

Now if some out of their curiosity shall despise them for their commonness, I must then retire myself to the refuge of that old

[2] *Dicteria, joci, sales*] bons mots, jests, witty sayings.

Adage, *Bona quo communia eo meliora:* If they prove good, they cannot be too common. Again, if any shall object and say, "I know that" and "This I have heard related," those I thus answer: If many have heard some of them, yet few or none (I dare presume) all. Besides, I do not challenge them for my own, but gathered from the mouths of others, and what is stale to me, may be to thee new. Accept them then as courteously as they are offered to thy perusal willingly, to make them familiar unto such to whom they are merely foreign, and to recollect the memories of those to whom they have been known but since forgotten.

I must ingenuously confess unto you that, had not the License[3] curbed my liberty, the leaves of this book had been more in tale and the Jests (for I know not how more properly to style them) greater in number. But as they are (for otherwise now they cannot be) if they be well accepted, I acknowledge them too few; but if not well received by many, too many.

ARCHEE

The Stationer to the Reader

Since, Reader, I before have found thee kind,
Expect this last impression much refined.
The coarser Cates, that might the feast disgrace,
Left out, and better served in their place.
Pasquil's Conceits are poor, and Scoggin's dry,
Skelton's merry rhyme, once read, but now laid by.
Hind's Jests are new, and Tarlton's they are stale.
These neither bark, nor bite, nor scratch, nor rail.
Banquets were made for Laughter, not for Tears.
Such are these sportive Taunts, Tales, Jests, and Jeers.

R[ichard] R[oyston]

---

[3] *License*] Since June, 1643, all books were required to be licensed by an official censor before publication.

Court Jests

7. *To Choose a Wife*

One being dissuaded from marrying such a woman because she was no wiser, replied, "I desire that my wife should have no more wit than to be able to distinguish my bed from another man's."

28. *Of Taking the Wall*

A contemplative Scholar, walking in the street and studying as he went, ere he was aware ran upon a Courtier and half jostled him from the wall. The Gallant was somewhat offended at it and roughly thrust him by, saying, "I do not use to give every coxcomb the wall."

The Scholar, looking up in his face, answered, "But I do, Sir," and so passed on.

45. *A Witty Put-off*

One being convented before the Governors of the place where he lived for getting his Laundress with Child, they said they wondered that a man of his place and gravity would so much overshoot himself. "Why should you wonder at that?" said he. "It had indeed been a wonder if she had gotten me with Child," and so put off the matter with a Jest.

47. *Book Writers Guilty of Felony*

The book of deposing Richard the second and the coming in of Henry the fourth, supposed to be written by D. Hayward[4]—who was

---

[4] *D. Hayward*] i.e., Sir John Hayward, *Life and Raigne of King Henrie IV* (1599).

committed to the Tower for it—had much incensed Queen Elizabeth. And she asked Mr. Bacon, being then of her learned Council, whether there were no treason contained in it. Mr. Bacon, intending to do him a pleasure and to take off the Queen's bitterness with a Jest, answered, "No, Madame, for treason, I cannot deliver my opinion that there is any, but very much felony."

The Queen, apprehending it gladly, asked, "How and wherein?"

Mr. Bacon answered, "Because he hath stolen many of his sentences and conceits out of Cornelius Tacitus."

60. *The Inventor of Purgatory*

They say in a tale of Sixtus Quintus that after his death he went to Hell, and the Porter of Hell said to him, "You have some reason to offer yourself to this place, but yet I have order not to receive you. You have a place of your own, Purgatory. You may go thither."

So he went away and sought Purgatory a great while, and could find no such place. Upon that, he took heart and went to Heaven, and knocked, and St. Peter asked who was there.

He said, "Sixtus Pope."

Whereunto St. Peter said, "Why do you knock? You have the keys."

Sixtus answered, "It is true, but it is so long since they were given, as I doubt the wards of the lock be altered."

66. *Archee Overreached*

Our patron Archee, the King's Jester, having before fooled many, was at last well met withal. For coming to a Nobleman to give him good morrow upon New Year's day, he received a very gracious reward from him—twenty good pieces of gold in his hand. But the covetous fool, expecting, it seems, a greater, shook them in his fist and said they were too light.

The Nobleman took it ill from him, but dissembling his anger, he said, "I prithee, Archee, let me see them again, for amongst them there is one piece I would be loathe to part with."

Archee, supposing he would have added more unto them, delivered them back to my Lord who, putting 'em up in his pocket, said, "Well, I once gave money into a fool's hand, who had not the wit to keep it."

67. *An Englishman and a Frenchman Courting a Lady*

An Englishman and a Frenchman going to visit a handsome Lady, the Frenchman, much taken with her feature at first sight, stepped forward before the other and kissed her—at which the English Gentleman, greatly incensed as being of his acquaintance, told him such manners savored of the French impudence and misbecame him here. But he thinking to excuse himself, and not well acquainted with our English phrase, replied, "No harm done, good Monsieur, for now I have kissed her before, you have good leave to kiss her behind."

69. *Short Dispatch*

Sir Amice Pawlet, when he saw too much haste made in any matter, was wont to say, "Stay a while, that we may make an end the sooner."

Camp Jests

11. *Two Ancient Companions*

Two old Soldiers and companions that had served in the Low Countries twenty-odd years together, in the last German war took pay under the King of Sweden. And while his Majesty lay with his Army before Frankfort, it chanced, as they two with some others were tippling, just as one of them was heaving up a great Bombard of Beer to fill his cup, it chanced, I say, that a bullet from the besieged wall struck the Jack out of his hand, and with it half his head off. The other, his ancient Familiar and acquaintance, seeing it, "Zounds!" saith he, swearing like a mad man, "the drink's all spilt."

College Jests

6. *Of a Scholar Married*

A Scholar that had married a young wife and was still at his Book, preferring his serious study before dalliance with her—at length, as she was one day wantoning whilst he was reading, "Sir," saith she, "I could wish that I had been made a Book, for then you would still be poring upon me, and I should never night or day be out of your fingers."

"So would I, Sweetheart," answered he, "so I might choose what book."

When she demanded of him what book he would wish her to be, "Marry, good wife," saith he, "an Almanac, for so I might have every year a new one."

17. *A Doctor's Answer*

A worthy Doctor, amongst many other charitable deeds, made a fair causeway at his own charge, to the great benefit of the Country, and being there one day in person and to visit the laborers, it happened that a nobleman rid that way and, knowing him, gave him a kind salutation. But withal, thinking to break a Jest upon him, "Mr.

Doctor," saith he, "for all your great charges and pains, I believe not that this is the highway to Heaven."

"I am of your mind in that, my Lord," replied the Doctor, "for if it were, I should have wondered to have met your Lordship here."

18. *Of a Doctor of Physic and a Servingman*

One thinking to put a trick upon an excellent Doctor of Physic had mingled the powder of a Brickbat with his water in his Urinal, which settling to the bottom shows just like red gravel that comes from the kidneys. This done, he showed it to the Doctor and told him it was his Master's water, who lay in grievous pain, desiring his worship's counsel, what would give him ease.

The Doctor chafed up and down and tried it by the fire, and in conclusion found out the fellow's knavery. Whereupon, cunningly closing with him, "Friend," said he, "wouldst thou have my advice to prevent this terrible disease growing on thy Master?"

"Yes, sir," replied the fellow. "That was the cause of my coming to your worship."

"Then tell him, all that I can prescribe at this time is that he eat no more Brickbats"—at which word he broke the Urinal upon his pate and so left him.

Cloister Jests

5. *A Gentleman and a Barber*

A Barber coming finically about a Gentleman was (as the most of them are) terrible full of talk. At length he found the leisure to ask him if he would be trimmed. "Marry, my friend," replied the Gentleman, "if thou canst possibly, do it in silence."

17. *A Drunkard and his Wife*

A Woman had a husband that used to come home often disguised, and sometimes to lie along the floor; and still when she offered to raise him from the ground he would not be removed, but answered, "The Tenement is mine own. I pay rent for it, and I may lie where I list."

Some few nights after, coming home in the like taking, and sitting in a chair before the fire, he fell asleep. The Woman would have waked him, but could not, and therefore went up to bed—in which she was scarce warm but the Maid cried out aloud, "Mistress, Mistress, my Master is fallen out of the chair and lies in the midst of the fire!"

Which she hearing, lay still, and answered, "Let him alone, for as long as he pays rent for the house, he may lie where he list."

City Jests

17. *Cuckold's Gilt Horns*

Secretary Bourne's[5] son kept a Gentleman's Wife in Shropshire, who lived from her Husband with him. When he was weary of her, he caused her Husband to be dealt with to take her home, and offered him five hundred pounds for reparation. The Gentleman went to Sir Henry Sidney,[6] to take his advice upon this offer, telling him that his wife promised now a new life and, to tell him truth, five hundred pounds would come well with him. And besides that, sometimes he wanted a woman in his bed.

"By my troth," said Sir Henry Sidney, "take her home and take the money, and then, whereas other Cuckolds wear their horns plain, you may wear yours gilt."

[5] *Secretary Bourne*] Sir John Bourne, principal secretary of state under Queen Mary, 1553–1567.
[6] *Sir Henry Sidney*] Sir Philip Sidney's father.

37. *Of a Captain with a Wooden Leg*

A Captain at the siege of Bergen that had a wooden leg booted over, had it shattered to pieces by a Cannon Bullet. His Soldiers crying out, "A Surgeon! a Surgeon for the Captain!"—"No, no," said he, "a Carpenter, a Carpenter will serve the turn."

43. *Of Tall Men*

Monsieur Cadenet, being sent from the French King to visit King James with his train of ruffling, longhaired Monsieurs, carried himself in such a light and flaunting garb that, after the audience, the King asked my Lord Keeper Bacon what he thought of the French Ambassador. He answered that he was a tall proper man. "Aye," his Majesty replied, "but what think you of his headpiece? Is he a proper man for the office of an Ambassador?"

"Sir," said Bacon, "tall men are like houses of four and five stories, wherein commonly the uppermost room is worst furnished."

61. *A Countryman Coming to Inquire After a Gentleman*

A plain Country fellow, coming up to London, was requested to inquire after such a Gentleman dwelling in such a place, and to deliver him a Letter. The Countryman comes to the house according to direction and asks for such a Gentleman. Now it fortuned that the Gentleman himself came to the door and, willing to have some sport with the fellow, told him that he had lost his labor; for the Party after whom he did inquire was hanged the last Sessions at Tyburn for a Robbery.

"For a Robbery!" quoth the Country fellow. "Now, fie upon him for a wicked man! Was he not content to be a notorious Cuckold (for so he was thought in the Country) but must he prove thief also?"

80. *Of a Madman in Bedlam*

A young woman, coming to Bedlam with others of her Neighbors to observe the fashions and behaviors of those wretched people, saw a man (as she then thought) somewhat more distracted than the rest, and taking compassion of him, supposing with herself that jealousy or some such like fancy had occasioned his frenzy, she asked him if he were not married. "Married?" saith he, looking steadfastly upon her. "No, indeed, Gentlewoman, I would have you to think I am not so mad yet."

103. *One that Wore but One Spur*

A Scholar, being jeered on the way for wearing but one Spur, said that if one side of his horse went on, it was not likely that the other would stay behind.

Country Jests

9. *A Silly Young Gentlewoman*

A silly Country Gentlewoman, being begot with child by one that was much her inferior, to save her credit accused the man of rape, whereupon the matter was had in question before a neighbor Justice of Peace—who, somewhat perceiving the matter, after he had heard her complaint how deeply she had been injured, as pitying her said, "Alas, poor Gentlewoman, I warrant this was not the first time the rogue ravished you."

She, to aggravate his crime, replied, "No, I'll be sworn he ravished me above twenty times"—which procured much laughter and the fellow's freedom.

47. *Hind's Fleet Mare*

Hind, sometime a butcher of Chipping Norton, riding somewhat hard overtook a Captain which was riding to his Troop, who desired Hind to bear him company to his Quarters. So as they rid, the Captain had a great fancy to buy Hind's Mare of him, and to ease his mind said, "Sir, if you will sell your Mare, I will give you any money for her, and a good horse to boot."

Hind being not stupid said, "Sir, if you will give me sixty pound and the Horse you ride on, you shall have my Mare. She is the fleetest Mare in England."

"Sir," said the Captain, "that is too much for her. But rather than I will leave her, you shall have my horse and fifty pound." So they agreed to ride each other's horse a little way.

But the Captain overtaking his Troop caused them to stand till he came back. So he rode on Hind's Mare from the place where the Troop stayed about a quarter of a mile, and only Hind to bear him company. So Hind alighted and gave the Captain his Horse and received his Mare again. Then said Hind, "Let me see what money you will give me to boot, Sir, for exchange."

The Captain, willing to have his Mare, pulled out of his pocket a Purse wherein was one hundred and threescore pounds in good Gold. Hind, seeing this, thought that delays would breed dangers, and to prevent it drew a private Pistol and set it to the Captain's breast and caused him to deliver his money.

So Hind, having his Gold, told him he would keep him company a little way, but it proved a little way indeed, for the next crossway, Hind bid him adieu. So the Captain went alone to his Troop, which might have had a Guard, but now he rides more guarded than regarded, for it is with him as with the old Proverb: "When the Steed is stolen, shut the Stable door."

79. *Of an Arrow Shot into a Swain's Nose*

A Countryman standing at a mark, an arrow lighted on his nose and spitted it through. At last the Archer coming to the mark to take up his arrow, the swain met him with it in his hand and asked him whether it were his arrow. "Yea," he answered, "where had ye it?"

"Marry, see here," replied the swain, pointing to his nose, "you have made me a proper nose, so you have. Indeed, if you serve me so any more, I'll break your arrow."

86. *A Wench's Honesty*

One was praising a wench's honesty, whom a stander-by knew to be a whore, wherefore he said to him, "Is she honest? Pray, had she never a child?"

The first answered him, "Indeed she had a child, but it was a very little one."

from A CHOICE BANQUET OF WITTY JESTS (1660)

248. *On Tobacco Shops*

One said Tobacco Shops of all other places were the most dangerous places to come into, because there were never any that frequented them but smoked for it.

255. *On Doctor Donne*

Doctor Donne, after he was married to a Maid whose name was Anne, in a frolic on his Wedding Day chalked this on the backside of his Kitchen door: "John Donne, Anne Donne, Undone."

298. *Hugh Peters' Sermon at Whitehall*

He, happening to preach one day in the Chapel at Whitehall, pitched upon these words: "Fear not, little flock. It is your Father's good pleasure to give you a Kingdom." Which words he handled very neatly, but seeing many Lobsters⁷ rush into the Chapel, he strays from his Text (a thing usual with him) and told them he had an errand to them in particular, and though his Text promised a Kingdom to the little flock in general—that is, to the Saints of Christ —yet he would promise that every one of them should have a Kingdom. "Yea, you shall have it, as sure as I can reach the top of the Pulpit," which he essayed to do, but could not by a yard or more, which caused many to go laughing out of the Chapel.

309. *Upon Jack Pudding*

Jack Pudding being asked why he played the Fool, answered, "Why not?" Whereas some play the fool for want of wit, he played the fool for want of money.

310. *On Three Scholars and an Ancient Man*

Three Scholars sitting in a Tavern very merry and jocund, an ancient, grave Gentleman looked in upon them, who (to show the quintessence of their wit) thus saluted him, saying, "This is our father Abraham"; another, "He is father Isaac"; the third, he was father Jacob. To which the grave Gentleman replied, "I am neither father Abraham, nor father Isaac, nor father Jacob. But I am Saul the son of Kish who went out to seek his father's Asses and here I find them and here I leave them."

⁷ *Lobsters*] soldiers.

312. *On King Charles and Archee*

King Charles ordered some thousands of Crowns to be delivered a French Monsieur to buy Horses with, whose skill therein was accounted extraordinary, and departed the Court with great splendor; which one of his Majesty's Jesters observing takes his pen and ink and puts his Majesty in his Catalogue of Fools, which not long after was found out by his Majesty and the reason demanded thereof. To which he thus answered, "Charles, thou hast given such a Frenchman so many thousand Crowns to buy Horses with, and if he return with either, I will scratch thee out and put him down for the fool indeed."

316. *On a Pedlar and Two Wolves*

A Scotch Pedlar coming for England was with the weight of his burthen and difficulty of passage through a thick wood constrained to sit down and open his Wallet, which was well filled with victuals —which he had no sooner fallen to but he was suddenly surprised by two Wolves who, drawing up towards him, he threw them scraps of meat, bread and cheese till all was gone.

Then the Wolves made a nearer approach unto him, to have devoured him after his victuals, which he seeing resolved upon this shift following: Taking out his Bagpipes to play on, as soon as ever they heard the noise thereof, away they run, even frightened out of their wits. Whereupon said the Pedlar, "A pox go with you both! Had I known you had loved Music so well, you should have had it before Dinner."

336. *On Ben Jonson and Sylvester*

These two notable and famous Poets endeavored to outvie each other in the making only one (and that best and truest) Verse, which was thus ended:

"I, Sylvester, lay with thy Sister."
"I, Ben Jonson, lay with thy Wife."

Whereupon Sylvester told him that was not a right Verse. "O," quoth Ben Jonson, "but it is true."

343. *Upon Parson Peters*

Master Peters once in the height of his zeal took occasion to reprehend the modish Gallants of the late times in these words: "Beloved, the apparel which men wear now makes them seem like Apes in their short Breeches, and your Gentlewomen must have their Gowns, forsooth, hang half a yard upon the ground to draw after them, a thing very unseemly. But let me advise you women to take up your Coats and you men to let down your Breeches. But pray mistake me not. I mean you women make your Coats shorter and you men make your Breeches longer."

355. *A Justice of Peace and a Bawd*

A Common Bawd was by a Warrant carried before a Justice of Peace for very many rude miscarriages and misdemeanors, but chiefly for keeping a public Bawdy House; who, being questioned of several matters laid to her charge, very confidently denied them, notwithstanding sufficient witness to convict her—which his Worship taking notice of, said, "Well, Gossip, you keep a Common Bawdy House, and I will maintain it."

"Truly, I thank your good Worship," answered the old Trader, "because I have very few such Supports, which I have need of."

377. *On a Fool and a Court Gallant*

A Court Gallant, walking with some of his friends in Whitehall (who was clad *a la mode*), seeing my Lord of Dorset's Fool in a new

Coat, told his friends he would go put a trick upon the Fool. So, walking up to him, he demands whose Fool he was. The Fool, well viewing him in his antic garb, replies to him presently, "I am my Lord of Dorset's Fool. Whose Fool art thou?" At which his friends laughed heartily, admiring the witty answer of the Natural.

380. *On a Citizen and his Wife*

A Citizen and his wife walking abroad in the fields and passing by a large Pond of Water, among other Discourse, "I would, wife," quoth he, "that all the Cuckolds in London were in the middle of this Pond."

"Sweetheart," quoth she, "can you swim?"

TALES AND JESTS OF
HUGH PETERS
(1660)

This book is largely responsible for establishing the legend of Hugh Peters as a comical preacher, a legend with slight basis in fact. Peters (1598–1660), son of a Cornish gentleman and educated at Cambridge, served first as a successful preacher in London. Forced to flee repression of Puritan practices, he became joint minister in the English Church, Rotterdam, along with William Ames, revered by Puritans as a second Saint Augustine. From this prestigious association, Peters emigrated in 1635 to Salem in New England where he succeeded the eminent Francis Higginson as minister and later became a member of the committee to found Harvard College. Still another mark of his high reputation was his being named to a three-man committee sent back to England in 1641 seeking financial support for the colony and the college.

Though England then boiled in civil war, Peters and his friends raised about £5000 for their colony's needs. This success led him to postpone returning to America in order to perform similar fund raising for the Independent party, then in a three-way struggle for supremacy against the Presbyterians and the Cavalier supporters of Charles I. The Independents, whose strength lay in the Army under Oliver Cromwell, quickly subdued all opposition and, executing the King, established a Commonwealth that lasted until 1660. With dissolution of the Commonwealth it was to be expected that Hugh Peters would be executed for the part he played as a conspirator against the King and as a member of the Commonwealth Establishment. He was hung, drawn, and quartered October 16, 1660.

It is hard to understand how we can accept the legend of his having been a buffoon preacher. It is easy to see how that legend grew. He was a butt of Presbyterian and Cavalier pamphleteers who caricatured his enthusiasm into buffoonery through parody and mock sermons. Neither his published sermons nor his own polemical writing show any humor at all. Various reports of his comical preaching seem to have been fabricated in the Opposition's propaganda mills, and seem to have picked up illustrative anecdotes as they made the rounds— sometimes from contemporary jestbooks, sometimes from distortions of fact. At his trial, when accused of having perpetrated blasphemous or scurrilous jests ascribed to him, he categorically denied them all. Yet shortly after his execution, The Tales and Jests of Hugh Peters *appeared in three variously titled editions, reprinting the jests from the trial and also compiling many more, a move perhaps calculated to justify his execution as a regicide but one that gave focus to the Hugh Peters legend.*

About a third of the jests are drawn, with only slight change, from Taylor's

Wit and Mirth. *The rest are from a variety of sources, including official publications: Jest 15, for example, is from an officially sanctioned pamphlet,* A Letter from Ireland, *September, 1649. Jest 44 is from a broadside,* Hosanna, *also of 1649. Jest 55 is from a report of Peters' trial. Despite such well-known sources as the trial report or Taylor's book, still the bookseller's dedication would have us believe these jests are based on personal observation, especially the " Pulpit flashes" assertedly taken down " by the pen of a ready writer" in a process such as described in Jest 59.*

(Wing P1721)

To the Reverend, his dearly beloved Brethren,
Mr. John Goodwin, Phillip Nye.[1]

BRETHREN,

I should do you and the Author an unexampled injury should I detain this Dedication from you, since necessity on the one side and equity on the other compels me to it: necessity in regard no other persons will patronize him; and equity because you have been co-partners with him in all his misdemeanors, so that you are by most well-Principled men termed A Trinity of Traitors. But our Author minding the Public good hath thus enrolled his name in the Catalogue of Wits and desires to wipe off all the obloquy people have cast upon him, by leaving these Remains to after-ages, that those which make him the subject of their discourses may, by remembering his Jests, forget his Crimes. He hath long enough been covered with the Knave's Coat and therefore now puts on the Fool's, for that, as Mr. Nedham[2] saith, is the only way to preferment and a Lady's Chamber. And without controversy, the Levite may laugh or cause laughter as well as the Layman. *Semel in anno ridet Apollo.*[3] The God of Wisdom

---

[1] *John Goodwin, Phillip Nye*] In June, 1660, Parliament debated whether they and Peters should be tried for treason. They were pardoned, but Peters was not.
[2] *Mr. Nedham*] Marchamont Nedham, Puritan propagandist and editor of the Commonwealth's official journal.
[3] *Semel . . . Apollo*] Apollo laughs but once a year.

may frolic it sometimes, why then may not he unbend himself with moderate mirth? *Non seria semper*[4]: he that with Heraclitus whines away his time, I judge more culpable than he that with Democritus shakes it away with laughter.

I have long time known this second Scogin and have been an often hearer of him, and I finding his Discourses so much of Wit and Mirth, could not but rake these embers together. There are amongst them several Pulpit flashes, for indeed they are collected out of many of his Sermons by the pen of a ready writer. They are the Cream of his Applicatory part. And since his Homilies would be too voluminous and probably impertinent, I have made this Publication that his Memory may survive his ashes, and you likewise to whom it is Dedicated have a share in his Immortality.

And, believe me, let the World say what it will, Archee was a fool to him, as appears by his fulfilling the Proverb, "Fortune favors Fools," for he got a good Estate; and so did our Author too, you'll say. But Fortune plays the Strumpet. He got it like a Fool and must lose it like a Fool. I cannot forget that Lesson he said the Heathen taught him, and indeed it concerns you all:

> —*Non Lex est justior ulla,*
> *Quam veris Artifices arte perire sua.*[5]

But you must know, "A Fool's Bolt is soon shot," and it is no matter what they say that matter not what they say. I am sure no Heathen could exceed him, for a Heathen in teaching him taught a man, but he would preach to Horses, "even till they broke their Halters." And, tell me, which is the hardest task, for a Heathen to make him cry or he to make a Dog laugh. I remember he was once in Company with some Ladies, and was extreme bashful, whereupon a Gentleman reproved him in this wise, "Fool, at 'em." And ever since, sprung up that Proverbial word, "Fool-a-tum." This being all, Dear Brethren, I remain,

Yours in the Lord (would I could say) Protector,

S. D.

[4] *Non seria semper*] Not always serious things.
[5] *Non Lex . . . perire sua*] A misquotation from Ovid, *Art of Love*, I, 655: *Neque enim lex aequior ulla est | Quam necis artifices arte perire sua:* There is no law more just than that the contrivers of death should perish by their own contrivances.

Jest 1. *How Mr. Peters being belated on a journey lodged at a Miller's house,
and what passed between him and the Miller*

Mr. Peters, being on a journey, inquired of a Miller whom he saw
standing on his mill, where he might have a lodging for himself and
conveniency for his Horse. The Miller answered he knew no place
thereabout; whereupon Peters traveled on his way till he came to a
little house which, as you shall hear anon, appeared to be the Miller's.
There he knocks. The good Woman coming to the door, Mr. Peters
desires her if she can to lodge him there. She tells him she had but
one bed in the house and therein lay her husband and herself, but
if he would be content with clean straw in the Barn he might have
that, and his Horse might stay there too, for she knew no other way
to help him.

Mr. Peters accepted the proffer and betakes himself to the Barn,
where he had not long lain but through a small cranny he spies a
man with a bottle of wine and a Capon, which was no sooner brought
but immediately a good fire was made, and down thereto it went.
Anon knocks the Miller. All the while the Dame was sore affrighted
and presently conveys away the Capon on the spit, puts out the fire,
hides her friend in a kneading trough hard by, and having thus with
abundance of celerity made a clear coast, she opens the door for her
husband. The good man, being weary, is presently desirous to be at
rest, and she as willing he should.

But Mr. Peters, seeing him betake himself to his bed, bethought
how he might be Master of that Capon, which he effected in manner
following: Leaving his Barn, he comes to the door of the House,
knocks, and straight there appears the Miller. "Honest friend,"
quoth Mr. Peters, "I enquired of you for a lodging, but you knew
of none, therefore I am content with this Barn. But being exceeding
hungry, I desire you by any means to refresh me with what you have.
I shall content you to your own desire."

"Indeed," quoth the Miller, "I have nothing but what I know
you can scarce eat, being a piece of brown bread and Suffolk cheese"
—so opens the door and lets him in.

Mr. Peters, being in, said, "Now, my friend, what if I should try a conclusion for some Victuals, thou'ldst not be angry, wouldst thou?"

"I angry? No, in truth, Sir, not I," quoth the Miller.

With that quoth Hugh, "When I was a youth I could conjure, and I think I have not forgot." So uttering some barbarous words and making strange figures with his fingers, saith he, "Look in such a place and see what there is."

"O, Sir," quoth the Miller, "I pray, Sir, don't Conjure. I would not by any means you should, nor dare I do as you command me."

"Prithee," saith Mr. Peters, "do so as I say and fear not. We shall have good cheer anon."

By these persuasions the Miller was wrought upon. He looks and finds a goodly Capon piping hot, which he brings forth. To this they both fall to, and were very well satisfied. But Mr. Peters, complaining of the smallness of the Miller's drink, would needs conjure again. So, doing as before, he bid the Miller look in such a place. The Miller looked and there finds a bottle of wine. This they drank—the Miller all this while admiring, and verily believed his guest had been a conjurer.

Having now eat and drank sufficiently, "Now," saith Mr. Peters, "but what if I should show you the devil that brought these good things?"

"O," quoth the Miller, "for God's sake, Sir, forbear. I never saw the Devil yet and I would not see him now."

"Nay," saith Mr. Peters, "do you do as I shall instruct you and you need not fear. Stand in the next room and when I stamp, then come forth."

With much persuasions, he went in. Being gone, Mr. Peters steps to the trough, wherein the kind Devil had hid himself, and uncovering it, saith he, "Go your ways and be glad you 'scape so." Out goes the man and Mr. Peters then stamps with his foot, whereupon presently appears the Miller. "Look," saith Mr. Peters, "see you where the Devil goes?"

"Good God," replied the Miller, "if you had not said it was the Devil, I durst have sworn it had been the Parson of our Parish." As indeed it was.

Jest 2. How a notable Parson put a merry jest upon Mr. Peters and Mr. T. when he was examined by them

A Country Parson being examined in order to his settlement in a Benefice, in which Committee sat Mr. T. and Mr. Peters, the latter being chairman he began to check the Parson for his former enormities, telling him how he had misspent his time in rioting and drunkenness, not regarding the good of Souls. To which the Parson humbly replied it was true he had been too negligent of his duty, but had repented and was become a new man and no man but had his failings, as we may read in the Example of the wisest men, Solomon, David, etc. They were polluted with the flesh and as the Apostle saith, "Such were some of you."

Mr. Peters, thinking this to be an affront cast upon himself, quoth he, "Here's a fellow abuses us to our teeth," and would by no means be persuaded to abide there any longer, but in anger went to an adjoining room. Mr. T., being there, went to him and advised him not to take exceptions at what was said—"For," saith he, "the man said nothing but what was Truth and Scripture, and you need not apply it to yourself more than another man."

At last Mr. Peters came again into the room but willed Mr. T. to examine the Parson, for he would not, whereupon Mr. T. asked him how he came to be converted. The Parson answered he supposed it was by reading, for of late he had given himself much to reading, hearing, and praying. "Why," saith Mr. T., "what Authors have you read?" The Parson replied he had read divers, as Nazianzen, Isidore, and many others.

"Which," saith Mr. T., "wrought upon you in reference to your conversion?"

"In truth, Sir," said the Parson, "that is very difficult to determine."

"But which do you think?" saith Mr. T.

"Why, indeed," saith the Parson, "I have read many, but I suppose the chiefest Piece that wrought upon my heart was *Mr. B. against T.*"

Mr. T., hearing him say so, was in as great a rage as his Predecessor and, taking Mr. Peters aside, told him he was now of his opinion. "Nay," saith Mr. Peters, "the man speaks truth, I believe. Nor have you any reason to be angry with him, for in reading *B. against T.* he reads T. himself and you know not but it might be your part of the Book that converted him."

But the Parson, having set them together by the ears, went out and never came before them any more.

Jest 3. *How Mr. Peters broke a jest upon a Lady*

Mr. Peters, by chance meeting a Lady of his acquaintance, asked her how she did and how her good husband fared, at which words weeping, she answered her husband had been in Heaven long since. "In Heaven!" quoth he. "It is the first time that I have heard of it, and I am sorry for it with all my heart."

Jest 4. *How Mr. Peters reproved Oliver Cromwell for sleeping in the Church while he was Preaching*

It being his turn to preach before the sometime Protector at 'the Chapel in Whitehall much about the time that his present Majesty was marching towards Worcester, he espied that the Devil had shut the casements of his Highness his eyes and lulled him asleep, whereupon, varying from his discourse in hand, quoth he, "We have now an enemy in this our land, a Potent one, and it is not unknown I suppose to any here that he daily approaches nearer us. But 'tis no matter. I preach but in vain while my Auditory sleeps. I hope he will come and take you napping."

Jest 5. *How Mr. Peters divided his Text at Saint Albans*

Mr. Peters, being another time to preach at Saint Albans, to that end ascends the Pulpit where, after he had prayed, he takes his Text out of Saint Mark's Gospel, chapter five, verse twenty-three, wherein are these words: "The unclean spirits entered into the swine and the herd ran violently down a steep place into the sea and were choked."

From which words he gathered these three Observations, taken from so many English Proverbs:

1. "That the Devil will rather play at small game than sit out."
2. "That they must needs go whom the Devil drives."
3. "That at last he brought his Hogs to a fair market."

Jest 6. *How Mr. Peters and his Neighbor discoursed of the wind*

Being at his own House in the Country when a great Tempest of wind rose, he takes an occasion to visit a Neighbor by him. And being somewhat merrily disposed, quoth he, "O, Neighbor, did you not see what a wind there was the other day?"

"No," said his Neighbor. "How should I see it?"

"Why," quoth Mr. Peters, "with thy eyes as I did."

"Pray tell me, then," said his Neighbor, "if you saw it, what was it like?"

"Like?" quoth he. "It was like to have blown my house down."

Jest 7. *How Mr. Peters inveighed against the pride of the English Nation*

The same man, inveighing violently against the pride of this Nation, broke passionately into this Expression: "Pride is the worm that consumes the best Fruit in this our Terrestial Paradise. For behold the Merchant's wife in her Satins, the Citizen's in her silks, and the Chambermaid, marry come up, she must glister in her silver-Lace—on the upper coat, half a dozen at least, on the next coat few less. Nay, their very smocks must be laced forsooth. Take up that and there sits Puss in her Majesty."

Jest 8. How Mr. Peters jested on his horse

Mr. Peters being in a chamber with a Friend and looking out at the window saw one riding on a horse in the street. "Do you," said he, "see yonder horse?"

"Yea," quoth the other.

"Then," replies he, "you may swear you have seen the best horse in England."

"How know you that?" said his Friend.

"I know it well," said he, "for it is my horse and I am sure he is the best, and yet I dare swear I have one in my stable worth ten of him."

Jest 9. How Mr. Peters examined a country Lad, and the jests that happened at that time

An unhappy boy that kept his Father's sheep in the country did use to carry a pair of Cards in his pocket, and with the same, meeting with companions, played at one-and-thirty (a Game so called) at which sport he would some days lose a sheep or two, for which his Father corrected him. In revenge whereof the boy would drive the sheep home at night over a narrow bridge where some of them, falling into the water, were drowned. The old man, wearied with his son's ungracious tricks, had him before Mr. Peters (he being a man busy and having some Authority in those parts where he lived).

Mr. Peters begins to reprove the boy in these words: "Sirrah, you are a notable Villain. You play at Cards and lose your Father's sheep at one-and-thirty."

The boy, using small reverence and less manners, replied it was a lie. "A lie!" quoth Mr. Peters. "You saucy Knave, do you give me the lie?"

"No," quoth the boy, "but you told a lie. For I never lost sheep at one-and-thirty, for when my game was one-and-thirty I always won."

"Indeed," said Mr. Peters, "thou sayest true. But I have another accusation against thee which is that you drive your Father's sheep over a narrow bridge where some of them are oftentimes drowned."

"That's a lie too," quoth the boy, "for those that go over the bridge are well enough. It is only such as fall besides that are drowned"—which Mr. Peters acknowledged for a truth, and being well pleased with these clownish answers, gave him a short advice and then dismissed him.

Jest 10. *How Mr. Peters and several Justices of the Peace sat two days about brewing small Beer*

Certain Justices of the Peace (with whom Mr. Peters was then accompanied), being informed of the frequent sin of Drunkenness within their Jurisdictions, met at a Market Town and sat two days to reform it, whereupon they commanded that from thenceforth smaller drink should be brewed. At which Order a mad Tosspot grieved, and having made himself half drunk, without fear or wit came to the Justices and asked them if they had sat two days about brewing of small Beer. One of them answered yes. "Why, then," quoth he, "I pray sit three more to know who shall drink it, for I will none of it."

Jest 11. *How Mr. Peters adviseth a Traveler to be accomplished*

A Friend of Mr. Peters being in discourse with him took an occasion to ask him this question: "When was the fittest time to journey?" Quoth he, "When you have a good horse, money in the purse, and good company."

Jest 12. *How Mr. Peters served the Parson of a hot Constitution*

Mr. Peters having desired a country Parson and Friend of his to give him a Sermon, the Parson consented, but Mr. Peters, being in a merry vein, resolved to make a jest, though he spoiled a Text. For, hearing that the Parson was of so hot a constitution that he would oftentimes preach in the Pulpit with his breeches down, he caused a Turf of an Ant's hill to be laid on the Pulpit bench.

The Parson, seeing the Turf, was well pleased, supposing it was laid there only as strowings to adorn his seat. So his breeches being down, he sits awhile, and when the Psalm was concluded he rises to his Prayer. All which time the Ants were very civil, till he had proceeded a good way, but then a War began, insomuch that by their biting and his scratching, some drops of blood was spilt upon the place, which caused him to break forth into these words: "The Word of God"—and, making a full stop, quoth he, "Good people, the word of God is in my mouth but I think the Devil is in my tail."

Jest 13. How Mr. Peters gave his opinion concerning Christendom

It was an usual saying of Mr. Peters that in Christendom there were neither Scholars enough, Gentlemen enough, nor Jews enough. And when answer was made that of all these three there was rather too great a plenty than a scarcity, he replied that if there were Scholars enough, so many would not be double or treble beneficed; if Gentlemen enough, so many Peasants would not be reckoned among the Gentry; and if Jews enough, so many Christians would not profess Usury.

Jest 14. How Mr. Peters rode through the Strand

Mr. Peters riding very fast through the Strand, a Gentleman coming by was minded to make him stop, and to that end called after him and coming to his speech saith he, "Sir, pray what Proclamation was that that was just now out?"

Mr. Peters, being angry to be stayed upon so frivolous a question, answered he might see that on every post. "I cry you mercy," said the Gentleman. "I took you for a Post, you rode so fast."

Jest 15. *How Mr. P. wrote a Letter from Tredagh[6] in Ireland*

Mr. Peters, being in Ireland at the taking of Tredagh, sends up a Letter to the Parliament whose substance was no more but: "The truth is, Tredagh is taken."

Yours,
Hugh Peters.

Jest 16. *How Mr. Peters described a Whore*

Mr. Peters discoursing with a Friend of his about what Effigies were the best to adorn a Room, his Friend told him that, among the rest he intended to buy, he would have a Courtesan exactly painted. "You may very well save that labor," said Mr. Peters, "for if she be a right Whore she will paint herself."

Jest 17. *How Mr. Peters lighted the Blind Harper*

Mr. Peters being in company with a Parliament man one evening, it so happened that a blind Harper, coming by and hearing their discourse, began to play. Upon which they willed him to come into the house. And having done, Mr. Peters called to his friend's Servant to light the Blind Harper out. To Whom the servant said, "Sir, the Harper is Blind."

"Why, then," quoth Mr. Peters, "he hath the more need of light."

---

[6] *Tredagh*] Drogheda, where 3,552 Irish were massacred in 1649. This is an actual letter read in Parliament on September 28, 1649.

Jest 18. *How Mr. Peters told a Tale of a Man, a Fish, and a Bird*

Mr. Peters, being in the pulpit at Christ-Church, came to the end of his Sermon, as the people did suppose. But he, perceiving them to make towards the door, wished them to lend their Attentions for a word or two more and he would conclude. The people, being then big with expectations, for the most tarried. He began as followeth:

"Beloved, in former time there were three creatures agreed to go on Pilgrimage together, by name a Man, an Eel, and a Swallow. They accompanied one another a great way, till the two latter were almost tired; wherefore, coming to a Wood, the Bird watches an opportunity and flies away. Now there remained only the Man and Fish, and they kept together still until they came to pass over a small brook. But the Fish, seeing the waters, gives a slip from the Man and was never seen after.

"Now the Man was left alone. But on he goes and, having passed the brook, espies on the other side several long rods. These he lays into bundles. Now, beloved, what think you these rods were for? I'll tell you. They were to whip such men as will make haste from a Sermon and return to hear a tale. So much for this time."

Jest 19. *Mr. Peters cheapened a close Stool*

Mr. Peters once cheapened a close stool, but the Shopkeeper asked (as he thought) too much for it but still commended his commodity, willing him to "Note the goodness of the Lock and Key"—at which he replied, "I have small use for either Lock or Key, for I purpose to put nothing in it but what I care not who steals."

Jest 20. *How Mr. Peters Jeered a Justice*

Mr. Peters riding on the way with a Justice of the Peace, to drive tediousness out of time the Justice said to him, "Suppose, Sir, that all the world were dead but you and I, and that one of us should be turned into a Horse and the other into an Ass, which of the two would you choose to be?"

Mr. Peters answered, "I shall give your worship the choice."

"Why, then," quoth the Justice, "I would be a Horse."

"Nay," said Mr. Peters, "let me entreat your Worship to be an Ass, for I would choose that above anything."

"Why?" said the Justice.

"Marry," quoth Hugh, "because I have known many Asses to become Justices, but I never knew a horse come to the like preferment."

Jest 21. *How Mr. Peters clothed Christ in a Buff Coat*

Another time he told his Auditory he had brought them Christ in a Buff Coat, saying, "Here, take him while you may have him, for if you refuse him this time, I'll carry him with me to New England."

Jest 22. *How Mr. Peters opened Heaven's Gate to a Committee Man*[7]

Preaching once in Ireland and discoursing on the times, it came into his head, with his Knuckle to hit against the Pulpit, intimating to his Auditory he had been in Heaven and answering the sound. Quoth he, "Who is there? A Cavalier? O, a Cavalier! You must not come here. You must to Hell, for you fight against the Parliament."

Then he knocks again and cries, "Who is there? A Roundhead? O, a Roundhead! You must come hither neither. You are factious and disorderly in opinions." So he knocks the third time and cries, "Who is there? A Committee Man? O, a Committee Man! He *must* come and shall"—laying his hands on the Pulpit door as if he would let him in.

[7] *Committee Man*] member of a select committee appointed by Cromwell or a Puritan Parliament.

Jest 23. *How Mr. Peters told a tale of his Friend*

Mr. Peters being merry with some friends of his entertains them awhile with this following story: Quoth he, "I knew a lusty Miller much given to the flesh, that never suffered any female to bring any Grist but he would endeavor to blow up their Chastities. And with whomsoever he was familiar, he would bargain that at the day of his Marriage each of them should send him a Cake.

"In process of time the Miller was married and, according to promise, they sent in their Cakes, to the number of Ninety-and-nine. His wife the bride wondered what was the meaning of so many Cakes. The Miller told her the truth of all without any dissembling. To whom his wife answered, 'If I had been so wise in Bargaining as you have been, the young men of my acquaintance would have sent me a hundred Cheeses to have eaten with your Cakes.'"

Jest 24. *How Mr. Peters described a Citizen*

He was wont to say a Citizen was a man all in earnest and in no point like a jest, because the Citizen was never bad nor the jest never good till they were both broke.

Jest 25. *How Mr. Peters showed one the way to Tame*

Mr. Peters journeying from Oxford towards London met on the way with a Gallant that rode excessive hard, who enquired of him if that were the way to Tame, meaning a place so called. But Mr. Peters, willing to mistake him, replied, "Yes, your horse, I'll warrant you, if he were as wild as the Devil."

Jest 26. *How Mr. Peters discoursed with a Tradesman*

Mr. Peters coming into a Tradesman's shop in London observed he Master to be very bountiful of his compliments and congees, whereupon quoth he, "Well said, honest friend. It is a good sign that thou will never break, thou dost bend so much."

Jest 27. How Mr. Peters reproved a young Scholar

Mr. Peters, hearing of some boisterous exercises used on the Sabbath day, and that a young Scholar whom he knew was frequently at cudgel-playing with the rest, he sends for this Scholar and told him how it suited not with his profession to use such an exercise, especially on such a day, and if he did not leave it, he would cause him to be ordered.

"Good Sir," replied the Scholar, "do not mistake me, for I do it on purpose to edify the ruder sort of the people."

"How so?" said Mr. Peters.

"Marry, Sir," said the Scholar, "what in the morning and evening they have learned, I soundly beat into their heads at cudgels for their better remembrance."

Jest 28. How Mr. Peters made an Ass of a Gentleman

Talking with a Gentleman that was rich and merry, the Gentleman said he had read a book called *Lucius Apuleius*, or the Golden Ass, and that he found there that Apuleius after he had been many years an Ass, by eating of roses did recover his human shape again. Mr. Peters thereupon replies, "Sir, if I were worthy to advise you, I would give you counsel to eat a salad of roses once a week at least yourself."

Jest 29. How Mr. Peters saved his License

Mr. Peters talking with some honest Countrymen about the affairs of his parish and happening to have his License in his hand, one of his Company seeing it, desires to look well on it. But perceiving it was in Latin, saith he, "O, I understand not Latin, but perhaps I may pick out a word or two."

"No, by no means," cried Mr. Peters, "I would not have my License picked, lest it should be spoiled."

Jest 30. *How Mr. Peters gave judgment of a Choleric Gentleman*

There was a Gentleman of a very hasty disposition, so that he would fret and quarrel perpetually and withal was a great Tobacco-Taker. This Gentleman in his anger beat and kicked his man extremely insomuch that the fellow ran away. And Mr. Peters, being an acquaintance of his Master's, he repairs to him, willing him to advise his Master to be more patient.

Mr. Peters said he would. "But," saith he, "so must you, for you know his conditions. For my part I think he is transformed into Brawn, for he is all choler"—and he supposed the reason of his Kicking was only because he took Coltsfoot in Tobacco.

Jest 31. *How Mr. Peters extolled the Army under Oliver*

It being ordered that Friday, December the 22, 1648, should be set apart for fasting, it was likewise ordered that Mr. Peters should preach on that day, as accordingly he did, without any more Audience than four Lords and twenty Commons. The subject of his Sermon was that of Moses his leading the Israelites out of Egypt, which he applied to the then Leaders of the Army. "But how," quoth Hugh, "shall the people in our days be led from their captivity? That," said he, "you shall know anon." Then clapping his hands before his eyes he leaned on his cushion for a while and suddenly starting up, saith he, "I'll tell you no more than hath been revealed to me:

"There is no way out of Egypt but by rooting up of Monarchy. And this Army must do it. This Army is the stone spoken of, cut out of the Mountain, which must dash the powers of the earth in pieces. But some object that the way we walk is without precedent. Alas we must act without and beyond precedents. Are not many things in scripture without precedent? What think you of the Virgin Mary? Was there any precedent that a Virgin should conceive? I tell you no. And this our Army hath done and shall do such glorious things as former ages never expected, the present doth admire, and the future will not believe."

Jest 32. How Mr. Peters visited the Earl of Pembroke

Mr. Peters, taking an occasion to visit the Earl of Pembroke, he salutes his Honor in this manner: "My Lord, I am come to see you and intend to dine with you, and because you should not want company I have brought one of the seven deadly sins along with me, viz. Colonel Pride, and have brought the Devil too, Colonel Dragon" —at which jest they all laughed and were well pleased.

Jest 33. How Mr. Peters wished his Auditory to beware of the Three W's

Mr. Peters, preaching in a country Village, exhorted his Congregation in this manner: "Beware, beloved, of three mischievous W's —Wine, Women, and Tobacco. But, you will object, Tobacco is no W. To which I answer, Tobacco must be understood under the notion of a Weed, and then it holds right."

Jest 34. How Mr. Peters called his Hearers Fools

Mr. Peters preaching in a strange place and having some information that the people suited not with his judgment, took this portion of Scripture for his Text: "O ye fools, when will ye be wise?"

"Which text," saith he, "admits of no divisions. For divide 'O' from 'Ye' I cannot. Or 'Ye' from 'Fools' (O, ye Fools!), that I am sure of, for you are such. 'When will ye be wise?' That the Lord above knows, for I am sure I do not nor ever shall."

Jest 35. How Mr. Peters took an affront on the Exchange

Mr. Peters walking at full 'Change time on the Royal Exchange, a certain person comes to him and, whispering him in the ear, says to him, "Mr. Peters, you are a Knave or else you had never gained so much wealth as you have."

"Say you so?" said he. "Marry, if you were not a fool, you would be a Knave too."

Jest 36. How Mr. Peters said he knew where his Majesty was

Mr. Peters was once heard to say that he knew where his Majesty was and, being desired to tell, said, "In Bedlam, sure enough, for unless he be mad he will not be in England."

Jest 37. How Mr. Peters inveighed against Citizens' Wives

Preaching in London, he exclaimed greatly against the Citizens' Wives. "Your City Mistresses," saith he, "must have their lapdogs to play with all day long, for want of children. And if by chance he lets fly an uncivil blast, then 'Out ye foisting cur! O, how he stinks!' Immediately after, he leaps into their lap again and to bed perhaps they both march together, and the happy cur is laid to snug where many an honest man would be with all his heart."

Jest 38. How Mr. Peters jeered a Rich Man and his Fat Wife

Mr. Peters being invited to dinner to a friend's house, knowing him to be very wealthy, and his wife as fat as he was rich, broke this jest at Table before them: "Truly, Sir," said he, "you have the world and the flesh. But pray God you get not the Devil in the end."

Jest 39. How Mr. Peters said he had been in Heaven

Another time, he told his Auditory he had been in Heaven and there were store of Roundheads; but going into Hell he found that so full of Cavaliers that if a Roundhead should chance to stumble thither there would be no room for him.

Jest 40. How Mr. Peters answered Oliver Cromwell

Being desired by Oliver Cromwell to repair to an appointed place there to preach, it suddenly fell a-raining, whereupon Cromwell offered him his Coat. To which he replied, "I'll not have it. For my part, I would not be in your Coat for a thousand pounds."

Jest 41. How Mr. Peters jested at his Friend's Hurt

Mr. Peters coming by one time where he espied a friend of his deeply cut in the head, who engaged too far in a foolish fray, he began to check him for his indiscretion. "But," saith he, "'tis too late now to give you Counsel. Come along with me to a Surgeon, a friend of mine, where I'll have you, see you dressed, and then bid you farewell."

Where being come, the Surgeon begins to wash away the blood and search for his brains to see if they were hurt. At which Mr.

Peters cries out, "What a mad man are you to seek for any such thing! If he had had any brains, he would never have ventured so rashly into so unlucky a Skirmish."

Jest 42. How Mr. Peters defaced a Shoulder of Mutton

Being invited to dinner, his Stomach invited him into the Kitchen to take a slice before dinner, where espying a Shoulder of Mutton, began to cut a piece of that and to deface it. At which saith the Maid, "O, Sir, cut not of that, because it is old."

"Say you so?" quoth he. "Then I will have a piece of it to choose, for age, you know, is honorable."

Jest 43. How Mr. Peters mistook in reaching to the top of his Pulpit

Mr. Peters, preaching immediately after the death of Oliver Cromwell, in his Sermon brought in this Expression, that he knew Oliver Cromwell was in Heaven as sure as he could then touch the head of his Pulpit—and reaching up, his hand came short thereof by half a yard.

Jest 44. How Mr. Peters advanced the Cause of Oliver

Master Peters, for the maintenance of the Army under his Master Oliver, used oftentimes to exhort the people to be liberal in their Contributions. And having used his utmost endeavors in London, he endeavored to stir up the well affected in several Counties, always intermixing somewhat of money in his Discourse. But, one time above the rest, having provided himself with a pair of breeches without pockets, only holes cut in places where the pockets should be, and his Auditory being most Women, he affrighted them exceedingly with the terrible Characters he gave the Cavaliers, and at length out comes a whole bunch of Rings which he had hung on his cod piece button.

And "My beloved," quoth Hugh, "these Rings the Women of such-a-Town gave me"—and shaking them a while in one hand, pretended to put them up. But, standing upright in the Pulpit, he took them through his breeches in the other, and "See here," saith he, "beloved Sisters, these the pious-minded Women of another Town gave me to subdue the wicked Cavaliers." By this piece of Sophistry he would preach his ignorant hearers out of large sums of money, which it may be supposed he treasured in his own coffers.

Jest 45. *How Mr. Peters went to Heaven and Hell*

Mr. Peters, in the midst of one of his Sermons, dives down and, rising up again, saith, "My beloved, where think you I have been now? I'll tell you. I have been in Heaven, and there's my Lord Bradshaw and many other worthy persons of Note." Then diving again, "Now," saith he, "I have been in Hell, and there were a Number of factious Parliament men"—and (that they might believe it to be true as that Gospel) showing a Paper-Book with Notes, bound up like a Testament.

Jest 46. *How Mr. Peters shared with the State*

He was wont after his Collections to carry all his treasure into one Room where there was two Chests. Then would he take one Bag and, flinging it into one of the Chests, "This," saith he, "for the State." And flinging another Bag into the other Chest, quoth he, "This for myself." This would he so frequently do that an ingenious fellow, his servant, noted it and to imitate his Master would commonly before he gave his Master his accounts, do the same—having provided himself with two Chests or Trunks, would cry, "This for my Master and this for myself," insomuch that in short time he had heaped up a great treasure, and taking himself to be somebody more than formerly, attempted to make love to a Gentlewoman related nearly to Mr. Peters. Whereupon Mr. Peters checks him for the presumption, saying she had a great fortune and was a pitch above him.

"Sir," quoth the servant, "I am not as despicable as you may think, nor shall her fortune exceed mine."

"Say you so?" saith Mr. Peters. "Make that appear and you shall have her."

"Why, Sir," quoth the Servant, "I have done as you taught me. You used to say, 'This for the State and this for myself,' so I would cast into your treasury one Bag and two into mine own."

"Sayest thou so?" replied his Master. "Believe me, I commend thee." And, clapping him on the Back, saith he, "Say no more. Thou dost deserve her." But whether they were married or not, my Intelligencer cannot inform me.

Jest 47. How Mr. Peters was served by the Butcher's Wife

Mr. Peters, ingratiating himself with a Butcher's Wife who was somewhat handsome, did with much entreaty gain her consent to be her visitor at midnight. And she ordered him to come at such-a-time and put his hand under the door where he should find the Key which should open a passage to her chamber. He comes at the appointed time, but this crafty woman, instead of the Key, had there laid a Trap. And Mr. Peters, looking for the Key, did un-luckily thrust his hand into the Trap and could not get it out till by his calling for help he was heard and disgracefully released.

Jest 48. How Mr. Peters prayed against the King's Arms

Praying in a Country village, he espied in the Church the King's Arms, whereupon he brings in these words, "Good Lord keep us from the yoke of Tyranny." And spreading his hands towards the King's Arms, saith he, "Preserve thy servants from the paw of the Lion and the horn of the Unicorn."

Jest 49. How Mr. Peters discoursed against Organs

Mr. Peters, discoursing of Church Ceremonies, broke into this expression: "'Ye must have Music too.' But indeed when as ye say, 'Lord have mercy upon us miserable sinners,' ye may well vary the words a little and let your Petition be, 'Lord have mercy upon us miserable singers.'"

Jest 50. How Mr. Peters preached three hours on a Fast Day

Mr. Peters, having on a Fast Day preached two long hours and espying his glass to be out after the second turning up, takes it in his hand and, having again turned it, saith, "Come, my Beloved, we will have the other glass, and so we'll part."

Jest 51. How Mr. Peters said the word of God had Free Passage

Discoursing of the advantage Christians have above Heathens and showing that they were guided only by Natural Instinct but we have the word preached to us, "And indeed," saith he, "the Gospel hath a very free passage amongst us, for I am confident it no sooner enters in at one ear but it is out at the other."

Jest 52. How Mr. Peters bought Cloth by the measure of his sword

Mr. Peters, being at a Linen Drapers buying Cloth, would not be contented with their yards or ells, but, drawing out his sword, told the Draper he would measure his Cloth thereby, or he would not buy—which the Draper, after he had viewed the sword, consented to and so they presently agreed.

Jest 53. *How Mr. Peters asked Grapes of Alderman Titchbourn*

Alderman Titchbourn, so formerly called, wrote a Book and entitled it, *A Cluster of Canaan's Grapes.* And Mr. Peters meeting of him asked him if his worship would be pleased to bestow a cluster of his Grapes on him, at which the Alderman answered, if he would come to his Vine (meaning his house) he should have his choice of all his store.

Jest 54. *How Mr. Peters Jeered the Poet Withers*

George Withers, having wrote a Poem in which he predicted the continuance of a free State, called it "The Perpetual Parliament." A little after, the Parliament was dissolved and Mr. Peters, meeting the said Mr. Withers, told him he was a pitiful Prophet and a pitiful Poet, otherwise he had not wrote such Predictions for a pitiful Parliament.

Jest 55. *How Mr. Peters gave his opinion of the three L's*

Being once conversing with several of his familiar friends, he was heard to say that England would never be right till one hundred and fifty were cut off. Everyone wondering where he would pick so many, at last one asked him who those were. He answered they were three L's and, each L standing for fifty, the number might easily be completed out of Lords, Levites, and Lawyers.

Jest 56. How Mr. Peters made himself Hewson's Father

Mr. Peters, meeting Colonel Hewson, merrily said to the Colonel, "How now, Son, where's your blessing?" But Hewson, not well conceiving what he said, asked what he meant. "Why," quoth Hugh, "I mean to teach you your duty. Know you not who I am? I am Hugh and, as I take it, you are Hugh's-son."

Jest 57. How Mr. Peters compared his late Majesty to Barrabas

He once preached a Sermon at Saint Margarets Westminster immediately after the Members were secluded (there being a Fast appointed in that place), where he chose for the words of his Text, "Not this man but Barrabas"—to whom he compared his late Majesty, inciting his Auditory to "Kill the King," withal adding that those Soldiers who assisted in that great work of Reformation had "Emanuel," that is, "God with us," written on their Bridles.

Jest 58. How Mr. Peters quoted the three fools in the Gospel

Mr. Peters, preaching on the neglect Christians too often had in duties, broke forth into this expression: "My Beloved, Observe, there are three Fools in the Gospel, for, being bid to the Wedding Supper, every one had his excuse.

"For the First, he had hired a Farm and must go see it. Had not he been a fool he would have seen it first, but he would be excused.

"The Second, he had bought a Yoke of Oxen, and he must go try them, therefore he likewise desired to be excused. He also was a fool because he did not try them before he bought them.

"The Third, he had married a Wife and without any compliment said plainly he could not come. He was a fool too, for by this he showed that one woman drew him away more than a whole Yoke of Oxen did the former."

Jest 59. *How Two Gentlemen put up a Bill to Mr. Peters*

On Sunday, January 21, 1648, being the time of that grand Trial and bloody murther of our Sovereign Lord King Charles the First of Blessed Memory, Mr. Peters preached at Whitehall upon Psalm 149, verse 8, of "Binding the Kings in Chains and the Nobles with fetters of Iron," applying his Text and Sermon to the late King and saying he had seen one joyful day and he hoped to see another tomorrow as good as the former.

There being at that time in the Church two Gentlemen who, as many more usually did, went rather to hear his Jests than his Doctrine, they hearing how bitterly he inveighed against his late Majesty and how he applauded the proceedings of the Army, being provided with Pen, Ink, and Paper on purpose to bear away some of his Pulpit Jests, immediately betake themselves to send him a line or two, which accidentally falling into my hands, I have here inserted:

> Sir, We return you thanks for this your pains,
> And hope you'll live yourself to wear the Chains;
> For, if our Genius don't at this time falter,
> Your merits well may claim both chain and halter.

This being wrapped close up, and he drawing to the conclusion of his Sermon, they deliver it to be handed to him, as though it were the Petition of some dying soul. But he, having read it, put it up and, as occasion served, made it now and then pass for a malignant Jest, notwithstanding at last it proved an earnest truth.

For now at last I shall conclude with the Author's death. He was indicted October 9, 1660, at Hicks Hall, and the Bill found by the Grand Jury of Knights and Gentlemen of Quality of the County of Middlesex. Such a Bench and such a Jury hath rarely been seen in that Court where that most learned Lord Chief Baron, Sir Orlando Bridgeman, gave him his charge—and being asked, "Guilty or not guilty," lift up his hands and his eyes (according to his custom) and said, "Guilty! No, not for ten thousand worlds."

However, after his Indictment was read and the Jury sworn, he saw a whole congregation of witnesses against him. Many things were by them asserted, relating to his guilt of being accessory to the spilling of his late Majesty's Royal Blood, and his moving and stirring up seditious rebellions in his Majesty's Dominions. To which Mr. Peters making no answer, the Jury gave their Verdict that Mr. Hugh Peters was guilty. Whereupon the sentence of the Court was that he should be drawn upon a Sledge to the place of execution and there be hanged by the neck till he be half dead, his bowels burnt, and his quarters to be disposed of according to order—which on Tuesday the 15th of October was accordingly done at the place where formerly Charing Cross stood.

Thus did he that called his sacred Majesty a Barrabas, a murderer, and seditious, die for murther and sedition himself, so that the snare which he laid for another hath catched hold of himself. In this we may see that, according to that of St. Augustine, "Justice hath leaden feet but Iron hands; and though vengeance treads slowly, it comes surely"—as hath appeared by this man (sometime my acquaintance) who was everything and indeed nothing, sometime fool and sometime knave, but what most commonly might induce to his benefit and advantage.

FINIS

NO JEST LIKE
A TRUE JEST
(ca. 1670)

James Hind the Highwayman, the hero of these jests, was a legendary rogue in his own time. He was notorious for robbing Roundheads and sparing Cavaliers and was something of a hero because of his forays against the Commonwealth. When he was caught and imprisoned in Newgate, in Novem-ber, 1651, jestbooks about him tumbled from the presses of friend and foe alike. From Newgate he published a Declaration *(November 15th) deploring "impertinent stories and new-invented fictions" about his career and officially authorizing George Horton to issue a collection entitled* The Pleasant and Delectable History of Captain Hind. *This was neither pleasant nor delectable but a cold narrative of the violent, vicious exploits performed by Hind and his men, so dull as to be most likely true. At the same time, however, Horton also issued a different kind of collection,* We Have Brought Our Hogs to a Fair Market, *featuring Hind performing "merry Pranks" and "witty jests." None of the fourteen jests in* The Pleasant . . . History *survived one printing, but five of the six jests in* We Have Brought Our Hogs *survived vigorously down to the* Dictionary *of National Biography.*

No Jest Like a True Jest *picked up the five jests from* We Have Brought Our Hogs. *Hind's* Declaration *from Newgate provided two more. The remainder may have been "new-invented," but all seem familiar from similar collections of jests about earlier rogues.* We Have Brought Our Hogs *is itself fabricated from earlier jestbooks, some well known in their own right. Jest 14 in* No Jest, *for instance, comes verbatim from* We Have Brought Our Hogs *which takes it from Paul Godwin's translation of* Histoire des Larrons *([London, 1638], pp. 12–18). In Godwin's trans-lation the hero is "a thief of Paris" and the physician's name is Alcander (and not Henry Van Veldes as in Jest 14). The difference is important in showing how Hind took on a halo of verisimilitude, for when Charles Johnson wrote of him in his* History . . . of the Most Famous Highwaymen *in 1734 he accepted the story uncritically even though he used Godwin's book for other portions of his* History.

The Hind who lived and died (hung, drawn, and quartered) was probably closer to the vicious Hind given us in The Pleasant and Delectable His-tory *than to the humorous, generous hero of* No Jest like a True Jest. *Yet the humorous Hind lived vividly in the jestbooks for more than a century. Issues of* No Jest *survive under various titles and guises from 1674, 1750, 1765, 1775, 1805, 1817, and 1820. Johnson's preface sums up this Hind they all knew and loved: "A Man as much talked of to this Day as almost any one of his Profession that ever lived, and who was distinguished by his Pleasantry in all his Adventures; for he never in his Life robbed a Man, but at the same time he either said or did something that was diverting"* (*p. 86*).

(Wing N1177A)

Chapter 1. Containing Hind's Birth, and how he first came to be a Highwayman

Captain James Hind (the subject of our ensuing discourse) was born at Chipping Norton in Oxfordshire. His Father, having no more Children, put him to School intending to make him a Scholar. But he minded his waggish pastimes more than his Book, which his Father perceiving, bound him 'Prentice to a Butcher. But he, having a running pate, soon grew weary of that also, and in conclusion ran away from his Master, comes to London, there grows acquainted with a company of roaring deboist[1] Blades who by their evil examples made him as bad as themselves.

To be short, as they seldom abounded with money, so they scorned to be long in want. When their stock grew short, they rode a-cutting for more. At last the knot was discovered, the Chief of them Hanged, and Hind (only) escaped, with the loss of his Horse. And now he sets up for himself.

Chapter 2. How Hind robbed a Gentleman on Foot, and furnished himself with a horse, money, and Clothes

Hind, having lost his Horse when he made his escape, was resolved to get one or to follow his trade on foot. His Master's misfortune grieved him much, yet he quickly cast it out of his mind. And now,

[1] *deboist*] debauched.

to color his knavery, he puts himself into the habit of a shepherd, with a long pike-staff on his neck, and so travels towards Banbury where in his way he espies a Gentleman coming down a hill, leading his horse in his hand. Hind, as[2] he took no notice of the Gentleman, went whistling the tune of an ordinary Psalm.

When the Gentleman came to the foot of the hill where Hind stood whistling his Psalm, the Gentleman inquired of him the time of the day. He answered him very civilly, but, as the Gentleman was getting on his Horse, Hind hit him with his long Pole such a stroke between the head and the shoulders that he made him tumble on the ground. Hind presently took his Money, Cloak, Horse, and Sword and left him his old Coat and his Pike-staff to beat on the hoof as he had done—giving him twenty shillings back to bear his charges. But to this day the Gentleman loves not the tune of a Psalm.

Chapter 3. How Hind was betrayed by two Whores who sent two Highwaymen to take his Money and how he robbed them

Hind, having gotten a good purchase in Gold, passed away the day very merrily, and towards night rides to an Inn which stood in a private road, where it seems some Highwaymen did use. After he had seen his Horse carefully dressed and fed, came into the house, where were two handsome Ladies by the Fire. He bespoke a good supper and invited them to it.

When supper was ready, he called for Wine and made them merry. They seemed very coy to him, but he, knowing their humor, pulled out of his Pocket a handful of Gold, singing, "Maids, where are your hearts become? Look you what here is." After much mirth, to Bed he went and, presently after, came in the two men that kept these two Whores, to whom they relate the courtesy of Hind and that he had abundance of Gold about him.

They resolve to watch his going and to follow him in the morning, but Hind, being wakeful, was up and mounted before these Lads

[2] *as*] as if.

were stirring. When they heard his horse prance, they looked out at the window and, seeing he had so good a Horse, were ready to fall out who should have him: "I will have the Horse," says one, "and you shall have his Money." "Nay, I'll have his Horse," says the other. In conclusion they quickly made themselves ready and rode after Hind.

When they had overtaken him, they asked him which way he rode. He answers them, "Toward Cambridge." They tell him they would be glad of his company. Now riding apace where no people was nigh, one of the Thieves sings, "Maids, where are your hearts become? Look you what here is."

Hind, seeing their intent and knowing he was betrayed, answers them in the same tune: "Now, you Rogues, you are both undone. Look you what here is"—drawing forth his Pistol and firing at one of them, by chance shot his Horse in the head who presently fell down with his Master's leg under him. The other, seeing this, betook himself to flight, but Hind quickly overtook him and made him deliver such Money as he had, cutting his Girths and his Bridle, made him work enough to catch his Horse again.

Hind now rides to the other Thief who lay but in little ease. He alights and pulls the Horse from his leg, and then helps him up and takes away his Money also, saying, "Is there but one Master Thief in England, and would you venture to rob him? Verily, were you not of my own profession, neither of you should have lived. But seeing you ventured hard for it, thou deservest something." So Hind gave him his Money back again to buy him another Horse, saying to him, "Disgrace not yourselves with small sums but aim high and for great ones, for the least will bring you to the Gallows." So Hind, shaking the poor Thief by the hand, left him to his Partner to catch the Horse, and bid him farewell.

Chapter 4. How Hind was enchanted by an old Hag for the space of three years

After Hind had robbed the two Thieves of their Money, it was his chance to ride to Hatfield where, lying at the George Inn, being the

Posthouse, he very merrily spent the evening with some Gentlemen that were there. In the morning early, Hind calls for his Horse to be gone, takes his leave of those Gentlemen that were stirring, and, as he rode along Hatfield, an old ill-favored Woman asked alms of him. His Horse presently stayed and would go no further.

"Sir," said the old Woman, "I have something to say to you, and then you shall be gone."

Hind, not liking her countenance, pulled out five shillings and gave her, thinking she would but, like a Gypsy, tell his Fortune, saying, "Good Woman, I am in haste."

"Sir," said she, "I have stayed all this morning to speak with you, and would you have me lose my labor?"

"Speak your mind," said Hind, whereupon the old Woman began thus: "Captain Hind, you ride and go many dangers, wherefore by my poor skill I have thought on a way to preserve you for the space of three years. But that time being passed, you are no more than an ordinary man and a mischance may fall on you as well as another. But if you be in England, come to me and I will renew the virtue of this charm again."

In saying these words, she pulled out of her bosom a little box, almost like a Sun Dial, and gave it Captain Hind, and said to him, "When you are in any distress, open this and that way you see the star turn, ride or go that way and you shall escape all dangers." So she switched him with a white rod that was in her hand and struck the Horse on the buttocks, and bid him farewell. The Horse presently leaped forward with such courage that Hind could not turn him to give her thanks, but guessing that it was her will it should be so, rode on his way.

Chapter 5. How Hind robbed a Gentleman in Yorkshire and afterwards came to the Inn where he lay, to sup with him, but did not

A Gentleman coming from York intending for London, by accident met with Hind, who soon made him deliver what he had. Hind gives him back twenty shillings to bear his charges till his own credit could better furnish him, so the Gentleman rode on his journey to the next Town, where he was well known by an Innkeeper there.

Being alighted from his Horse, he desires the Host to get somewhat ready for his supper, so the Gentleman went to his Chamber. In the meantime in comes Hind and asks if there were any Gentlemen that went for London. The Host answered there was one Gentleman alone, and he would be glad of any good company. So Hind went up to the Gentleman's Chamber and saluted him.

The Gentleman said, "Sir, sit down, and I will tell you how I was robbed today—and I durst have sworn that you had been the man, but that I see your hair is short and his hair was long."

"Sir," said Hind, "do you know his Horse?"

"Yes, very well," said the Gentleman.

"To satisfy you," said Hind, "you shall see mine." So Hind went down and fetched his horse out of the stable and asked the Gentleman if that were the Horse.

He answered, "Aye, aye, that's the Horse!"

"Then," said Hind, "I cannot sup with you tonight, if you know my horse better than myself"—so bids him good night.

Chapter 6. How Hind robbed two Gentlemen's Servants, caused a Parson to be apprehended for a Highwayman, and escaped himself

Hind, being informed of a purchase, as he rode espied some Gentlemen drinking at an Alehouse on horseback, having sent their Servants before. Hind passed by them, but riding at a good rate quickly overtook the Gentlemen's Servants who rode but easily.

Hind by their portmanteaus saw there was Money in them, bid deliver the Money or he would be their death. They, being not used to fight, yielded unto him. He, seeing their delays would breed danger, with his dagger knife cut open their portmanteaus and took out the Money and, tying the bags together, laid them before him and rid full speed away. One of the Servants rode to acquaint their Masters, who presently pursued Hind.

Hind met a Parson and said to him, "Sir, I am liked to be robbed. You must stand to it now for your own good as well as mine. They would have this Money from me which you see. Come, sir, be of good cheer! One honest man will scare ten Thieves. You shall have one of my Pistols." So Hind gives the Parson a Pistol ready cocked and charged, and bids him fire at them that came first, "while I," says he, "ride down to the next Village and raise the Country people to be our help."

The Parson, having taken a cup too much at a wedding, was pot valiant, and rid up boldly to the Gentlemen and fired his Pistol at them, but being too far off did no execution. He rid nigher and flung his Pistol at one of them, that he had like to have knocked him off his Horse. The Gentlemen seize on him and take him prisoner. The Parson cries out, "Spare my life and you shall have all my Money!"

"No, sirrah," said the Gentlemen, "we will have you hanged. What! a Parson and rob on the Highway!"

They presently hale him to the next Justice of Peace, which was very near. When they came before the Justice, they told him that they were robbed of two hundred pounds and that this Parson was one of the Thieves. The Justice marveled that such an apparent testimony should come against the Parson of his parish.

The Parson by this time was come to himself and desired the Justice to give him leave to speak for himself. Being licensed to speak, he said to the Justice, "Sir, you have known me this twenty years and no man can say I have wronged him of a penny, much less this which is laid to my charge.

"Sir, I shall tell you so much as I know of the business: As I was riding in my way home, I met a man who had two bags of Money before him, who told me that Thieves pursued him, and he desired my help, saying that I need not fear, for one honest man would beat ten Thieves, so he gave me a Pistol charged, cocked, primed, and bid me fire at the first that came while he raised the Countrymen to assist us. So when these Gentlemen came down the hill, I rode up to them and fired my Pistol among them, and when I had so done, I flung it at this Gentleman's head, thinking they had been Thieves. Sir, this is all I know of the matter."

The Justice laughed to see the Parson of his parish apprehended for a Highwayman, but he passed his word for his appearance the next Assize—who, when he was brought before the Bench, was cleared. But he made a vow never to fire Pistol more.

Chapter 7. How Hind robbed a Gentleman of thirty pound that would give twenty pound to see him

Hind overtook a Gentleman as he rode on the road, and they fell in discourse. So the Gentleman was saying he would give twenty pounds to see Hind, but as they were riding, the Gentleman fancied Hind's Horse. "Sir," said the Gentleman, "what Money shall I give you to exchange Horses with me?"

"Forty pound," said Hind.

"I will give you thirty pound in gold," said the Gentleman, so Hind said, "Sir, ride him." So the Gentleman gave him thirty pounds in gold and his Horse.

But as they rode along, there was a ditch. "Sir," said Hind, "leap him over this ditch."

"I cannot," said the Gentleman.

Hind desired the Gentleman to alight. So he got on his own Horse and leaped over the ditch. And when he was on the other side, he said, "Sir, you would give twenty pound to see Hind, and now you have seen him. But the other ten pound was for riding my Horse. So now I think you have seen enough of him and so farewell."

Chapter 8. How neatly Hind robbed a Parson of forty pound in gold which he had hid in the Collar of his Doublet

A Parson riding from Coventry towards London, by petty thieves was robbed of his silver, but having forty pound in gold about him, resolved to go on his Journey. And as he rode, Hind overtook him and asked the Parson which way he traveled.

The Parson told him that he intended for London, "But," says he, "I was almost prevented, for today I was robbed of five pound in silver, and the Knaves left me but five shillings."

"Sir," said Hind, "I was robbed of a little silver today, for a man were as good to let them have it quietly as endanger one's life to resist. But I was cunning enough to hide my gold in my boots beforehand."

"Nay, I believe," said the Parson, "that mine is as safe, for I have quilted it in the Collar of my Doublet."

Hind was not a little glad when he heard where his gold lay, but being near their Inn, they supped together and went to bed. In the morning, the Parson called Hind up and told him he would be glad of his company. After breakfast they rode together. Hind asked the Parson if he could guess what trade he was of. "No," said the Parson.

Then said Hind, "I am a Cutter, for I must cut the Collar of your Doublet off before I shall come to your money." Having so done, he left the Parson forty pound lighter than he found him.

Chapter 9. How Hind served two Bailiffs and a Usurer

Hind, riding through a little Town in Warwickshire, saw a tumult in the street, so he rid up to them to know the occasion. One told him that an honest Innkeeper was arrested for twenty pound and that the man was undone if he had not some relief speedily.

Hind goes to the man and asked him if he would give him any security if he should pay the money for him. The poor man, being much overjoyed at this unlooked-for news, told him he would make over all he had for the security. So Hind had the Usurer and the Bailiffs into the house, desired the Bond, paid the Usurer all he demanded, giving the Bailiffs their fees, and canceled the Bond. Hind sent for one to make over the Innkeeper's goods to himself, which being done they departed.

Hind, being not unmindful to inquire which way the Usurer was to go, went after him and overtook him in a convenient place. "Friend," says he, "I lent you twenty pound even now, but I must needs have it again."

The Usurer said, "You paid me so much money on a bond."

"Sir," says Hind, "it is no time to dispute it now." So Hind took from the old Usurer his twenty pound and twenty more which he had got by Usury, and rode back to the Inn and gave the Host his writing again and five pound in money, telling him he had good luck by lending to honest men.

The Usurer came after to the Innkeeper, thinking to get some Money of him, but the Innkeeper did beat him almost to death, saying: "You rogue! I am engaged in all that I have for the payment of the money, and if you be robbed must I pay you again? I will, I will." So this was all the Usurer could get.

Chapter 10. How Hind robbed a Captain upon Chalkhill in Buckingham-shire

After a day or two Hind rode into Buckinghamshire, where he was acquainted with many Gentlemen, and passing away the time till he his opportunity served, it was his chance to ride towards Chalkhill. Hind espied a little before him a Gentleman and his Servant who were alighted to walk down the Hill. The Captain gives his Horse to his man and bids him stay at the Stile till he came down.

The Captain, having occasion to untruss a point, stayed under a little Hedge. Hind watching his opportunity rid softly till he came near the Captain and, seeing him in good clothes, rid hastily up to him and bid him deliver. The Captain was amazed at this present occasion of Hind, who all this while held a Pistol at his breast and bids him dispatch. "For it is not my custom," said he, "to stand maundering, but I demand. And look you make no longer stay."

The Captain desired him to forbear till he was trussed up. Hind, giving him so much leave, said, "Your Money, sir." The Captain, seeing it could not be helped by delays, delivers him thirty pieces of gold.

Hind said, "Sir, I take this in part. I shall not be too mercenary upon you at this time." And so he rode down the Hill where the Captain's man stayed with his Master's Horse. Hind said, "Sirrah, is that your Master on the Hill?"

He answers him, "Yes, sir."

Then said Hind, "I seldom take anything from the Master but I give the Servant something." So giving him ten shillings, "Here is somewhat for thee," says he, "to drink my health. I prithee tell thy Master my name is Hind."

Chapter 11. How Hind robbed a Gentleman of 150 pound

Hind travelling up and down the Country met with a lusty young fellow whom he had formerly known, and asking him many questions, among the rest said, "Jack, if thou wilt live with me, thou shalt have Money at command, or anything thou wantest." Jack knowing partly his trade gave consent. Hind presently bought a good Horse for his man, and furnished him with Clothes, a Sword, and small Pistols.

Being well fixed, away they traveled towards Nottingham, and as they rode they chanced to come into an Inn where a Gentleman and his man were newly come before them. Hind rides by the stable door where the Hostler was taking off the other Gentleman's Portmanteau. The Hostler said, "It is but a little Portmanteau, but it is very heavy."

Hind, well eying it, said to his man, "Jack, inquire cunningly which way this Gentleman travels tomorrow." So Hind went in, and when supper was ready, they went to supper together.

After the Gentlemen had supped, the Servants fell to and Hind's man gives the other Gentleman's Servant a pint of sack, and after supper Jack gives him some Spanish tobacco, and now they begin to be great acquaintance, so they go together unto the stable to see their horses dressed.

Jack asks the Gentleman's Servant which way they rode in the morn. He told him towards London. "My Master," says Jack, "rides that way, too, I think."

Now Jack hath as much as he desired, went to see what his Master wanted. Hind bids his man get his slippers ready and pull off his boots; which being done, he takes his leave of the Gentleman and goes to bed. When he came into his chamber, he asked his man which way they went. Jack tells him.

In the morning Hind rides first. The Gentleman stays behind to eat his breakfast. After he had done, he rode on his Journey. And riding by a Wood where Hind and his man lay in Ambush for him, Hind rides out to the Gentleman and with his Cane slaps him over the pate, saying, "Have I nothing to do but to wait on you, Sir?" Jack takes off the Portmanteau, saying, "'Tis heavy, Master."

"Sir," said Hind to the Gentleman, "you are ill beloved in the Country. You cannot get gold for your silver." Jack rides back to the Gentleman's Servant and strikes him over the pate, saying, "You Rogue, must I spoil my Horse to carry your Portmanteau? Must I? Must I? You Rogue you!"

So Hind and his man rid away (leaving the Gentleman and his Servant looking one upon another, almost amazed at this sudden accident) sparing no horseflesh till they were far enough from the Gentleman, for they rid all the byways, that it had been hard for anyone to follow them. And being at a place where they knew themselves safe, they looked in the Portmanteau, where they found 150 pound. This they put up as a good morning's work.

Chapter 12. How Hind served a Committeeman who disguised himself for fear of robbing

A Committeeman having occasion to travel towards London for to buy many Commodities, hearing that there was robbing on that road, fitted himself with an old gray Coat, out at the elbows, and an old Mare, with boots instead of stirrups hung at a saddle that was not worth threepence, and a bridle of the same price. Now rides he merrily, thinking no Highwayman would set on him. But Money ill got will be ill spent, for he chanced to meet with Hind, who asked what he was. He answered that he was an old man going to get relief among his friends.

Hind gave him a piece of gold, and bid him drink his health and be merry at his Inn. The old Miser, thinking to please Hind, coined two or three great oaths presently and said he would be drunk with drinking his health.

Hind parted from him, and the old man went to his Inn and set up his Mare, then called for half a pint of sack. And after the first glass was down, he began to say that he escaped the greatest danger that ever he was in, "For," said he, "I met with Hind and, instead of robbing me, he gave me a piece of gold and bid me drink his health. But I'll see him hanged before I'll spend one penny for his sake. Hang him, Rogue, he robs all honest men. Only Cavaliers he lets them go. I'll put his gold amongst my own. I would have given ten pound to have been rid of him when first I met with him." So, after a short supper, went to bed.

Hind came to the Inn, using to lie there as a Traveler not known. The Host was telling him in what fear an old Committeeman was today, saying he had met with Hind, who gave him Money to drink his health, but he said he would see him hanged first, and called him Rogue a thousand times.

Hind went to bed, and let the old man travel first in the morning. And about an hour after, Hind rides after him. When he had overtaken him, he asked the old man if he drunk his health.

"Aye," said he, "I was never so drunk in my life as I was the last night, for I drank the King's health, the Queen's, the Prince's, and your health ten times over."

Hind said unto him, "Friend, I have found you in many lies, and now I will make you call me Rogue for something." So Hind made him untie his greasy Snapsack where he found fifty pound in gold and his own piece besides. Now the Committeeman to cheer up himself resolved to borrow so much Money of the State before he went another Journey. Hind said, "The sooner you get it, the better for me if I meet with you again."

Chapter 13. *How Hind robbed a Gentleman in Hyde Park*

Hind, being well horsed, went one evening into Hyde Park to see some sport, and, riding up and down the Park by the Coaches, spies a bag of Money by a Gentleman—to whom Hind used some discourse about the Race that was to run. But the Race beginning, the Gentleman caused his Coach to stand still that he might judge which horse ran best. Hind's head being not idle, rode to the Coach, took the bag in his hand, and rode away.

The Gentleman presently missing his Money cries out, "Stay him! Stay him! I am robbed!" Many rode after him, especially the Captain whom he robbed at Chalkhill, who pursued him hard.

Hind, riding by St. James's, said to the Soldiers, "I have won the wager." But holding his bag fast, his cloak fell off, which he left for them that came next. He, riding the way by Soho, left them. But when he came to his Companions he said he never earned an hundred pound so dear in his life.

Chapter 14. *How Hind put a trick upon a Dutch Mountebank in Holland*

Hind, having committed many robberies, was constrained to leave England and to go for Holland. Now being in a strange Country and not having that command to rob on the Highway as he had in England, fell into want of Money. So, hearing of a rich Mountebank that went about quacking of it, how he never went without store of Money (his name was Henry Van Veldes; he was somewhat fortunate in Cures, therefore by everyone desired), this Mountebank going to visit his sick Patients in divers parts of the City having received divers sums of Money for his particular Cures, was watched by Hind. And as he passed through a by-street, he runs to him as in great haste and salutes him in a kind manner thus: "Sir, I have heard much of your renown in Cures of dangerous consequence, and since it is my happiness to meet with you, I live not far from this place, if you please to go along with me to my house, I have a Wife much troubled with a flux in her belly for these fourteen days, and you by your experience may do her much good if you please to give her a visit. I humbly request you to go along with me, and what content you desire I shall willingly satisfy."

This Bell sounded well in his ears. Well, he goes with Hind to his Lodging, and in the way he gives Hind comfortable answers, saying, "God forbid I should neglect that little skill I have, to do your wife any good I can." Upon these Compliments, Hind leads him from one street to another till at last he got him within his Lodging, which was so contrived that it was some distance from other Houses.

Having locked the door upon him he takes in one hand a Pistol, in the other a great empty Purse, and furiously looking upon the Mountebank, he said, "Sir, here is my wife," meaning the empty Purse. "She hath been a long time troubled with a flux in her belly and you are the only man that can remedy and find out a means to cure this disease, else I by the help of this Pistol am resolved to remedy it."

This Mountebank, seeing himself thus cunningly and suddenly surprised, began suddenly to cry out, but was presently silenced by the sight of the Pistol, and fain for fear to let go his own Purse to cure Hind's which had the flux. But according to his wonted charity, seeing the man in this trembling condition, he restored him some part of his Money again, promised to convey him to his Lodging, and rid with his Pistol cocked for fear of an outcry, and in the mid-way left him to find out his Chamber himself.

Chapter 15. *How Hind went into Scotland to the Scotch King at Sterling and how he was apprehended in London*

Hind, being ever weary of staying long in a place, shipped himself for Scotland. When he was landed he went and presented his service to the King at Sterling. The King, being informed who it was, had some discourse with him and commended him to the Duke of Buckingham, then present, to ride in his troop because his life guard was full. He came into England with the same Troop, was in the engagement at Warrington, came to fight at Worcester and stayed till the King was fled. Hind, being in the City, saw the Gate full of flying persons. He leaped over the wall, on foot (by himself only) traveled the Country and lay three days under bushes and hedges because of the Soldiery.

Afterwards he came to Sir John Packington's wood where he lay five days, and from thence he came on foot to London and lodged five weeks very securely. But upon November 9, 1651, a discovery was made of Captain Hind's frequenting one Denzy's, a Barber over against Saint Dunstan's Church in Fleet Street, who went in the name of Brown.

This information was communicated to certain Gentlemen belonging to the Right Honorable Mr. Speaker, who with great care so ordered the business that there was no suspicion at all. To his Chamber door they came, forced it open, and immediately with their Pistols cocked seized upon his person and carried him to Mr. Speaker's house in Chancery Lane, and so secured him for that night.

The next day being Monday, by order from the Right Honorable the Council of State, the said Captain Hind was brought to Whitehall, who was examined before a Committee, and divers questions put to him concerning his late engagement with Charles Stuart, and whether he accompanied the Scotch King for the furtherance of his escape.

To them he answered that he never saw the King since the fight at Worcester, neither knew he of his getting the field, but was glad to hear he had made so happy an escape. After some time was spent about his examination, 'twas ordered he should be sent prisoner to the Gatehouse till the next day. So the next day by special order from the Council of State, he was brought from thence in a Coach, with iron bolts on his legs, Captain Compton and two other Messengers belonging to the State guarding him. And about two of the clock in the afternoon, he was put into Newgate, where he lay till the next Sessions.

Chapter 16. Containing the conclusion of the story and Captain Hind's last farewell at Worcester

On Friday the 12th of December, 1651, Captain Hind was brought to the Sessions House in the Old Bailey, where divers questions were propounded unto him by Mr. Recorder concerning his life and conversation. He answered, what he confessed before the Council of State the like he acknowledged to that honorable Court, protesting his innocence in any matter of fact or crime since the year 1649 within any of the Parliament's Dominions.

So he was dismissed from that place and on Monday the 1st of March, 1651, he was carried in a Coach from Newgate to Reading, whereupon the Wednesday following he was arraigned before the Right Honorable Judge Warberton for killing one Poole, his companion at Knowl, a little village in that Country. After evidence given in against him, he was found guilty of manslaughter and condemned to die. But the next morning, the Act of Oblivion being sent acquitted all former offenses, only the Indictment for High Treason against the State, and for that fact carried to Worcester and there he was hanged, drawn, and quartered upon Friday, September 24, 1652.

> Thus Fate this great Derider did Deride
> Who lived by robbery, yet for Treason died.

FINIS

Selections from

WILLIAM HICKS

OXFORD JESTS

(1671)

The little we know about Captain William Hicks is what Anthony à Wood tells us in Athenae Oxoniensis *(1691), and the only reason Wood says anything about him is to make sure we do not confuse him with a proper Oxonian of the same name. For though Captain Hicks claimed to be of Oxford, Wood knew him as a "sharking and indigent fellow" not connected with the University. Born in Oxford and bred a tapster, he had left town during the Civil War and now resided at Deptford as a woodmonger and sometime trainer of militia (thus the captaincy). Wood says further that the Captain wrote his several books of verse and jests "meerly to get bread and make the pot walk," but he does not explain how one so poorly educated could have acquired such facility in rhyming or in compiling and reworking jests from so wide a range as the* Oxford Jests *displays.*

In effect this is a pool of the best English jests current since the fifteenth century. Here Scogin, Sommers, Peters, and Hind bob alongside Erasmus, More, and Poggio. But Captain Hicks is not merely retelling old tales. He distills his 583 jests to minimum length, using stock characters and settings for economy, preferring declarative statements to either dialogue or dramatic forms, often neglecting form entirely in order to emphasize the point. Many of his jests are more properly what his title page calls "joques," which proved so popular that Oxford Jests *remained in print until 1640 when the* Jests of Joe Miller *(1739) monopolized the market.*

(Wing H1891)

from *To the Reader*

Then for its original and growth, at present know that some part of it was collected from those that have writ formerly of this Subject; but so as that (under correction be it spoken) most of them did deserve correction, for some were so concise that, without addition, they signified little to the purpose; others so impertinently large that they as much needed Subtraction. Another part, and that the greatest, was received from the lips of the most refined Wits in Oxford (being the place of my Nativity), which is reason enough for its Denomination. . . .

3.

A pretty Maid having her Valentine pinned on her sleeve, a Gentleman said, "Sweetheart, is your Waistcoat to be let?"

"Yes," says she, "'tis to be let alone."

"Well," says he, "I am content to let your Waistcoat alone, but not your Petticoat, if you please."

17.

The Italian Proverb is "Three Women make a Market with their chatting." "Zounds!" says a Fellow, "if my Wife had been there, it had been a Fair."

33.

One lent his neighbor his Ass for two days, but he kept him a week. And going to ask for him, he told him he was not at home. And as he spoke, the Ass brayed in the stable, at which he was angry. "Neighbor," says he, "will you believe your Ass before me?"

87.

One parting a Fray was cut into the skull. Says the Surgeon, "Sir, one may see your brains."

"Nay, then I'll be hanged," says he, "for if I had any brains I had never come there."

90.

A Miller had wooed abundance of Girls, and did lie with them, upon which he refused to marry them. But one Girl he did solicit her much, but all would not do. Then he married her, and told her on the Marriage night, if she would have let him done as the rest did, he would never have had her. "By my troth, I thought so," says she, "for I was served so by half a dozen before."

152.

A Gentlewoman that used to plaster her face to repair Nature, was invited abroad. But one advised her not to go, "For we shall be very merry, and you cannot laugh for fear of showing two faces."

202.

An Oxford Scholar, having been ten days at Cambridge together, it seems they kept him drinking so all night that he never could rise before dinner; and being asked how he liked Cambridge, said, "I like the place well enough, but that there are no Forenoons in't."

215.

A Gentlewoman being with child, her Husband was carving at the Table a couple of Coneys and, beginning with the flaps, his Wife called to him, "Pray, Husband, give me a flap o' the Coney."

"What!" says he, "before all this company, Wife?"

234.

A Student newly married, being abed, calls for his book. His Wife, wondering at it, calls for her wheel also. "How now," says he, "what is the matter?"

"To spin," says she, "that you may reel. For if you had not been drunk, you would never have studied to conceive by Book."

237.

A Wench coming to be Confessed, confessed abundance of her sins, but the chief was lying with men. "Well," says the Friar, "Whoredom is a thing which doth much displease God."

"Faith," says she, "I am sorry for that, for I am sure it pleased me."

241.

A Captain having a Mistress before Colchester Siege and having there eat nothing but Horseflesh for eleven weeks together (for indeed there was nothing else to eat), after his coming home would fain have been dabbling with his old Mistress again. She said no, for though she had a mind to be got with child, yet she was resolved never to be got with Colt.

242.

A Hall in Cambridge is called Catherine Hall, and an old Lady meeting with a Cambridge man asked him how her Nephew behaved himself. "Truly, Madam," says he, "he is a great student, and holds close to Catherine Hall."

"I vow," says she, "I feared as much, for the Boy was ever given to Wenches from his infancy."

261.

Another Wench complained to a Justice that such a one would have refreshed her. "Thou meanest," says the Justice, "ravish."

"Yes, Sir," says she, "I meant so indeed."

"I warrant," says the Justice, "this Rogue has ravished thee many times before this?"

And she, to aggravate the matter, said, "Yes, Sir, at least twenty times before now"—which saved his life.

274.

In the Rump's time, the Troopers kept a Guard at St. Paul's Church, and an Essex man coming to Town heard that Troop was then upon the Guard which quartered at their Town. So he went in and found the man that Quartered at his house. "O, Landlord," says he, "how de'e?"

"By my troth," says John, "I am glad to see this blessed Reformation in London, for in our Town we can't get the people to Church, but here the very horses come to Church."

277.

A Fellow in a Cook's shop in France filled his belly only with standing by whilst the meal was dished up, and the Cook would be paid for a meal. So it was left to the decision of the next Passenger, which happened to be an Idiot, who said that the man's money should be put between two dishes, ringing it for a time, and the Cook should be content with the jingling of the money as the man was satisfied with the smell of the meat.

304.

A drunken Fellow named John Tompson, driving his Cart towards Wells in Somersetshire and being fast asleep in his Cart, his two Horses were stolen away. He awaking said, "Either I am John Tompson, or not John Tompson. If I am John Tompson, then I have lost my two Horses. If I be not John Tompson, then I have found a Cart."

329.

One affirmed that he had seen a Cabbage so big that five hundred men on horseback might stand under its shade. "And I, for my part," says another, "have seen a Cauldron so wide that three hundred men wrought therein, each distant from the other twenty yards."

Then the Cabbage-liar asked him, "For what use was that Cauldron?"

Says he, "To boil your Cabbage in."

333.

A rich Bumpkin had a son something simple, yet he would have him made a Priest. So he, having spoke to the Bishop before and desired him to be favorable to him, being come the Bishop said, "Noah had three sons, Shem, Ham, and Japhet. Now, who was Japhet's Father?"

"Truly, my Lord," says he, "I never learnt that yet."

But coming back again, his Father hearing of it, said, "Has not Cole my Dog three Whelps, Rig, Trig, and Tribal, and must not Cole be the Sire of Tribal?"

"O, Father," says he, "now I have it." So the next day he went to the Bishop again and the Bishop asked the former Question, "Who was Japhet's Father?"

"Why," says he, "Cole, my Father's Dog."

334.

A Gentleman coming hungry home called for a Dinner. His man told him it was newly struck ten. "Puh," says he, "don't tell me of ten by the Clock, when it has struck twelve by my stomach."

346.

Bishop Bonner told Henry the Eighth if he sent him on such a rough Message to the French King, he'd take his head off. "If he does," says he, "I'll take a thousand of his subjects' heads off!"

"Aye, Sir," says he, "but I question whether any of them will fit my shoulders."

366.

A Woman having played false with her Husband he thereupon grew extreme melancholy. And being asked what was his distemper, "Truly," says he, "I am only troubled with a bad liver."

384.

Two fighting together in a frosty morning, one struck the other's head off, but, fearing the Law, took up the head again, being reeking hot, and clapped it on, which immediately was frozen on. Then they both went to an Alehouse to drink, and he whose head was fastened, his nose began to drop and he, going to blow his nose, his neck being thawed by the great fire, threw it quite into the fire— which saved the other's life. *Probatum est.*

389.

A Maid was to be sworn before a Paritor,[1] and he told her if she told a lie, it would be her damnation—at which she hummed and hawed a great while, for she was to tell whether she was Maid, Widow, or Wife. But she, considering of it, said, "Though I was never married, yet you may write me down young woman."

396.

A Wench was got with child and her Mistress would know who got it. She said, "Nobody."

Says her Mistress, "You Whore, do you think any Woman can be with child without a man?"

"Why," says she, "may not I have a child without a man as well as a Hen lays eggs without a Cock?''

399.

A young Parson having been three miles off to Christen a child in Oxfordshire, coming home again, lost his way in the Forest of

---

[1] *Paritor*] summoner of ecclesiastical court.

Whichwood. It being a very cold and rainy night, at last he lighted upon a poor Cottage and desired any lodging or Haycroft to lie in and some fire to dry him. The man told him that his Wife and he had but one bed, and if he pleased to lie with her, so. If not, there was no other. So after supper, being weary with coming so far afoot, he went to bed.

In the morning early, the man rose to go to Witney Market, and at the end of the Forest met some of his neighbors going to Market also. Then he fell heartily a-laughing, and was asked the reason. "Why," says he, "to think how shamed the Parson will be when he wakes and finds himself abed with my wife."

400.

A married man having got a Wench with child was told by the Justice that he thought such a man as he would not have defiled his bed so. "You mistake, Sir," says he. "There was no defiling of the bed in the matter, for it was done in the field."

401.

Another man was accused for getting his Maid with child, and that he should go into his Maid's bed to do it. He to excuse it swore that he never went into his Maid's bed, for the bed was his own.

408.

An ingenious man was riding into the Country and, having rid four or five miles, he began to complain that his foot was sore and that his boots hurt him. He bid his man pluck off one of his boots, which he did and felt all about but could not find where the hurt was.

"Sir," says he, "here's nothing hurts you on this foot."

"Then prithee," says he, "pluck off the other boot, for I am sure one of them hurts me."

409.

One swore that he had traveled so far that he had laid his hand upon the hole where the wind came out. "Puh," says the second,

"I have been further than that, for I have been at the furthest end
of the world and drove a nail quite through it."

"Puh," says the third, "but I have been further than you both,
for I was then on the other side and clenched that nail."

412.

A Doctor being newly married to a pretty woman and loving her
exceedingly, she had a desire to go into the Country to see her
Friends, and desired him to ride before her on a horse. And on the
way as he was riding before her, she called to him to kiss her. And
though he was before her, yet he kissed her behind.

425.

A Gentleman was all in mourning for his Father which died a
month before. And as he was riding before some Ladies, his horse
having a crimson Velvet cloth on with a rich Saddle, the Ladies
asked him why that was not black too. "O," says he, "the father of
my horse is not dead yet."

438.

A great eater, having a lusty piece of roast Beef set before him, he
began to cut sometimes at one end and sometimes at the other. The
Woman desired him to cut it handsomely and in one place. "Peace,"
says he. "It is no matter at which end I begin, for I intend to make
an end of it all before I go."

448.

A Fellow was blaming his Sweetheart, telling her he heard she
was false to him with another man. She, to clear herself, used many
imprecations bidding him, if it were so, to mark her end. "Nay, for
that," said he, "I shall not so much mark your end as I shall mark
your middle."

454.

Another time [Hugh Peters] would preach in a Corporation
where he found some little opposition by the Mayor. But at last by
the intercession of some zealous Women he was admitted, where to

be even with the Mayor, in his Prayer (after he had made Intercession for Oliver and some other of his Patrons) he proceeded to the
Mayor, who by trade was a Butcher, in these words: "Lord, thou
hast likewise commanded us to pray for our enemies. Herein we
beseech thee for the Right Worshipful the Mayor and his brethren.
Grant that he may knock down sin like an Ox, and quarter iniquity
like a fatted Calf, and that his horn may be exalted above his
Brethren."

477.

Another going by Saint Paul's Church was saying that it was like
to a Trunk with a Hatcase upon it. "Nay," says another, "I'll tell
you what it is most like, and that is, that if it be not speedily re-
paired, it is like to fall."

481.

Scogin being in France took upon him to be a Priest, and had a
number of people come to him to be confessed, one whereof was a
Shepherd whom Scogin asked if he had kept the Commandments.
The Shepherd said, "No."

"What hast thou kept then?" said Scogin.

"Why," said the Shepherd, "I never kept anything but sheep in
all my life."

482.

Another who came to him to be confessed, told him that he had
stolen a Halter. "Well," said Scogin, "to steal a Halter is no great
matter."

"But," said the Fellow, "there was a horse tied at the end of it."

"Aye, marry," quoth Scogin, "there is something in that. There
is a difference between a Horse and a Halter. You must therefore
restore the owner the Horse, and when you have done that, come to
me and I'll absolve you for the Halter."

494.

One owing money was by his Creditor arrested and clapped into
prison, of which he complained very sorely, saying that he had

trouble enough to borrow the money and had not need to be troubled to pay it.

501.

A Farmer being for his means made a Knight and his Wife thereupon growing very fine, one said that his Worship was very much in fault, in spoiling a Good-wife to make a Mad-dame.

509.

A Country fellow pressed in the late wars, having been at a fight and being asked what exploits he had done there, he said that he had cut off one of the Enemy's legs. And being told that it had been more manly if he had cut off his head, "O," said he, "you must know that his head was off before."

543.

A Quaker having took a Lodging at the Red Lion at Brainford, the house being full, a damning Blade came up into the room and would have Hectored him out but the other told him 'twas his room and by yea and nay he should not come there. The Hector then began to thunder out his oaths and to strike him, but the Quaker being a stout fellow returned him his blows double and treble, and at last kicked him downstairs. With that, the Master of the house sent up the Tapster to know what caused the noise above. He told him, 'twas nothing but that "yea and nay" had kicked "God damn me" downstairs.

546.

A Gentleman dancing in a ball, a Lady found fault with him that he straddled too much. "Madam," quoth he, "if you had that betwixt your legs that I have betwixt mine, you would straddle more."

569.

A Quaker that had taken one of his female Saints to wife, but about a fortnight after, he found she had given him a lusty clap that he became very ill, insomuch that another Quaker came to him and asked him how he did, he said, "Not well."

The other, mistrusting how it was with him (he having given her the clap before), told him he'd go with him to a Surgeon that should cure him. Being come, the Surgeon asked him what was his distemper. He said he was not well.

"I ask you, what's your distemper?"

Still he said he was not well.

Then the Surgeon, being a choleric Fellow, said, "What a pox is your distemper!"

"Aye, that, that, that's it!" says he.

Selections from

ABEL BOYER

THE WISE AND
INGENIOUS COMPANION
(1700)

*Abel Boyer (1667–1729), a Huguenot refugee resident of London since
1689, was French tutor to the youthful Duke of Gloucester, for whom he prepared a plain and simple French grammar-rhetoric textbook which was
published in 1694 as* The Complete French Master. *This text included
four sections of reading matter with French and English on facing pages,
among them a section that included 25 jests, ancient and modern.* The Wise
and Ingenious Companion *expands these 25 into 191 ancient and 151
modern jests, separated by three tales—the " Widow of Ephesus," one from*
The Golden Ass, *and another from a modern French romance. His aim is
still pedagogical, and he prefaces the new collection with an essay on the name
and nature of jests as well as their proper use and application.*

*Boyer's interest is chiefly linguistic, as befits a great lexicographer who
compiled the standard French-English dictionary (1699) unsurpassed for
more than a century. But he is a pedagogue at heart, for even his* Dictionary
*is distinguished by its designating given words as "vulgar," "figurative,"
"proverbial," etc., so that students may know not only what the words mean
but under what circumstances they are most fitly used. This same concern is
carried over to the preface of* The Wise and Ingenious Companion *which,
after distinguishing the kinds of jests, offers guidance for their proper use. In
both these precepts and his practice, Boyer rounds off the seventeenth century
with a utilitarian flourish, while his emphasis in distinguishing between what
is said and how it is said promotes a new standard for jests: what oft was
thought but ne'er so well expressed.*

(Wing B3918)

A Prefatory Introduction; concerning The Excellency, Nature,
and Use of wise Sayings, witty Repartees, Jests, and pleasant
Stories

Sentences, witty Repartees, and Jests have ever been esteemed by
all civilized Nations. The Ancient Greeks and Romans have shown
what account they made of them, by their care of Collecting and
Quoting them. Julius Caesar made a Collection of the Jests of his
Contemporaries; the famous Historian Plutarch is very exact in

recording all those of the illustrious Men of whom he writes the Lives, wherein he has been imitated by Diogenes Laertius in his lives of the Philosophers, and among the Moderns, my Lord Bacon, Guichardin, and several others have enriched their Writings with them.

These Testimonies carry so much weight with them that we cannot but join our approbation with that of so many illustrious Persons. The only Question is how to make a good Choice and not confound true Wit and Sense with abundance of low Thoughts and dull and vulgar Jests which are imposed upon the World; and this I have proposed to do in the following Collection.

The Ancients under the names of Apophthegms comprehended what we call wise Sayings, generous and noble Sentiments, Jests and witty Repartees. However, according to our Notions, the Apophthegm thus differs from a Jest or Repartee that the first is generally Grave and Instructive, whereas Jests and Repartees instruct us and make us merry at once. Nay, sometimes these are merely diverting, and sometimes sharp and Satirical.

The French call *Bons Mots* all those witty Sayings and ingenious Replies which are the result of a true Judgment and of a happy and quick Imagination.

Now the first and most certain Rule to know a true Jest from a false Thought is that it may be translated into another Language without losing anything of its Sense and Pleasantness, for then it is certain that it runs upon the Thing expressed in it and not upon a Pun or Quibble.

Puns and Quibbles are what we call playing upon Words, or Equivocations. They are known by this, that being turned into another Language they lose that resemblance of Sound wherein their subtlety consists. And as they affect the Ear more than the Mind, we must take care not to mistake them for true Jests. The pretended Beauty of Equivocations is only owing to Chance, which makes one and the same Word to signify several Things, and therefore their double Application is generally forced. But suppose it were true, a Jest is still imperfect when it runs upon the Expression and not upon the Thought.

I confess an Equivocation may be allowed of when it offers two different Ideas to our Mind, one of which is in a proper and the other in a Figurative Sense. But as for those miserable Puns and Quibbles, which are nothing but an empty jingle of Words, the French have branded them with the infamous Name of *Turlupinades*, and they ought to be banished the Conversation of polite and well-bred Persons, as only fit to entertain the vulgar Sort.

Jests and witty Repartees have ever been more frequent among the Ancient Grecians than any other Nations, which may be ascribed, first, to the quickness of their Wit, their deep Learning, and good Education; secondly, to the constitution of their Government—for living for the most part in Commonwealths, they were not constrained in their Fancy by the Respect due to Sovereigns and those whom they make sharers of their Authority in Monarchical States, wherein the different degrees established among Men do often keep Inferiors from speaking their Thoughts about the *Ridiculum* of those above them.

We may draw a double advantage from true Jests, for besides they serve to make us merry and revive now and then a fainting Conversation, several of them are full of good and wholesome Instructions, applicable to the different Exigencies of Life, both in a public and private Fortune.

As for Stories, they differ from Jests in that they express their Subject in its full Latitude and generally leave nothing to be guessed at, as Jests do. They are sometimes divertingly Instructive, but their chief aim is to make the Hearers merry by relating sometimes a concurrence of Comical Accidents, sometimes a piece of Simplicity or Ignorance, and sometimes Malicious Tricks that have been put upon anyone to make sport for others. In all these we must use the same Caution as we have mentioned about Jests; that is, we must take care not to confound good Stories with many pieces of low Buffoonry which tickle mean and vulgar Ears by their smuttiness, daubed over with paltry Equivocations.

Now the use a Gentleman ought to make of Jests and Stories is, never to quote them but when they come pat and apropos to the Subject, and before those who are disposed to hear and be merry with them, without courting the occasion of being thought a pleasant and jocose Man; for Persons of a nice discernment will presently take notice of those nauseous Affectations—and, as the judicious

LaBruyere has it: "That Man who endeavors to make us Merry, seldom makes himself to be esteemed."

We must also observe never to usher in Jests or Stories with formal Commendations, which will prevent our hearers from being agreeably surprised; for 'tis by this surprise that the Pleasure they give is principally excited. Likewise, when we begin to tell them, we must not begin to laugh ourselves if we intend to make the Company laugh; for those who promised us Mirth beforehand are seldom so good as their Words, and how silly and ridiculous does that Man look who laughs by himself at a cold and threadbare Jest whilst the rest can hardly force a Smile to keep him in Countenance. Lastly, we must avoid telling a Jest or Story several times over to the same Persons, an impertinence which makes the Conversation of old People so very distasteful.

Before I make an end of this Introduction, I shall obviate an Objection which some supercilious Critics will be apt to make against this Work; viz., that most of these Apophthegms, Jests, Repartees, and Stories are already known to Persons of good Education and to Men of Learning. To which I answer that, granting this to be true, yet 'tis hoped they may be glad to find them here again just as we are pleased to hear a fine Tune over and over, provided it be well Sung. But besides, this Collection is so vastly Rich that it is hard if not impossible for any single Reader to know all it contains, and not be either instructed or diverted by something that will be new to him. To which I must add that my chief Design in this Collection is to facilitate the Learning of the French Tongue to the English, and that of the English language to Foreigners, and upon that score I have taken particular care to make both Languages answer one another as near as their different Idioms would allow.

Ancients

16.

The Emperor Augustus, endeavoring to find the reason of the great likeness which a young Grecian bore to him, asked him whether his Mother was ever at Rome. "No, Sir," answered the Grecian, "but my Father was many a time."

19.

A certain Soldier came in a great Fright to Leonidas and told him, "Captain, the Enemy are very near us."

"Then we are very near them too," said Leonidas.

There was another that came to tell him that the Enemy were so numerous that one could hardly see the Sun for the quantity of their Arrows, to whom he answered very pleasantly, "Will it not be a great Pleasure to fight in the shade?"

23.

Maecenas, Augustus's Favorite, being entertained at Dinner by a Roman Knight, towards the end of the Meal began to take some Liberties with his Wife. The Knight, to make his court to him, instead of showing any jealousy of it, counterfeited Sleep. But seeing one of his Slaves going to take away something from the Cupboard, "Sirrah," says he, "dost thou not see that I only sleep for Maecenas?"

43.

Memnon, King Darius's General, in his War against Alexander hearing one of his Soldiers belch out many injurious Words against that great Enemy, he gave him a great blow with a Halbert and told him, "I pay thee to fight against Alexander and not to abuse him."

46.

Antigonus, hearing a Poet call him Son of Jupiter, "My *valet de Chambre*," said he smiling, "who empties my Close-stool knows but too well that I am but a Man."

49.

Some Body twitting Hiero the Tyrant with a stinking Breath, he chid his Wife for not telling him of it before. "I thought," answered she, "all Men's Breath smelled like yours."

50.

One asked Charillus why at Lacedemon Maids went barefaced when Married Women were veiled. "Because," answered he, "the first look for Husbands and the others are afraid to lose them by Jealousy and Divorce."

51.

Diogenes seeing over the Door of a new Married Man these written Words, "Hence all Evil," said he, "After Death, the Physician." The same Philosopher perceiving one Day some Women hanged on an Olive tree, "Would to God," cried he, "all other Trees bore the like Fruit."

63.

Two Criminals accused one another before the same King. This Prince, having patiently heard them both, said, "I condemn this Fellow presently to depart my Kingdom and the other to run after him."

70.

The Ambassadors the Athenians had sent to Philip being returned to Athens, commended that Prince for his Beauty and Eloquence and his being able to drink much. "These Commendations," said Demosthenes, "are little worthy of a King. The first of those advantages is proper to Women, the second to Rhetoricians, and the third to Sponges."

169.

Metellus, who was born of a Woman of great Liberties, pretending to joke upon Cicero about the meanness of his Birth, asked him who his Father was. Cicero, instead of giving a direct Answer to the Question, waived it cunningly by telling him, "Thy Mother has made that Question harder for thee to answer."

177.

Those of Numantia, a very warlike People, having been defeated and put to flight by Scipio, the old Men reproached them severely with Cowardice, saying, "Are not these the same Roman Sheep which we have so often beaten and drove before us?"

"Yes," answered a young Man, "these are the same Sheep, but they have changed their Shepherd."

183.

Servius Geminus, going one day to see Lucius Mallius, a very skilful Painter, and seeing his Children who were extremely ugly, he could not forbear telling him that he wondered he did make so fine Pictures and get so ugly Children. To which Mallius pleasantly replied, "Don't be surprised at it, for I draw the Pictures in the Day and get the Children in the Night."

193. *A Story taken out of Apuleius's* Golden Ass

A Laboring Man that worked hard for his Livelihood at the Forges had a very handsome Wife, though none of the most virtuous. This Poor wretch going out one Morning as he used to do, gave opportunity to an extravagant young Blade to slip into his House where, being in close conflict with his Wife, the Husband unexpectedly returned. But finding the door fast, little suspected what had been done in his absence, he therefore within himself began to extol his Wife's Chastity and by a Whistle gave her notice of his coming. She, in Cases of this Nature being not a little Politic, soon disengaged herself from her Spark's embraces and with a great deal of unconcern hid him in an old empty Tub that stood in the corner of the Room—which done, opening the Door in a fury, she accosted her Cuckold after this manner:

"Is it thus, thou senseless Drone, that thou providest for the wants of thy Family thus sauntering with Arms across, whilst I must labor both Day and Night to supply the wants occasioned by thy Idleness? O! how much happier is my Neighbor Daphne, who has nothing else to do but be merry with her Lovers."

To which the frighted Husband replied, "What great harm is there, poor Chicken? Though our Master has no work for me today, by reason of attending his Law-business, yet I have provided for thy Dinner. Dost thou see that old Tub there that serves for nothing but to encumber our Room? Why I have sold it, Honey, for Fifteen pence, and the Man that bought it will be here presently to fetch it away. Come, lay aside thy Work and help me to cleanse it, for I would not by any means but deliver it sweet and wholesome into his Hands."

Hereat the Wife began to laugh heartily, and being furnished with a Stratagem from the occasion, cried out, "Bless me! What a rare Stock-jobber have I got to my Husband that could find in his Heart to let that go for Fifteen pence which I, though a Woman that never stirs abroad, have made shift to get half a Crown for!"

The Husband not a little pleased with his Wife's Bargain, forthwith demanded what Sot it was that had offered so much. "A Codhead, you may be sure," replied the Wife, "and to prove him such, he is just now got into it to see what Profit he is like to make."

Here the Gallant finding his Cue, peeped out and cried, "Good Woman, would you have me tell you the Truth? This Tub is exceeding old and very full of Cracks. You ought not in Conscience to have so much for it as I bid you." Then turning to her Husband quoth he cunningly, "And you, honest Man, whosoever you are, prithee lend me a Candle a little, that I may scrape out the filth and know whether it be for my turn or no, before I pay my money, if you think I come honestly by it."

Hereupon our subtle Vulcan, little dreaming of the design upon him, presently fetched a Candle and coming up to him said, "Prithee, stand aside a little, Friend, and let me see what I can do, for 'tis but reason you should have it as clean as may be." Then stripping himself and delivering the Candle to his Wife, he crept into the Tub and begun to work amain on the dried Lees whilst the crafty Lover did as much on his Consort, whom he had laid athwart the Vessel.

All this while the good Woman, leaning over her Head to light her Husband, amused the poor Man by showing him that "here" and "there" and "there" were places to be cleansed. But at length both labors being ended, the contented Cuckold, having received the half Crown, thought himself further obliged to take the Hogshead on his Back and carry it to his Friend's House.

Moderns

II.

The famous Molière being dead, many Poetasters writ Epitaphs upon him. One of them went one Day and presented one of his own making to a Prince much renowned for his Wit. "Would to God," said the Prince, receiving the Epitaph, "that Molière presented me yours."

21.

A Lord having pitched upon an ignoramus to be his Library keeper, "That's the Seraglio," said a very witty Lady, "committed to the Custody of an Eunuch."

41

Alphonsus King of Spain, hearing that those of Sienna who, during the War of Italy, remained Neuter, had been plundered by the Soldiers of both Parties as soon as the War was ended, said that they were like those who live in the middle Stories of a House, that are incommoded by the Smoke of those beneath, and by the Noise of those above them.

43.

A Man of War crying up before Sigismundus Military Employments and vilifying Magistracy, "Hold your tongue," said the Emperor to him, "and learn that if all Magistrates performed their Duty we should have no occasion for Military Officers."

68.

A Venetian Ambassador at Rome went through Florence and waited on the late Duke of Tuscany. This Prince complained to the Ambassador that the Republic had sent him a Venetian whose Conduct during the time of his residence at his Court he was not satisfied with. "Your Highness," said the Ambassador, "ought not to wonder at it, for I can assure you that we have abundance of Fools at Venice."

"So have we at Florence," answered the great Duke, "but we don't send them abroad to treat of public Affairs."

107.

Two Friends who had not seen one another a great while, meeting by chance, one asked the other how he did. He said he was not very well, and was Married since he saw him. "That is good news, indeed," says he.

"Nay, not so much good news neither," replies the other, "for I have married a Shrew."

"That is bad," said the other.

"Not so bad neither," says he, "for I had two Thousand Pounds with her."

"That's well again," says the other.

"Not so well neither, for I laid it out in Sheep and they died of the Rot."

"That was hard indeed," says his Friend.

"Not so hard neither," says he, "for I sold the Skins for more Money than the Sheep cost."

"That made you amends," says the other.

"Not so much amends neither," says he, "for I laid out my Money in a House and it was burned."

"That was a great loss indeed!"

"Nay, not so great a Loss neither, for my Wife was Burnt in it."

116.

A modest Gentlewoman being compelled to accuse her Husband of defect and being in the Court, she humbly desired the Judge that she might write what she durst not speak for Modesty. The Judge gave her that liberty and a Clerk was presently commanded to give her Pen, Ink, and Paper; whereupon she took the Pen without dipping it into the Ink, and made as if she would write. Says the Clerk to her, "Madam, there is no Ink in your Pen."

"Truly, Sir," says she, "that's just my Case, and therefore I need not explain myself any further."